Praise for

VOICES FROM THE HENNESSY PRESIDENCY

"Voices from the Hennessy Presidency takes a novel approach to telling university history. There could be no better way to understand John Hennessy's legacy than through the voices of the university leaders he recruited and mentored. Their stories from Stanford beautifully reflect the strength of Hennessy's leadership style. By fostering collaboration and bridge-building across disciplines, Hennessy and his team developed new models for organizing the 21st century's research university. Stanford benefited enormously, as did universities across the nation and around the world."

—Susan Hockfield, PhD, MIT President Emerita
and Professor of Neuroscience

"These extraordinarily candid and comprehensive perspectives on the sixteen years of John Hennessy's Stanford presidency provide an invaluable resource for understanding an enormously consequential moment in the University's history. Indeed, they offer rare insights into the complex, uniquely American institution that is the modern university."

—David M. Kennedy, Donald J. McLachlan Professor of History, Emeritus,
at Stanford University and Pulitzer Prize-winning
author of *Freedom from Fear: The American People in Depression and War*

"Voices from the Hennessy Presidency delivers fresh insight into a transformative and consequential moment in the history of Stanford, Silicon Valley, and American higher education. Fascinating, forthright, and immensely valuable."

—Margaret O'Mara, Scott and Dorothy Bullitt Professor of American History,
University of Washington and author of *The Code: Silicon Valley and the Remaking
of America* and *Cities of Knowledge: Cold War Science
and the Search for the Next Silicon Valley*

"Leading a university is one of the most rewarding—and complex—jobs in the world. This book reveals why John Hennessy, 10th president of Stanford, was so good at it. It comprises interviews with a range of administrative leaders whose expertise John relied on as he led Stanford through crises, triumphed over intractable problems, and refocused the university's research enterprise on making a global impact. *Voices from the Hennessy Presidency* not only highlights John's courage, integrity, humility, and genuinely collaborative spirit, but also draws much deserved attention to the extraordinary team of leaders who helped him transform Stanford into one of the greatest research universities in the world."

—L. Rafael Reif, President, MIT

"Oral history ably reveals the intricate leadership that transformed Stanford University during John Hennessy's sixteen years as president. Interviews with the president, provost, vice provosts, institute directors, deans, and chairs of the board of trustees provide insights into the challenges he faced, the decisions he made, and the teamwork he inspired."

—Donald A. Ritchie, author of *Doing Oral History*

"As a fellow university president and a Stanford graduate, I have deep admiration for John Hennessy. This insightful volume of interviews with John and the team that surrounded him shows that his presidential leadership was characterized by an exceptional focus on innovation and the obligation of universities—through research and education—to address human suffering. President Hennessy marshaled his colleagues to address global challenges, and he did so with great political skill and clear-eyed attention to the ethical and moral aspects of them as well."

—Peter Salovey, President, Yale University; Chris Argyris Professor of Psychology, Epidemiology & Public Health, Management, and Sociology

"Over many decades, Stanford has progressed to the highest ranks of research universities. The Hennessy years, however, were truly transformational, comparable to the origins of Silicon Valley in the Sterling/Terman era. Among many important developments in these sixteen years, Stanford became a powerhouse in interdisciplinary, problem-oriented research in a multitude of critical areas: environment and climate, medicine, biotechnology and the life sciences, applications of materials science, and many more. This book captures all this through the eyes of the University's leaders, the key people who worked with President Hennessy—if you like, the engineers of this transformation. It is an important document in the history of American higher education."

—A. Michael Spence, former dean of the Faculty of Arts and Sciences at Harvard University and of the Stanford Graduate School of Business; winner of the Nobel Memorial Prize in Economic Sciences

"It is no small feat to lead a university that is revered the world over. I have known Dr. John Hennessy for decades and have witnessed first-hand the qualities and character that made him such a fine university president. John provided inspirational leadership and unwavering devotion over his 16-year tenure that not only upheld Stanford's long-standing reputation, but propelled the institution forward with a dynamic vision of greater global impact. *Voices from the Hennessy Presidency* captures the greatness of the Hennessy era with a unique insider perspective and offers invaluable lessons and insights for all of us working to benefit humanity through the pursuit of research, scholarship, and education."

—Henry T. Yang, Chancellor, University of California, Santa Barbara

VOICES *from*
the HENNESSY
PRESIDENCY

COLLECTED INTERVIEWS WITH
STANFORD UNIVERSITY LEADERS
2000—2016

Edited by Eric Knight

STANFORD HISTORICAL SOCIETY

Published by Stanford Historical Society
P.O. Box 20028
Stanford, CA 94309

This work was supported by a grant to the editor from the Australian-American Fulbright Commission and funds from the Stanford Historical Society.

Cover and interior design – Glen Edelstein, Hudson Valley Book Design
Publishing strategy – Holly Brady, Brady New Media Publishing

Photographs – by Linda A. Cicero/Stanford News Service, except as noted:
    photo of Carla Shatz – Lee Abel
    photo of Bob Joss at press conference – Steve Castillo/Stanford News Service
    photo of Patricia Gumport at GRAD Day reception – Ved Chirayath
    photo of Jim Clark, John Hennessy, and Carla Shatz – Heideh Fattaey
    photo of Bing Concert Hall exterior – Jeff Goldberg for Ennead Architects
    photo of Denning House exterior – Natalie Marine-Street/Stanford Historical
        Society
    photo of Stephen Quake and Jessica Melin with Deans Pizzo and Plummer –
        Norbert van Groben

Hardcover with dust jacket: 978-0-9847958-5-7
Hardcover with laminated case: 978-0-9847958-7-1
Ebook: 978-0-9847958-6-4

Library of Congress Control Number: 2022946518

Typeset in 11.5/16 Baskerville
Printed in the USA

CONTENTS

FOREWORD
John Hennessy

As I look back on my sixteen years as president and read through the insights of the incredible colleagues I had the good fortune to work with, I am reminded of a phrase that appears at the end of my inauguration speech: "The challenges before us are many, but the opportunities are unbounded..." During my tenure we certainly faced a variety of challenges, which required our attention and efforts to overcome, but those activities were dominated by a relentless goal to move Stanford forward in new ways.

Underlying that effort to increase our excellence and enlarge our contribution to the world was the belief that if we could clearly articulate a vision of Stanford's greater role in the world, we could use the combination of endowment growth and anticipated philanthropy to take the university to a new level. We could grow the institution, but we needed to do it strategically with a focus on enlarging our contribution. Universities have an unusual hurdle, not typically faced by other institutions: they are both the keepers of the past as well as the pursuers of the future. As my predecessor, Gerhard Casper, said in his inauguration speech: "Even after 100 years—or, for that matter, 500 years—the days of a university are always *first* days." Our challenge was not to grow incrementally and uniformly, not just to preserve what had made Stanford great, but to build new efforts in areas of global need and to make a great university even greater.

To achieve that goal we wanted to bring the many elements of the university together to build something where the whole was greater than the parts. That goal required a degree of collaboration among the deans and the schools they led. The provost and I were very fortunate to find deans who would both lead their schools forward and also see themselves as university citizens, contributing to making the entire institution better. Together with the other academic leaders (vice provosts and institute directors), we managed to take the university to new levels. That teamwork and focus on excellence pervaded not only the academic efforts we undertook, but also our efforts in managing the university's finances and our ambitious plans for new facilities. We also had the active support and counsel of a fantastic set of trustees and board chairs, who were all dedicated to the university and ambitious to help make it even better.

Reading through these interviews, I was reminded of how truly blessed I was to have the opportunity to work with such an incredible team, all dedicated to taking Stanford to new heights. I would like to deeply thank Eric Knight and his team for their extraordinary efforts to collect and edit these interviews. I hope that this work will both serve those interested in the history of those years as well as provide insights to my colleagues throughout academia.

INTRODUCTION
Eric Knight

Stanford University occupies a unique place among the world's great universities. Not only are its research and teaching considered among the best in the world, but it is also located at the epicenter of one of the most consequential ecosystems in modern economic history: Silicon Valley. Much has been written about the symbiotic nature of this relationship—but mostly from the perspective of the students who have graduated from Stanford University. What about the stories of those who have led Stanford University? What of their vision for the university, and the strategies and investments they implemented to enable others to have this impact?

JOHN HENNESSY AND HIS PRESIDENCY

This book is a collection of edited interviews with key figures from the presidency of John L. Hennessy, president of Stanford University from 2000 to 2016. A Turing Award–winning computer scientist, dean of Engineering, provost, and entrepreneur, Hennessy led Stanford during an unprecedented time in the university's history and during a digital revolution that put Silicon Valley at the foreground of the world's technology economy.[1]

Hennessy achieved extraordinary things for Stanford during his tenure. He engaged in transformational fundraising to reimagine the educational experience, to establish ambitious new structures to support interdisciplinary research discoveries, and to support the largest building program in Stanford history to date. However, these achievements can only be understood in the context of the team he led. This book amplifies the voices of some of those figures. Serving Stanford University at different points during the Hennessy presidency, the interviewees in this book are leaders in their own fields. This book covers their contributions to Stanford University during the Hennessy presidency and the remarkable and aligned vision they developed and shared. Their energy and judgment, combined with the support of others not interviewed in this book—staff, trustees, donors, alumni, students, and members of the wider community—helped drive Stanford University's incredible success during the first two decades of the twenty-first century.

A few key facts are worth noting about Stanford University during the Hennessy presidency. In the fall of 2000, the year Hennessy became president, Stanford had 16,228 students across undergraduate, graduate, and other cohorts, and 2,625 faculty. By the fall of 2016, when Hennessy finished his tenure, these population sizes had modestly increased, consistent with the broad approach taken at Stanford over the preceding decades. At the same time, Stanford's endowment during this period grew significantly. The endowment's market value in 2000/2001 was around US$8.886 billion, as recorded in the Stanford University Annual Financial Report. By 2016/2017 this number had risen to US$22.4 billion.[2]

This growth in wealth was significantly stimulated by the Stanford Challenge, launched in October 2008 as an ambitious five-year plan to fund a new model of research and teaching on the environment, human health, and international affairs, among other issues. By the end of the fundraising campaign in December 2011, Stanford had raised $6.2 billion, exceeding its original target of $4.3 billion. This money was used to fund 130 new endowed faculty appointments, 360 new fellowships for graduate students, $27 million in seed grants for faculty and students to pursue various innovative research agendas, more than $250 million for need-based undergraduate scholarships and the renovation or construction of 38 buildings that enhanced Stanford's campus. These investments supported the creation or scaling up of multidisciplinary initiatives such as Stanford Bio-X and the Woods Institute for the Environment, and the advancement of major new initiatives in research and teaching, such as new data-driven approaches to K–12 education policy and the formation of a new field known as "optogenetics."

CHAPTER SUMMARIES

The chapters in this book are edited interviews. Each interview was recorded, transcribed, edited for clarity, organized with key topic headings, and presented back to the original interviewees for validation. They are presented here in four thematically related sections—the president's immediate team, chairs of the board, deans, and cross-institution leaders—roughly in chronological order based on when those leaders commenced their roles.

PART ONE includes interviews of President John Hennessy and Provost John Etchemendy—or "John and John," as they were commonly referred to—and Jeff Wachtel, who served as chief of staff to President Hennessy throughout his tenure.

Chapter 1: John Hennessy (President of Stanford University, 2000–2016) reflects on his approach to transforming Stanford's landmark institutions, including the hospitals and Medical School, and his commitment to interdisciplinarity across the entire institution. He speaks about some of his key principles in leading the university and his vision of the role of university leaders in shaping public affairs.

Chapter 2: John Etchemendy (Provost of Stanford University, 2000–2017) recalls his time growing into the provost role and building his vision and approach to leadership. He also reflects on challenges that faced U.S. higher education during his tenure, including the global financial crisis.

Chapter 3: Jeff Wachtel (Special Assistant to President John Hennessy, 2000–2016; Executive Director, Knight-Hennessy Scholars Program, 2016–2019) describes his role as chief of staff and how decisions were made in the President's Office. He reflects on the use of discretionary funding to seed projects, how the culture of entrepreneurialism energized the office, and the ambassadorial duties he fulfilled for the president.

PART TWO captures the views of chairs of the Board of Trustees at Stanford during the Hennessy presidency with the exception of Burton McMurty (member of the Board of Trustees, 1997–2007; chair of the Board of Trustees, 2004–2007) who passed away in 2018. These interviews capture the culture of the university's governing board, important discussions, and the board's relationship with both President Hennessy and the institution more broadly.

Chapter 4: Isaac Stein (Member, 1994–2004 and and 2006–2016 and Chair of Stanford's Board of Trustees, 2000–2004) covers his role as a trustee and then chair of the board. He reflects on the contributions of Etchemendy and Hennessy during their tenure and in particular the fundraising efforts of the board. He also recalls the discussions behind campus planning, including the possibility of a New York campus.

Chapter 5: Leslie Hume (Member, 2000–2012 and Chair of Stanford's Board of Trustees, 2008–2012) shares her insights on the inner workings of governance at Stanford and how the board approached its role of supporting the president. She reflects on the creation of the Stanford Challenge and how the board dealt with a range of issues, including the prospect of expanding its footprint to New York.

Chapter 6: Steve Denning (Member, 2004–2017 and Chair of Stanford's Board of Trustees, 2012–2017) talks about the impact of the global financial crisis on the operations of the board and the fundraising endeavors pursued during this time. He also reflects on the end of Hennessy's tenure and the conception of the Knight-Hennessy Scholars program.

Part Three covers leaders who served as deans during significant portions of Hennessy's tenure. Each took on leadership at different stages during the presidency and with difficult goals during their terms of office.

Chapter 7: Jim Plummer (Dean of the School of Engineering, 1999–2014) reflects on the significance of increased undergraduate interest in computer science during his term as dean of the School of Engineering and the emergence of open searches for faculty appointments. Plummer also describes curricular innovations for preparing the engineers of the future, the creation of the Hasso Plattner Institute of Design, or d.school, and the unique manner in which the Department of Bioengineering is structured at Stanford.

Chapter 8: Bob Joss (Dean of Stanford Graduate School of Business, 1999–2009) recalls the challenges of moving from business to academic leadership. He reflects on the role of teaching in leadership, his contributions to the internationalization of the school, and his efforts to integrate a formerly isolated Graduate School of Business with the rest of the university, including programs to train future university leaders.

Chapter 9: Phil Pizzo (Dean of the Stanford University School of Medicine, 2001–2012) reflects on the strategic planning processes he used to overcome the financial deficit that he inherited and improve the School of Medicine's status, both in the eyes of the university and in the global rankings. He describes the challenges of building a new leadership team and strengthening Stanford's clinical expertise while upgrading medical education facilities and building innovative interdisciplinary research programs.

Chapter 10: Pam Matson (Dean of the School of Earth, Energy and Environmental Sciences, 2002–2017) describes the processes underlying Stanford's pursuit of interdisciplinarity during the Hennessy administration, including how funds from the Stanford Challenge and changes to recruitment and appointment strategies led to the transformation of the School of Earth, Energy and Environmental Sciences. She also reflects on how university leadership, faculty, and alumni combined to effect change in Stanford's approach to the environment and sustainability.

Chapter 11: Deborah Stipek (Dean of the School of Education, 2001–2012, 2014–2015) recounts her transition from the UCLA faculty to her role as dean of the School of Education. Reflecting on the balance between achieving disciplinary excellence and making real-world contributions to the practice of education, she recalls new fundraising and policy initiatives, programs to support educational leaders and a charter school, a key partnership with the San Francisco Unified School District, and more

Chapter 12: Larry Kramer (Dean of Stanford Law School, 2004–2012) reflects on his work in deepening the engagement of the Law School with the rest of the university and building consensus with his faculty, including by appointing a "cabinet of deans" to strengthen his leadership team. He explains the significant challenges involved in shifting the Law School's academic calendar, his emphasis on joint degrees, and how Stanford worked to strengthen practical experiences for students through improving its clinical education programs and integrating public interest law into the curriculum.

Chapter 13: Richard Saller (Dean of Humanities and Sciences, 2007–2018) covers the significant influence of the senior leadership team, especially John Etchemendy, in supporting the School of Humanities and Sciences. He describes his efforts to improve trust and administrative responsiveness within the school, which helped in retaining key faculty talent, and showcases efforts to facilitate university-wide collaboration, including the establishment of ChEM-H.[3] He also reflects on efforts to strengthen Middle Eastern and Asian Studies and the challenges of expanding Stanford's global presence.

PART FOUR includes interviews with leaders in cross-institutional initiatives under the Hennessy presidency, including research administration, undergraduate education, property, and finance.

Chapter 14: John Bravman (Vice Provost for Under-graduate Education, 1999–2010) describes changes to undergraduate education at Stanford, from the vision of President Gerhard Casper and the Commission on Undergraduate Education through the establishment of the Office of the Vice Provost for Undergraduate Education, to various programmatic initiatives carried out during John Hennessy's administration. He recalls traveling across the country to raise funds for undergraduate education and reveals his role in building residential education at Stanford through Freshman-Sophomore College.[4]

Chapter 15: Harry Elam (Vice Provost for Under-graduate Education, 2010–2020) offers details of his journey to the drama faculty and his contributions to the shaping of undergraduate education at Stanford, describing a career that fruitfully unites scholarship, teaching, theater directing, and administration. He provides insights into changes in first-year and general education requirements at Stanford, efforts to increase faculty engagement with the process of undergraduate education, and a move toward an undergraduate experience that is adaptable, experiential, and focused on learning objectives and critical thinking skills.

Chapter 16: Patricia Gumport (Vice Provost for Graduate Education and Postdoctoral Affairs (2006–2019) describes the creation of a new vice provostial office at Stanford tasked with improving Stanford's already excellent graduate education. She brings into focus the challenges of effecting institutional change in a highly decentralized function and highlights the collaborative approaches she used to advance diversity, reframe the student-advisor relationship, and address affordability issues for graduate students and postdocs, increasing their salaries and taking the necessary step of expanding graduate housing.

Chapter 17: Ann Arvin (Vice Provost and Dean of Research, 2006–2018) describes the university's complex and innovative research administration apparatus, revealing how Stanford's rich history and a forward-looking policy helped to shape a new wave of interdisciplinary programs during the Hennessy presidency. She highlights some of the challenges of the role, including establishing and funding the shared facilities and infrastructure needed to pursue this agenda.

Chapter 18: Carla Shatz (Director, Stanford Bio-X, 2007–Present) tells the story of the origins of this unique interdisciplinary research center, its successful seed grants program, and the construction of its purposefully designed home, the James H. Clark Center. She discusses her recruitment as the director and reflects on the connections, mindset, and research success incubated by Bio-X.[5]

Chapter 19: Jeffrey Koseff (Founding Co-Director, Stanford Woods Institute for the Environment, 2005–Present) reflects on the early days of building the Woods Institute for the Environment, including the range of academic and institutional challenges facing the founders and the valuable outputs the institute created. He recalls the decision-making structures and approach to funding that fueled the growth of the institute and enabled its ability to make a global impact.

Chapter 20: Randy Livingston (Vice President for Business Affairs, Chief Financial Officer, and University Liaison for Stanford Medicine, 2001–Present) reflects on taking on the role of chief financial officer after his many years in the private sector advising in Silicon Valley. He describes the immense structural changes to the fiscal risk management practices and enterprise systems at Stanford. He reveals his approach to navigating the financial challenges during his term, from the dotcom bubble to the global financial crisis.

Chapter 21: Bob Reidy (Vice President of Land, Buildings, and Real Estate, 1997–Present) reflects on overcoming the underlying challenges of managing the real estate and investment opportunities at Stanford as the vice president of Land, Buildings, and Real Estate. He showcases his key role in developing interdisciplinary hubs across campus including his prominent work with the Bio-X program, the arts district, and the Medical School to support cross-disciplinary engagement across Stanford.

Concluding Remarks

This book offers a firsthand account of Stanford University's leadership under the Hennessy presidency. However, its significance extends beyond Stanford: the insights captured here are relevant to academic and university leaders around the globe and for future generations of leaders at Stanford University.

Three broad themes emerge. The first is the importance of strong team dynamics. Across the interviews, a picture emerges of a team bound by a unified purpose. Many leaders highlighted similar achievements, articulated shared visions, and spoke about aligned values they deployed to make tough decisions. Each perspective adds nuance to the broad consistency on display during the Hennessy administration.

Second is the application of an entrepreneurial culture in a university setting. Nowhere are innovation and entrepreneurship more prized than in Silicon Valley. The Hennessy presidency brought that culture to university leadership. The interviews reflect bold moves, transformative ideas, and ambitious plans, but also the tensions entailed in operationalizing this within a university context. Their methods were bold and innovative, too—with seed funding, mergers between groups, start-up activities, and innovative research endeavors all part of the mix of activity.

Finally, the interviews reflect a relentless drive toward excellence. The leaders in the Hennessy administration did not simply seek to leave a mark on their teams or disciplines. They sought to leave a mark on society. Each exemplified this higher purpose in how they went about their role and their quest to collaborate beyond traditional lines. Moreover, nothing less than a twenty-year horizon was in their sights.

ACKNOWLEDGMENTS

These interviews were collected in early 2020 during a visit to Stanford University on a research sabbatical funded on a Fulbright senior fellowship. In retrospect, it was a blissful time. By the time COVID-19 disruptions had sent California into lockdown in March 2020, most of the interviews had been completed. Interviews were conducted in a semi-structured manner, with questions following each interviewee's tenure in their position: how they came to their role, their early challenges, what they sought to achieve, and how these initiatives came to pass.

I approached Stanford as something of an outsider, an Australian academic leader interested in Stanford's role in the world and the leadership principles it applied over multiple generations. My understanding of Stanford's history was aided by a number of important books on key figures in its history, such as *Fred Terman at Stanford* by C. Stewart Gillmor and *Creating the Cold War University* by Rebecca S. Lowen. John Hennessy was generous enough to accept an impromptu invitation to reflect on his presidency and from there to issue an invitation to key figures in his administration. As their accounts unfolded, it quickly became apparent that their insights, wisdom, and experiences were relevant, not only to university administrators and those interested in the history of Stanford, but also to those leading complex, multifaceted institutions around the world.

The idea of a collection of interviews was made possible with the support of the Stanford Historical Society. In particular, the support of Oral History Program Manager Natalie Marine-Street has been crucial to realizing this project. From the outset, she has demonstrated a commitment to and interest in oral history and the significance of the Hennessy presidency to Stanford's history. She has played a crucial role in cross-editing many of the transcripts and readying the manuscript for publication, and she also conducted the interview with Jeff Wachtel. The society's Publications and Oral History committees offered important editorial and project management advice and supported the effort financially. Special thanks to committee members Karen Bartholomew, Linda Cicero, Elena Danielson, Andy DiPaolo, Charlie Junkerman, Roxanne Nilan, Susan Schofield, and Jan Thomson. Thanks are also due to Linda Cicero, Emma Frothingham, Pamela Moreland, and Sunny Scott for their assistance with photos, and to society board member Michele Marincovich who conducted one of the interviews from which the Harry Elam chapter is drawn. Kara Gehman provided excellent editorial work and insights during the project's earliest stages. With her publishing expertise, Holly Brady helped to bring the project to the finish line.

A NOTE ABOUT ORAL HISTORY

Natalie Marine-Street
Oral History Program Manager
Stanford Historical Society

The interviews collected for *Voices from the Hennessy Presidency* provide rich first-person accounts from leaders in higher education and essential figures in the history of Stanford University. In each chapter, an individual voice shines through, allowing us to dwell for a time in the particular, variegated world of the storyteller. The interviews provide a glimpse of the networks that brought people to Stanford, the circumstances that enabled their actions here, and the past experiences that shaped their encounters when they arrived. They offer, as well, a rare chance to learn about motivations, paths not taken, and the contingencies—chance happenings, sometimes breathtaking or even ridiculous—that affected their own careers and institutional outcomes.

In addition to these individual textures, we can discern in this collection narrative patterns, collective agreements, and language that tellingly recur across interviews. Together, these interviews provide not only a sense of the opportunities and challenges facing the university in the early decades of the twenty-first century and the strategies pursued by members of the leadership team but also the values, mores, and other connective tissues that held a varied and decentralized enterprise together. Like the university John Hennessy envisioned, the interviews here are, indeed, more than the sum of their parts.

Oral history interviews are compelling primary sources used in many kinds of historical accounts. They excel at plumbing lived experiences and subjective perspectives and should be an essential part of the modern historian's research toolkit. Just as historians evaluate all forms of evidence, they should ask of oral histories: When was the source created? How close was the creator to the events in question? What did their vantage point allow them to see, and what could they not see very well from where they stood? What might have intervened between historical events and the time of the interview to influence a narrator's account? As I tell my students, when we are in the realm of oral history, we are walking on the tricky terrain of memory, one marked by pools of deep reflection, new realizations, and misunderstandings, with strange outcroppings that invite deeper explorations. Oral history is a generative methodology that does and should prompt questions.

The accounts that follow emerged largely in conversation with Eric Knight, a noted scholar of organizational theory and strategic management and a senior university leader in Australia. While the questions Professor Knight asked are not included in the text, his influence remains salient. A different interviewer may have elicited different responses. The tenor of these narratives reflects a particular intersubjectivity that includes the relationship between the parties, the circumstances in which the interviews occurred, the nature and the rhythm of the questions asked.

The interviews collected in this volume represent, of course, only a partial view of Stanford during John Hennessy's presidency. By design, Eric Knight's project sought the perspectives of those at the upper levels of leadership at Stanford, aiming to understand the behavior of those with institutional power and the contexts in which they operated. While not all institutional actors appear here, a diverse array of voices reflecting on the university's history can be found in the Stanford Historical Society Oral History Program collections and other collections housed in the Stanford University Archives. Those carefully preserved and widely accessible interview collections speak to the strong legacy of oral history at Stanford. Since the mid-1970s, with the Stanford Historical Society and the University Archives as catalysts, faculty, staff, alumni, and students have collaborated to document the multifaceted histories of the university using the methodology of oral history. The extensive archive that has resulted benefits researchers in many disciplines, speaking not only to the history of the university and the perspectives of its senior leaders but also to the evolution of teaching and research in higher education; the intersections between Stanford and the Silicon Valley; changes in student life and expectations over time; and the life narratives of scholars whose contributions have changed the way we see the world.

To learn more about the oral history program and collections, please visit the Stanford Historical Society's website at https://historicalsociety.stanford.edu.

PART ONE

UNIVERSITY LEADERS: INSIDE THE PRESIDENT'S OFFICE

CHAPTER 1

JOHN HENNESSY

President of Stanford University (2000–2016)

John L. Hennessy was Stanford's tenth president. In 1977, he joined the Stanford faculty as an assistant professor of electrical engineering. A successful entrepreneur, he helped transfer the technology that was the subject of his research to industry by cofounding MIPS Computer Systems in 1984. He served as chair of the Department of Computer Science (1994–1996) and dean of the School of Engineering (1996–1999) before being appointed provost in 1999 and president in 2000. He currently serves as chair of the board for Alphabet, Inc., Google's parent company.

Moving in a New Direction

To be a great scholar, you have to be willing to reinvent yourself. Maybe you take on a leadership role, maybe you go into a new field. Steve Chu, for instance, moved into biophysics after being a solid state condensed matter physicist for many years because he thought there were so many opportunities in the field.[6] Prior to becoming provost, and then president just a year later, I had tried out a variety of smaller leadership roles. Thank goodness I did those because I wouldn't have been prepared, nor would I have been willing to take the really bold step of accepting the provost position if it required skipping a lot of the intermediate steps. I knew I was moving in the direction of a career as a leader, but I didn't think that much about what would come next.

Partnership with Provost John Etchemendy

When they selected me as president, John Etchemendy was actually the faculty co-chair of the search committee. I had known him earlier because we had served on a university committee that Gerhard Casper had organized, focused on technology and education. He was the chair, and I was on that committee.

When I needed to choose a provost, I talked to some of the trustees that I knew and a few of the other leaders around Stanford. They were certainly impressed with John's breadth.

His field complemented mine in that he is a philosopher in the humanities. I felt it was important—particularly for someone coming from Engineering—to have somebody from the School of Humanities and Sciences, from the core of the university. I went and asked John if he'd do it, and he said yes.

Early on, we discovered that we think and reason in a similar fashion. He's a logician, and I'm a computer scientist. We work things through in logically similar ways, so we had common skills for reaching decisions together. It was a good match from a style viewpoint. We also developed a trust of one another. He and I had a general rule that, except for ceremonial university activities where everybody leading the university had to be there, we would try to avoid overlapping. We would coordinate our schedules so that we did not need to be in the same place at the same time. We communicated. We typically met twice a week, and that helped ensure that we always knew where the other person was on a topic, where we were moving, and where we were going. That allowed me to focus more of my attention outside the university, on fund-raising in particular, while he focused more of his attention inside the university.

Early on, we were communicating about relatively small things. Over time, we got more comfortable knowing that we could navigate issues that came up without consulting on everything. If a crisis arose while I was traveling or if something else was going on and we weren't able to meet as often, we had enough understanding of each other's thought process that we could navigate during those periods of time. Being a logician, John realizes that you can't know everything, so you're going to have to make some decisions that are instinctual.

He has another characteristic that was really important to complement me: he has the patience of Job. He is the most patient person I have ever met. In some situations, it was obvious what the right thing to do was, and it was obvious we were going to get there, but there was some resistance to be mollified and brought along. He would meet with people; he would meet with them again; and then he would meet with them again, just so that no one could say, "I didn't have the chance to express my views. I didn't understand what the provost would do." He is a more patient person than I am. I'm a person of action. Probably because he's a philosopher, he is willing to realize that some things just require deliberation—thinking about it and letting it settle in. That made an enormous difference on a number of key things where we needed to move the university to a place that 80 percent of the people wanted to go, but 20 percent were hesitant. If 20 percent of the people are against you in a university—even 10 percent—they can completely stop you. John was really good at bringing people along, communicating again and again and again, and willing to go to yet another meeting to deal with the issue.

Besides having great taste in terms of faculty and overseeing faculty appointments, he became an expert on the university's budget and guiding the budget process. When we were in office, the university budget was probably close to $3.5 billion, not including the hospitals. That's a gigantic thing to wrap your head around. The fact that John learned how to do that early on and then became a master of it really meant that I didn't have to worry constantly about the critical issue of the university budget and the allocation of resources. So that worked great.

I think one of the reasons I was able to do the job for so long was that I had a great provost for so long. One of the things that makes it difficult for a president is if you have to bring in a new provost every few years and then bring the new provost up to speed. If you look at top research universities, John is one of the few provosts who has ever served that long. His tenure as provost was the longest in Stanford history.

Stanford leaders past and present at John Hennessy's inauguration as president of Stanford University in October 2000. From left, Provost John Etchemendy; former university presidents Richard Lyman, Donald Kennedy, and Gerhard Casper; Hennessy; and Board of Trustees' President Isaac Stein.

INITIAL OPPORTUNITIES AND CHALLENGES

When I became president, I put issues at the university into two piles: opportunities and challenges. My predecessor had really tried to reshape the undergraduate experience and had raised enough expendable funds to do several experiments. He established freshman seminars and what we call Sophomore College, where sophomores return three weeks before the beginning of the fall quarter and take one intensive course during that time. The university had also increased exposure to undergraduate research and resources to support writing and presentation skills. It was really about trying to take the first two years and make them much more rewarding, as opposed to just sitting in one large Econ 1 lecture. Those experiments were highly successful, both with students and with faculty. Faculty really liked teaching these courses to small groups of undergraduates who were really interested in the subject matter.

The opportunity was to build on that success, to think about what would complement it in students' junior and senior years. This could be accomplished primarily through the expansion of undergraduate research opportunities, so students could take more advantage of being at a research university. We also needed to raise the funds to sustain all of these innovations permanently. My predecessor, Gerhard Casper, had started this effort raising a nucleus fund for a campaign. At my inauguration, we announced that we would launch a billion-dollar campaign for that, the Campaign for Undergraduate Education, which at that time was the largest campaign ever focused on undergraduate education.[7]

Addressing the Concerns of Women Faculty

One of the issues I encountered in my provostial year was a set of concerns by women faculty about possible systemic discrimination. In fact, we had a group of women faculty that had filed a federal complaint about such behavior by the university.

I think the group peaked at sixteen in number. The origins of this were complicated. For any institution that has a federal contract, which the university does, there is a separate agency (the Office of Federal Contract Compliance Programs) that worries about fair employment issues and affirmative action. The Clinton administration had brought a new set of people into that agency, who had a strong credo of affirmative action. As provost, Condi Rice had made a point that we have affirmative action when we hire faculty, but we don't have affirmative action when we consider tenure cases; we have one tenure standard for everyone. A group of women faculty had argued to Provost Rice that there was systemic discrimination, and the head of the Office of Civil Rights gave a speech in which she said that Condi's statement showed discrimination. That argument erupted into a number of complaints.[8]

After the complaints had been filed with the Office of Federal Contract Compliance Programs, I invited every single woman faculty member to lunch and met with about a dozen to fifteen at a time. Once I worked it through, I concluded that their claim that there was a systematic problem was not right, but there were pockets of problems. For example, even though the university had policies, let's say around maternity leave or sabbatical usage, some groups were discouraging women faculty from taking advantage of them. In addition, the surgical side of the Medical School had an earlier history of sexist harassment. However, no data showed systemic discrimination. In fact, we already had processes such as annual salary reviews to ensure disparities were not disproportionately disadvantageous to women.

Some individuals withdrew their complaints once they saw that their concerns were not being rejected out of hand, that somebody was at least listening. Where there's smoke, there's sometimes fire, especially in a large complex institution. You want to catch it before it's a wildfire.

Eventually, we resolved all of those issues, and the complaints were closed out by the government, although this process took about two years of hard work by the Stanford team, led by our highly capable General Counsel Debra Zumwalt. (Debra would be my general counsel for my entire tenure as president and was a trusted counselor, often dealing with the most confidential and delicate crises.) I learned so much during these conversations with my colleagues that the periodic lunches with random groups of faculty from across the university became a mainstay of my 16 years as president.

Transforming Stanford's Hospitals and Medical School

The other big problem we had is the one that contributed to my predecessor probably staying a shorter amount of time than he intended. When I took the provost job, I thought he was going to stay three more years, until he finished ten years, but he announced a decision to step down shortly after I started as provost. One very trying event was the ill-fated merger of the Stanford and UCSF hospitals. In the late 1990s, our adult hospital was losing a lot of money. For example, one year it lost approximately $50 million. The university couldn't sustain those losses. The hospital is a wholly owned subsidiary but financially independent, the finances are not consolidated, but we worried that eventually the hospital would break through the firewall and draw down resources from the university.

One of the problems with high-end, high-acuity hospitals is that the cost of building a team to perform heart transplants, for example, is enormous. You've got to have enough highly skilled and compensated medical people with some duplication of talent, because when people need heart transplants, you can't wait until the surgeon gets back from vacation. We had two heart transplant teams—one for adults and one for children—and UCSF had the same thing. The idea was to merge the two hospitals, combine services: let one hospital perform cardiac surgery for children and let one perform it for adults. That was the plan. Because it was a complicated merger, and UCSF is a public institution, you couldn't announce it publicly. You had to do all the work in the background and then make it a fait accompli. That was the only way to get through the politics.

It turned out that the situation at UCSF was worse financially than had been determined when we did our due diligence (due to a need for long delayed work on the facilities and the clinical IT system). In addition, there was a lot of faculty resistance to the merger. Once the universities announced that they were going to get rid of an adult heart transplant group here, or another kind of group there, that didn't go over well. Then, the chancellor of UCSF who had negotiated the arrangement left for the Harvard Medical School, and the merger went downhill very quickly. The politicians got involved, and they also objected to it. Given the problems, the merger had to be taken apart. My predecessor, Gerhard Casper, took on that burden, together with Mariann Byerwalter, the CFO.

While that was a necessary step, it did not solve the problem: we still didn't have a financially viable hospital, so we had to get it on solid footing. One of the issues was that the roots of our Medical School were primarily in biomedical research. We were deep on the basic research side, but not as deep in high-end clinical care. The dean of the Medical School had been running the hospital. At one level, that sounds like a great idea, but the skill set to both oversee a medical school (focusing on faculty, education, and research) and also oversee a major clinical hospital is extremely rare. So, our hospital was losing a fortune, at least compared to the rest of the university. I also felt that the hospital had consumed too much of President Casper's time relative to the rest of the university. We had to make some changes so as to avoid a financial disaster as well as getting stuck in a quagmire.

First, we hired a new dean, Phil Pizzo. Phil came to his first trustee retreat, and I said, "The topic of the retreat will be reforming the hospital and its economics, or bringing in an external firm to run the hospital, or even selling it." That caused everybody to kind of sit up and focus. While I put that question out there, the answer I wanted was not that we were going to close the hospital, or that we were going to bring in an outside provider. It was: we need to fix this, because we can't afford to lose $100 million a year in running the hospital. That really sharpened everybody's focus in a way that we hadn't been successful in doing before.

In the end, we fixed the situation. We fixed it pretty quickly, actually. We brought in a new CEO for the hospital that was focused on the business of running the hospital and making the hospital successful. Universities are generally not good at management, and a hospital needs excellent management. On the academic side, we have another set of values, another set of objectives, besides economic efficiency. But on the business side of the university—everything from how you borrow money, to how you run a hospital, to how you construct buildings—every dollar you waste is a dollar you can't use for the academic side.

And yet, we resist this notion that some parts of the university need to run with the same discipline we'd have in running a business.

We had to restructure, too. Initially, the hospital CEO was reporting to the dean, who had a difficult job in balancing the demands of the faculty with the demands of the patient population and the hospital staff, which are sometimes in conflict. The faculty would like more money for their research and their education programs, and the hospital staff would like enough money to really improve the quality of care. We restructured that so that the dean and the hospital CEO reported as independent entities. The hospital board became less advisory and more operational because they had power to appoint and oversee the hospital CEO, and we recruited new board members who were knowledgeable about the finances of the healthcare system.

Given the history and all of the things that had gone wrong, we wouldn't have been able to get a CEO of the quality we wanted if that person was going to report to the dean. We were lucky. Martha Marsh was the first person we appointed into that role, and she did a great job of reforming the hospital and turning it around.[9] Phil Pizzo was an active participant in that. He was a researcher, but he was also a clinician and he believed equally in the clinical mission. He and Martha really transformed things.

The academic side had never been in serious trouble. We had always had great basic science departments. Our clinical departments were more mixed. Some of them were really top notch, but some of them were less distinguished. That was a question of making great faculty appointments and recruiting excellent chairs. In medicine, the department chairs are there for long periods of time and have financial oversight as well as

13

faculty appointment oversight. We had some great chairs, but we had others that were less than great. Phil Pizzo really transformed the quality of chairs that we had in the school, and that led to strength in the clinical programs.

Two things early on gave me some confidence. First of all, the new department chairs were really serious about making their departments not only academically high quality, but financially stable. That was a key thing. Phil also launched the effort for Stanford to become a comprehensive cancer center.[10] We were one of the few top-ranked medical schools in the country that wasn't a comprehensive cancer center at the time. It's a lot of work and a high bar to get that designation, and no one had ever taken the time and energy to pursue it before. Phil launched that effort and recruited leadership for it, and we were successful.

And then on the hospital side, Martha really got serious about focusing on feedback and the experience of patients. That made a big difference. The medical outcomes were good, but people didn't feel well-treated. I still remember I got a phone call from a CEO in the Valley who blasted me about the treatment his wife had had, and his decision to transfer her to another hospital. I said to the leadership, "If you want to end up closing this hospital, you just have a few more cases like that and your reputation will be destroyed. Nobody will come here."

When I initially told the trustees, several years later, "We're going to go out and raise money for a new hospital," they said, "It's never going to happen because you don't have the community support for it." Turning that community support around was really key. It was a team effort that did it. Since then, we've rebuilt the hospital, and it's phenomenally successful.

One other person who was really a hero was Mariann Byer-walter.[11] Mariann had been a trustee, and Gerhard Casper had tapped her to be chief financial officer of the university. She was chief financial officer for about five years. When I came in, I asked her to stay until we hired a new CFO. She had overseen the merger with UCSF and its decoupling, so I asked her to become chair of the hospital board when we restructured it. She was a great partner because she understood what needed to happen for the hospital to realign itself and be successful financially. I had a board chair who understood that the hospital board had two roles: a role of overseeing the financial management of the hospital so that it was running well, as well as a traditional philanthropic role. She understood that both roles were important if the hospital was going to survive. When Randy Livingston succeeded Mariann Byerwalter as CFO, I asked him to be the university representative to the hospital boards, and he did an excellent job bringing his perspective and helping financially to coordinate the hospitals and university.

TACKLING LONG-TERM ISSUES

The Campaign for Undergraduate Education took off very fast with the head start that Gerhard Casper had initiated. It was pretty clear we were going to be able to finish it quickly and that with the changes we had put in place and the additions we had planned to do, we were going to cement a very strong position in undergraduate education, as strong as any research-intensive institution can have. We started asking, "What else do we want to do? What are the things we should be doing?"

It was a time when it was clear that given the scale of the problems we faced around the world, universities were going to have to play a bigger role, not a smaller role, in looking for solutions and preparing people to grapple with those problems. We spent a lot of time with the deans thinking through what we wanted to do, and then with a small set of trustees who served as the advisory group who helped hammer out a plan. Whenever I'm trying to conceptualize a new vision, I like to try it out, eventually get it down into words—a thought paper or a presentation, it doesn't matter. But getting it into that form makes it concrete in my mind and gives me something to share. That initial six-page thought paper became the plan for the Stanford Challenge and where we were trying to take the university.

We asked: What are the really big issues that will take decades to address? Not twenty years, but forty years. Think of something where you're going to make a commitment that's going to be forty or fifty years at a minimum, because twenty years is the set up and take down time in a university. It takes twenty years to implement something new and take it down if it's wrong. So, we said think forty to fifty years on anything you want to do. For example, the environment/sustainability, human health, peace, security, democracy—those are really big long-term issues.

Then we identified areas in which the university could build on existing strengths. Not necessarily that we had everybody we needed or all of the bridge builders, but a core group of people who would bring strength, and where bringing them together in some organizational structure would actually improve Stanford's position and visibility in the field. We ultimately raised billions to fund interdisciplinary research and teaching efforts in those areas.

Structuring for Interdisciplinarity

We grappled a lot with structure. For the interdisciplinary efforts, we primarily ended up with a matrix structure. We decided not to take apart the academic departments. First of all, there would have been a big political battle, but more importantly, we viewed the departments as the preservers or guardians of quality inside the institution with respect to faculty appointments. So, we proposed a matrix organization, where billets or halves of billets, for example, might belong to an interdisciplinary center, but they would have to partner with departments in order to realize those appointments. Bio-X, the Woods Institute, they're all structured like that. That's worked out pretty well. It's not perfect. There are some places where it's hard to get the partnership to work.

Bio-X chair Matthew Scott addresses hundreds of Stanford community members and supporters during the dedication of the James H. Clark Center, the home for Stanford's pioneering Bio-X interdisciplinary research center, in 2003. Also onstage, from left, President John Hennessy, Board of Trustees Chair Isaac Stein, and Clark, who donated $90 million for the center's construction.

There were a few barriers to collaboration that we had to eliminate or reduce. One was the reluctance that faculty members in field X and field Y had to collaborate, because both of them already had achieved success. If they stuck to their own fields, they still could get additional funding—they were well enough established. We had to figure out a way to get them to work together and incentivize a research collaboration. That really began with Bio-X and the Bio-X Seed Grants Program, which rewarded innovative interdisciplinary initiatives with two years of start-up funding. Bio-X was sort of our icebreaker to figure out how to do these things. That model worked so well that we could just clone it as we went around to the other activities. My guess is we were investing less than 10 cents on the dollar in return for future research funding. That's been tremendously successful, so we replicated the seed funding model, having determined that it would scale appropriately.

Second was getting people to think about how to make joint appointments—including joint appointments of junior faculty—in ways that would work and would be successful. The fact that we had figured out how to do this with Computer Science and Electrical Engineering and then applied that across the rest of the School of Engineering, meant that we could then begin to think about how to make that work in other parts of the university.

I remember Pam Matson said something really insightful when we were planning the environmental initiative. She said, "You should give them half-billets to appoint jointly with existing departments and programs in the university because that will do two things. First of all, they'll have to find a partnership with a disciplinary-based program. Also, it will help change the disciplinary-based programs, moving that department in the direction of this bigger opportunity, and the way we want to go." And she was right. It has. That was key, thinking about how to make these joint disciplinary-based appointments.

The primary issue with joint appointments is the double jeopardy problem. Faculty with joint appointments have to get tenure in two fields. We came up with a scheme in EE and CS. We said, "We're going to appoint junior faculty, but the faculty member can choose which department will review their tenure case." Once their tenure case is reviewed, the other department votes, but the only thing the department is voting on at that point is whether or not this person should retain a joint appointment in that department. So, if the second department votes no, then the person gets tenure in the department they selected as their primary department. If they vote yes, then that's fine: they still have a joint appointment, and they get promoted. I don't think we've ever had the second department opt out of a joint appointment.

Another key to reducing barriers is a kind of funny one. I tell people not to worry about the nickels and dimes when they're playing big stakes in terms of moving the university. It's very easy when departments agree on a joint appointment, for example, to argue over whether or not the department is getting its full half-share of this individual. If they're only getting 40 percent, they tend to worry about that 10 percent of faculty time that they're not getting. It's very easy to nickel and dime over these little things. We had to overcome that. Otherwise, the Bioengineering Department—which is a collaboration between the School of Engineering and the School of Medicine—could have never started because the way the Engineering School and

Medicine think about faculty time and financial resources is so different. Don't worry about these little things. Because overall, if working together you hire a great faculty member and that person goes on to do spectacular work, there'll be enough glory to be shed on both departments and both departments will reflect that aura.

The other thing we learned along the way is the importance of leadership in interdisciplinary endeavors. You have to have the person who's going to be the leader who is going to say: "I'm on the line. I'm responsible. I'm going to put some of my personal research time on hold, my teaching on hold, to take on this greater mission." That turns out to be critical. If you don't have it, it just doesn't work.

More Than the Sum of Its Parts

What matters to academics is often space and billets (i.e., faculty slots). They're both precious resources, and sometimes we focus too much on local optimization (e.g., what's best for an area or department), not thinking about the bigger picture. We were able to get people over that hurdle by helping them think about Stanford as a whole. We were blessed to have a set of deans who thought about not only what was in the interest of the school that they were looking after, but also what was in the interest of Stanford as a whole. That was key to making changes and to building new efforts.

Another key for us as we began to think about the future of the university was to say, "Look, we don't want to be seven schools that don't intersect and don't interact, because what's the value of being a university then? You might as well be seven different colleges and split out and separate."

Bob Joss was very articulate about strengthening the connection between the Business School and the rest of the university. For example, every school has a flag that we use at commencement; the Business School flag has a griffin on it. The commencement flag was the only time we ever used that symbol. But the Business School had removed the university logo from their business cards and replaced it with the griffin logo. It said in giant letters, "Graduate School of Business" and in little tiny letters down at the bottom it said, "Stanford University." Dean Joss reversed all that and established a number of new collaborations. They had had some with Engineering previously, particularly around the center on manufacturing that his predecessor had started, but he strengthened a lot of those connections. One of the more fascinating things was that he became a big advocate for one of the initiatives we ended up starting later in the process: a focus on strengthening the arts at Stanford. He was a champion for it. You want to see magic and changed minds? Get your dean of the Business School to talk about the importance of the arts in the education of MBA students. It was a dream come true.

The dean of the Law School, Larry Kramer, made changes that integrated law students with other parts of the university. He was a champion for Law School students getting an additional degree. He said, "Law school is really only two years long, but it's required to be three years, so you have enough time to do something else. Go do something in environmental studies. Do something in technology." He enacted a big change that made that possible, which was to move the Law School to the quarter system. The Law School was still on semesters; the rest of the university was on quarters. Larry led that effort, which required a deft touch and great patience, but the change made it much easier for students to pursue joint degrees because then their academic year schedules were the same. The rise in joint degrees was really exciting to see. Figuring out how to bring all the parts of the university together was critical to our vision and the notion of one university.

On Billets, Tenure Decisions, and Faculty Appointments

In general, we viewed it as the job of the deans to reallocate billets within their schools. We would not typically take a billet from Humanities and Sciences and send it over to the Engineering School because of the growth in the field of computer science. Instead, the president and provost would be working with the dean, helping to raise additional funds for new billets. That general model dates back to an earlier time. During Gerhard Casper and Condi Rice's administration, there was a financial crisis that they responded to by not replacing retirement billets. Crises should never be wasted. What happened subsequently is that the schools didn't necessarily go back to the pre-crisis allocation. When a school's billets were re-funded, which generally meant through fundraising, the billets could be redirected by the dean. Some of the growth in Computer Science certainly came from that ability to move billets around.

We were fairly flexible with respect to junior faculty appointments. If a department had a strong case for a junior faculty appointment and believed that it was a good appointment and provided strong supporting evidence, we would generally be fairly permissive about letting the department assess the level of risk they were willing to take for a particular candidate. Sometimes they would take a higher risk on a candidate that was either an underrepresented minority or woman or was in a field that they really wanted to move into. Those things are fine.

Obviously, tenure is a big decision. That's the one that much of the deliberation would focus on and where the provost would be, in the end, a key decision maker. I think of tenure cases as falling into one of three piles. You can identify easy "yes" cases right away. Easy "no" cases are ones the department should not put forward. We tried to encourage the departments or the deans to make those tough decisions on their own. We pushed back on a small number of cases. There were some departments that had a habit of taking a straw poll. If the straw poll was in favor of tenure but a split vote, they would then agree to take a unanimous poll in one direction. But, of course, when people up the line read that case, they say, "Come on. There are things wrong with this, and you're not reflecting it." So, we tried to have a more transparent, honest system.

Of course, the hardest tenure cases are those in the middle, the ones that are right on the edge. I don't think there's any easy formula for looking at those. Sometimes the provost would do some extra due diligence. Sometimes the provost would send the case back and say, "I want additional letters from people to understand this case better." Ideally, the individuals closest to the candidate—their own department or the school—would make the tough decisions. That's clearly much better. You don't want to just be the veto person at the top.

Generally, our view was that a senior-level appointment should be extremely compelling, both in terms of quality and programmatic issues. If you're going for a senior-level appointment, that person should be critical—a department chair or an appointment in an area that is strategically critical to the university as a whole. Often, the president or the provost would end up meeting with those candidates. Generally, the departments have very high thresholds around those senior appointments, so it is more a question of "we're in recruiting mode" and trying to figure out the recruitment package. What the president and provost are often on the hook for, particularly for a senior appointment, is the starter package, because they're large. I think probably our largest packages were well into several million dollars in cases where the person was initiating a new program or building a new capability. That obviously is far beyond the resources that a department or even a school could manage on its own. Our strategy was everybody contributes. Before you come to the president, go to the department, go to the dean. Then you can come to the president or provost, so that everybody's got some skin in the game.

I think both the provost and I had a preference for junior appointments except where there was a leadership component that was desperately needed. We did that because people who come to the institution and grow up in it have a sense of loyalty and commitment to the institution that they simply don't have if they moved here two years ago.

DIFFERENCES ACROSS
ACADEMIC DISCIPLINES

Clearly the degree to which collaborative and solution-oriented approaches get traction varies across disciplines. The social sciences are undergoing dramatic transformation. The age of big data is changing their ability to do experiments and propose solutions to things in a way that they've never seen. Doing an experiment to investigate whether or not a school reform or local policy initiative is working was just impossible in the past because it took years or decades before you could evaluate the effect of the change. Now you can do it by running the experiment in reverse, finding surrogates from an earlier time to estimate the impact. Data-driven analysis is dramatically changing the social sciences.

It's been much harder to get some of the humanists engaged in seeking solutions. The humanities disciplines are trying to understand what their relevance is and how they can bring their disciplinary skills, which are often about deep understanding of complex human problems, to bear. They're not usually solution creators, but they bring a depth of analysis and knowledge to understanding how an approach may work in a particular setting. They've traditionally not been collaborative in their research model—a single-authored monograph is the standard publication unit, but they have a lot to contribute.

The role of graduate students is also very different across the university. If you think about engineering, which is the most graduate student–intensive discipline, it's a team. It's you and your graduate students. Whatever you're doing, especially if you're an experimentalist like I am, you're building stuff all together. At the other extreme, you have the humanities, where basically graduate students work solo. Faculty in engineering would be shocked if they saw how humanists worked with their graduate students. The faculty member certainly has oversight over the final thesis, but it's not anywhere near the collaboration that exists in engineering. Science and medicine are somewhere in between those extremes, closer to engineering than the humanities.

Evaluating faculty productivity across the disciplines has been one of the more interesting things for me. For example, in engineering or science, you think of people as most productive in their thirties, maybe early forties and then by that time they advance, they are overseeing a large group and providing wisdom. When they are just starting out, they'll get a best paper award or some other junior faculty award, so you have a pretty good indication of where people stand. While I couldn't give you a strict ordering among faculty, I could give you a lattice that shows where people were in terms of their stature and research contributions. But it's just the opposite in the humanities. People often do their greatest work when they're in their fifties or even sixties sometimes. It's hard to do the evaluations for careers that really are going to peak twenty years down the road. The work that I got the Turing Award for, I did basically from the time I was thirty-two to thirty-seven. Steve Chu's work that won the Nobel Prize, he did when he was in his early thirties. David Kennedy started his Pulitzer Prize-winning book when he was in his fifties and finished it in his sixties. Same thing for Jack Rakove's book. You have to have the patience to understand that difference and the difficulty it creates in how you evaluate people.[12]

So there are really cultural differences that are rooted in what careers are like in those disciplines. You have to understand those, respect them, and ask, "How do we move forward? How do we make any department better?"

I remember when I was in my presidential interview, one of the questions that came up was, "What would you do to make our humanities departments better?" The truth is, I'd only been provost for one year, and I didn't know the right answer. But it turned out there was somebody who knew the right answer, and that was John Etchemendy. When I was interviewing him for the provost job, he said, "During your interview, you gave this one answer about humanities that really wasn't very good." I said, "Yes. Well, what would you do to make the humanities better, John?" He said, "You make them better by making one great appointment at a time." That stuck in my head. That's certainly what you do in engineering, too, of course. You can create some other incentives, but in the end, it's the quality of the faculty appointments that are going to determine how good that department is.

EFFORTS TO EXPAND THE UNDERGRADUATE STUDENT BODY

For us, there were two issues related to increasing the number of undergraduates at Stanford. One, which the provost and I were very moved by, was the moral argument: the population of qualified students has expanded significantly, and Stanford hasn't expanded its undergraduate population. Why not? Second, in the U.S., state funding for public universities was decreasing (on a per capita basis), thereby preventing them from preparing more students. Although we felt that two-pronged argument was very strong, I'd say that it did not carry the day. Among our trustees, some bought it, but some didn't. Nor did it resonate with the faculty. Their view was, "So you add another 10 percent of students. It doesn't make any difference." My view was, "I'm going to talk to potential parents of that 10 percent and see what they think!"

In the end, what won over the trustees was that the graduate population had continued to expand, since it was not centrally controlled. The university that a current trustee had been at 30 years earlier had been maybe 55 percent undergraduate, 45 percent graduate students. Those ratios had been reversed: it had become 55 percent graduate students to 45 percent undergraduate students and was on its way to 60:40 if you gave it enough time. We either needed to start expanding the undergraduate class, or we were going to lose the opportunity to do it because we were going to have populated the campus with graduate students.

The other argument that helped, which I found very compelling, was our desire to have more international students in each class. If I could make that happen without taking fewer U.S. students, it would be a lot easier to sell to alumni who have to support it in the end and help us with the financial aid issues.

We started a faculty task force to look at expanding undergraduate enrollment, and then we had the 2008 financial crisis that set that back. Since then, we've done a little expansion. The other element to consider is: How big can you let the undergraduate population get before you lose some of the intimacy that is Stanford? Enrollment is about 7,000 now; it could be 8,000. It can't be 20,000, that's for sure.

In the future, I think we'll find other ways to leverage the university's capability rather than expansion. The residential, four-year undergraduate experience is deeply ingrained and won't change. Furthermore, there's not a lot of support for a B+ Stanford undergraduate education, such as might happen at a remote campus. You've got to scale differently. How do you best use the resources of the institution? Could you imagine a mechanism where you use faculty or graduate students in a different way, and could you use online education to replace the lecture hall? Perhaps the flipped classroom ideas are the right direction.

One of Stanford's biggest teaching successes is the Intro CS course. It has about 600 students a quarter and ranks in the top five courses in the university, partly because of the way it's taught. There are conventional large lectures, which are outstanding. Equally important are the section leaders who are undergraduates who have recently taken the course and done well, and taken another course to prepare them to teach. Each section leader works with a group of ten undergrads. The big problem in a programming course is if you miss a concept in week 2, you are in real trouble, since week 3 builds on week 2. You can avoid that pitfall when there are only ten people around the table working on a problem, talking about how to solve it. It works phenomenally well. Perhaps this is a model for expanding Stanford's reach.

ROLE OF UNIVERSITY LEADERS: "SERVING THE WORLD"

I think there are some similarities between political leadership and university leadership. I remember the former president of the University of Oregon who had previously been state attorney general—wonderful guy. He said, "University presidents are like politicians in that you have to run for sheriff." You're basically in a semi-elected office in a university. When you look at the failures of university presidents, ignoring scandals where there is misbehavior, most presidents fail because the faculty revolt. It's much more rare that it's a trustee or regent mismatch with the president; it happens, but it's rare. You cannot compel a tenured faculty to do something; you don't have a lot of sticks in a university, but you have a few carrots. So, in that sense, university leadership does model some of the difficulties that politicians have. Like some other leadership roles, you have a complex objective function, especially compared to a corporation. In a university, you are striving for excellence and optimizing the university's reputation across many dimensions and over a long time span.

Another similarity is how leaders respond to crisis situations, which are bound to occur. A lot of political leaders that I've read about have faced really big crises, such as civil wars. How a leader faces up to those difficult situations and figures out how to navigate them is important. One Silicon Valley CEO told me that the real test of leaders was not how they operated in good times, but how they lead in tough times.

One of the biggest challenges in university leadership is the breadth of constituencies that you serve: undergraduate and graduate students, faculty and staff, alumni, employers, and local and national political leaders. You have many stakeholders, and they have a particularly long-term focus. Corporations for many years focused primarily on their shareholders, but that is changing with the so-called stakeholder model. These days

CEOs and boards are not only thinking about their shareholder's interest, but also about the interests of employees, customers, and the community in which they live. In the business world, had leaders maintained a focus on long-term value and outcomes, we wouldn't have gotten so focused on quarterly returns and shareholder returns. A few corporations were smart enough to protect against that to some extent, but even so, all business leaders feel some pressure from quarterly returns. Although university leaders certainly like short-term outcomes, it is the long-term trajectory of the university that matters most.

There's a really negative trend that's occurred, not only in U.S. politics, but globally. One of our alums who was a four-term senator said to me, "When I first went to the Senate, I went not only as a representative of my state but also as a servant of all the people in the country. Now I'm asked to represent just the people in my party in my state." And that's a real difference. There's this great quotation by Abraham Lincoln. When he ran for his first elected office in the House of Representatives, he said something to the effect of, "I'd love for you to vote for me, but I will represent all the people of Sangamon County whether or not you voted for me." Now we are in this political deadlock because people don't cross the aisle anymore. They vote in the narrow interests of what somebody says is in the interest of their party.

By contrast, university leaders increasingly serve the world. They have the advantage in that they are not beholden to a political party. In an earlier time, I think universities had influence in Washington at that level. This occurred during the Obama administration when a number of people moved into government service from the university setting. There was engagement there, as there was during the Clinton era. But if you go back to the World War II and post–World War II eras, university presidents were often important allies who helped national leaders create plans for dealing with the crisis and for the future.

It's certainly not like that anymore, though maybe there's a new alliance on the horizon. Maybe it's the people at the university who are trying to figure out sustainability, working with the State of California, working with the Chinese government, working with other communities at different local levels, and working with NGOs. There may be a different model emerging for how we get things done and how universities improve our world. Maybe the partnerships don't cover entire countries. Maybe it's more localized. You work bottom-up. You work with communities. You go to a state like Florida or a city like New York that's going to be under water if they don't do something about climate change, and you begin to think about new alliances.

You cannot manufacture your way out of the climate crisis. If you think about the sustainability problem, I have no doubt that technology is going to be part of the solution. But it is not going to get there fast enough and at scale soon enough without policies that help push new sustainable technologies along and that also limit the use of nonsustainable technologies that were subsidized in an earlier era. This presents a new challenge for our universities: We know how to capitalize on a scientific discovery or a technology that can make an important contribution if it is commercialized. Policy is a much harder thing. How do you get that policy change to occur? I suspect we will need to form new alliances with NGOs, with governments at all levels, and with corporations, if we are to address some of the toughest problems we face.

CHAPTER 2

JOHN ETCHEMENDY

Provost of Stanford University (2000–2017)

John W. Etchemendy is an American logician and philosopher who served as Stanford University's twelfth provost. He succeeded John L. Hennessy to the post on September 1, 2000, and stepped down on January 31, 2017. He is the Patrick Suppes Family Professor in the School of Humanities and Sciences. He received his PhD from Stanford University in 1982 and joined the Department of Philosophy as a faculty member in 1983.

Background

I had done some administration at Stanford prior to becoming provost. I was senior associate dean for the humanities and arts in the School of Humanities and Sciences (H&S). I had stepped down from that and had gone back to my department and had no desire to go back into administration. In fact, at one point the then president and provost, Gerhard Casper and Condi Rice, asked me to be dean of H&S and I refused. I was not interested in doing more administration. I had done administration for five years, and that was plenty. I wanted to go back to research and teaching and my department, which I did. I was chair of the department, so it's not as if I was not doing some administration. But I thought I was done doing wider university administration.

Anyway, at some point a search committee was put together to find a successor to President Gerhard Casper. When we do search committees here at Stanford, it's the trustees' responsibility to appoint a president. Our trustees have a tradition—which I think is very good—of forming a committee that consists of half trustees and half faculty. They also have a few students. That's not always done at universities. But I think it's a very important thing that our trustees do because so much of the success of the president is determined by the faculty and whether the president is respected by the faculty.

The chair of that committee is a trustee, but they ask one of the faculty members to be the co-chair—actually, a chair and a vice-chair is what they call it. Anyway, they asked me to do that. I was the vice-chair of that search committee for the new president. The search for a president takes an awfully long time—many months. I don't remember how long it took, but it was probably on the order of five months of work.

In the course of doing that, it opened my eyes to a number of things. First of all, you get to know the university much more broadly than you might otherwise because you have faculty on the committee from all over. You also interview faculty and you see the breadth of the university in ways that you might not have otherwise, and you realize that Stanford is a very impressive university. That allowed me to appreciate the university in a way that I hadn't so much before.

The second thing you do is you talk to a lot of peers in higher education around the world, partly because you want to get input from them, and partly because you're looking at possible candidates, too. In the course of doing that, you come to realize how important leadership is and how much of an effect and impact the president of the university can have, good or bad. That's something that is not always obvious to faculty. So, during this year on the search committee I came to appreciate and love Stanford in a way that I might not have before. I've always been a Stanford partisan, but I began to appreciate the importance of leadership.

I say all of that because it was that experience that prepped me for becoming provost. After we selected John Hennessy and he agreed to be president, he obviously had to find a new provost. The way Stanford did a search committee for the provost at that time is that they never interviewed candidates. They presumably talked to a lot of people and got input, but I certainly wasn't one of them. I gather the committee recommended to John that he ask me to be provost. John called me in one day. I already knew him as a faculty member, and I had gotten to know him a bit better as part of the search committee. Anyway, he called and said, "John, could you come in and talk to me tomorrow?" I had no idea what he wanted to talk about, but he asked me whether I would be provost. It was a complete surprise. Had I not had that experience on the search committee that year, I don't know what my answer would have been.

As it was, I found it was an easy answer, and the reason for that is you can have an effect on the institution. However good my research is, I'm a logician—I'm not going to cure cancer, for example. The impact of my research, however positive it was, would be dwarfed by the potential impact of what I could do as provost at this university if I could just improve this university a little bit. At that point, it was an easy decision, and so I agreed to be provost.

Growing into the Provost Role

The role of provost at Stanford is a lot of work. Every provost is a chief academic officer. I was also the chief budget officer, so I was responsible for the budget for the whole university, both administrative and academic. I also did the capital planning, so all the decisions about what buildings were built and where they were built and so forth came under me. It was a pretty substantial role.

The learning curve was kind of vertical. The only thing that I really knew how to do was faculty appointments. I had done that as a department chair, and I had been on the advisory board, which is a committee that looks at all appointments and promotions across the university. That was the part of the role that I understood and knew how to do.

However, the first budget I ever created in my life was a $3 billion budget. That's a very significant learning curve. Obviously, capital planning I had not done before. And you're overseeing an incredibly diverse university. You have everything from the Athletic Department to the dean of religious life, to the hospital, to the Medical School. The learning curve was vertical. It was three years before I really felt I understood what I was doing.

What happens in the interim? Why doesn't the university fall apart? The university doesn't fall apart because you have great staff in place, and staff bridge that divide—whether it be the budget office or the people in charge of land and buildings, and so on. Eventually, you come to understand the process well and you start making decisions, but that takes a few years before you get to that place. So, it was hard. The first year almost killed me, literally.

BUILDING THE LEADERSHIP TEAM

When you become provost, you inherit the deans and vice provosts that are in place. A university is unlike, say, if you become president of the United States and you appoint all of the cabinet members and so forth. You don't have a clean slate. You work with the people that are in place, and you make changes incrementally. At Stanford, we generally have deans on a five-year contract, and then they can be reappointed a second time. In some exceptional cases, they can go on for even more than ten years, but we try to limit it to about ten years and sometimes we limit it to five years, which is good, because you don't want to suddenly have to appoint a whole bunch of new leaders.

Let me tell you something about what I think we achieved. Particularly in the early years, one of the most important things that John and I achieved was getting a leadership team that really pulled together, that viewed themselves as university leaders first and foremost and, secondarily, in charge of a particular school. That's unusual. I had known a lot of universities where, say, the dean of the law school or the dean of the medical school will see themselves as first and foremost the leaders of their school, and the relationship with the rest of the university is often contentious. They often view it as a zero-sum game; they are in it to make sure that they get all the resources they can for their school, and that's at the cost of other deans. That creates a lot of tension and in-fighting.

We had a fair amount of that at the beginning. We did not have deans that viewed themselves as co-authors who were part of the university leadership. What I did was select a new group of deans and made sure that they were people who understood that the goal was to build the strongest Stanford that we could. We expected them to be a team willing to help each other. Building the strongest university that we could would enable us to build the strongest schools. For example, part of what makes the Law School strong at Stanford is that you can tap into the entirety of the university. It's the same with the Medical School. It is strong in part because of the strength of the university as a whole and the fact that you can draw on Stanford's strengths in engineering or in law or in business.

I used to say when I started that our goal was to build one university as opposed to a collection of schools. I think the main mechanism we used to do that was to ensure the deans didn't view their roles that way. We slowly replaced those deans with people who we very explicitly chose based upon whether or not they understood that they were joining as members of a university leadership group, as opposed to a school leadership position. That's actually one of the best things that John and I did.

Think, then, about what we built on top of that. A lot of people notice that we have very effective interdisciplinary work at Stanford. We have interdisciplinary research institutes across different schools, and that is made possible by the fact that there is not this competition between the schools. There aren't these battle lines between schools.

Another example is when a dean is recruiting a faculty member. Often, when one school is recruiting a faculty member, their spouse may be a faculty member in another discipline. If the dean for that other discipline is willing to help make that hire, then you can get people to Stanford who you wouldn't otherwise be able to get. So, the kinds of cooperation we got between the deans really helped to build the strength of the faculty.

VISION FOR THE UNIVERSITY

When John and I started, we didn't have a vision for the university. It's hard to have a vision for a place so big and diverse as a university, particularly when we had inherited a very strong institution. We wanted to make it stronger, but that in itself is not a vision.

One of the first things we did was launch what we called a needs assessment. It was a year-long process where we asked, "What do we need at the university to make it the strongest university possible?" Through that process, a couple of things became apparent. One was that one of the great strengths of Stanford, which not many universities have, is that we have a breadth of strong disciplines across the board. Secondly, we're located on a very compact campus. Harvard has an amazing breadth of strengths, but you have one school that's on the other side of the river and another that's a little over here, and the medical school is spread around Boston. So, you don't have the kind of compact campus that we have at Stanford. In addition, we have nice weather, and so it's easy to walk from one part of the campus to another. That has a big impact on people's ability to collaborate. For somebody in the Law School to collaborate with somebody in the Medical School, they can easily walk from one place to the other in ten to fifteen minutes, even though they are on opposite sides of the campus. That's quite an asset that we have that distinguishes Stanford from a lot of places.

So, how do you use that asset? One way is by promoting interdisciplinary work, because we are in such a good position to do that. In the course of the needs assessment, we had one committee that was looking at the main requirements for each of the schools, so the schools could discuss their needs, and whether we needed a building for such and such. But then we also had a committee looking at the university more globally, and what kinds of initiatives the university should pursue for the future. That committee came up with a number of different suggestions, in particular, the main interdisciplinary pushes that we ended up deciding to pursue. It was a combination of all of these things that led to the interdisciplinary focus that arose.

Structures to Support Collaboration

Something that people actually don't notice or don't recognize from the outside is that at so many universities, there are barriers to interschool collaborations—whether they be in research or teaching—because the individual schools are financially separate. At Harvard, for example, each school is "a tub on its own bottom." It has its own finances. It collects its own tuition and collects its own indirect cost recovery. Or at a place like Penn [the University of Pennsylvania], all of the funds are collected from each school and are allocated via what is called a resource-based management calculation. That can be a disaster for a university because it erects barriers against any kind of cross-school collaboration. For example, if you have faculty members from two schools who want to collaborate by co-teaching a course, you have to first negotiate who gets credit. Who gets the tuition for the students to take that course? You have to have some way of allocating that tuition to the various faculty that are teaching in that course. If you get a grant and you have principal investigators from two or three schools, you have to figure out how to allocate the indirect cost recovery to the various schools.

Those are very difficult questions. It puts a barrier in place; it puts a friction in place for anything that crosses the school boundaries. That is one thing that we have managed to completely get rid of at the university. Most of the funding comes in centrally, and then it's allocated based on the school's needs. So, the school comes to the provost and says, "This is what our goals are. We have a certain amount of money that we can put toward those goals. We would like to ask for some incremental general funds to allow us to pursue them." For historical reasons, the funding models for the School of Medicine and the Graduate School of Business are more formulaic, more like the Penn model.

The benefit of this is that every school and every administrative unit comes through the same process. It comes to the provost. I had a group reporting to me that examined all the budget requests and made recommendations. The decision making at the end is not done by any kind of counting of how many students are being taught, or counting where the grants are sitting, or anything of that sort. People don't have to worry about that and that takes away those barriers.

Once you've taken away the barriers, then the "cat food model" works.[13] The question therefore becomes: How do you provide the additional incentive to faculty? Based on the above, I've taken away the barriers for interdisciplinary work. How do I actually make it happen? It's fairly easy to do it via fairly simple incentives.

Having said that, there are important subtleties here. We provide incentives, but this is not an incentive-based system. It is not as if we provide funds based on any kind of incentive measure. What are people's incentives? First of all, you hire people who come with their own incentives: they want to do research, and they want to teach. If they don't have those built-in motivations, then you don't give them tenure. When you do have top people, then you just let them thrive and you provide what you can, but you don't do it by incentive. You don't say, "If you teach more, then I'm going to hire more people." You leave that decision up to the department chair.

Funding Building Projects on Stanford's Campus

The question of sequencing, and hence prioritization, of building projects is a multifactor kind of consideration. Sometimes it has to do with when we can tear down an existing building in order to replace it with another. You have to work things out logistically, purely logistically.

Another thing that can determine the priorities is the availability of funds. Our goal in building an academic building is generally, if you can raise half of the money from donations, then that's very good and then the rest you can do with debt or with reserves. So, your goal is to ideally raise about half of the funds for any building from donors. You do this based on what is possible. With some buildings, you can raise 80 percent of the funds from a donor, and in rare cases, 100 percent from a donor. The Knight Management Center at the Graduate School of Business is a good example. It was 100 percent funded through donations. The Stanford Institute for Economic Policy Research's new building was also 100 percent donor funded.

The more you can do that, the more you can allocate university resources to things that are more difficult to raise funds for—such as some things in the School of Humanities and Sciences, and even some of the things within Engineering, which require more of a subsidy.

In the case of our buildings plan, one of the pressing needs that John and I had when we started was that we had an aging science and engineering and medical campus. So, we had what we called the SEMC project: the Science, Engineering, and Medical Campus. That included all of the buildings that now are in the engineering quad. It included the new biology building, the chemistry building, and several new medical buildings—part of the payment of that depended upon the availability of donors.

RESPONSE TO THE GLOBAL FINANCIAL CRISIS

The financial crisis transpired quickly as these things go, given that universities move at a fairly deliberate pace. It was pretty clear at a certain point that we were going to have to make cuts and that those were going to be fairly significant. We didn't know exactly how much the cuts would have to be. But it was clear to John and me very early that it was going to be toward the big end. The endowment went down about 25 percent, and that meant that there was going to be an overall budget cut of about 10 to 15 percent to the overall funding for the university.

We decided we needed to do that all at once. The way the endowment works is there's a smoothing function, so we could have let the endowment pay out. Ordinarily, if we had used the regular smoothing function, the payout would have declined each year for about five to seven years, about 4 to 5 percent each year. So, we could have taken a series of 5 percent cuts and done it that way, and it would have eased the blow in some sense. But we decided very early on that we weren't going to do that and that we were going to make the cuts in effect all at once.

That choice was guided by the following considerations. First of all, if you take, say, a 20 percent cut, and you do it all at once, you make different cuts and you think more strategically than if you take four 5-percent cuts. If you drag it out and do smaller cuts, you try to do belt tightening. You start by saying, "We're going to stop doing parties, and we're all going to be very careful about the Xerox paper. Everybody is going to buy their own whatever." But those are generally not sustainable cuts, because the spending all comes back. And then the following year you try to do a little bit more, and in the end, you get to an unsustainable position that is not strategically driven. We believed that the right way to make cuts was to look at what you do and say, "What piece of what we do can we do without?" and cut that piece as opposed to cropping it. The only way you're going to do that is by thinking strategically and doing a major cut rather than the succession of slices. We decided that was what we were going to do. That was the first reason: that the cuts would be more strategic.

The second reason was that if you drag out the cuts, you're going to end up four, five years out and you're going to be cutting and the economy is going to be great and all the faculty are going to be saying, "Why are we cutting? Why is this university doing this? The economy's great. What's going on here?" When you take the larger cuts right after and during the financial crisis, people are behind you. One of the things we did was we froze salaries. John Hennessy and I took 10 percent salary cuts, and the deans voluntarily took 5 percent salary cuts, and then we froze salaries across the board of everybody in the university.

We have 13,000 employees. I did not receive one complaint about that decision. Why? Because people understood that it had to be done. People saw that we were taking cuts ourselves, but people understood the need to stop spending. We wanted to do the cuts when people understood and would back the cuts, not down the road when people would resent them and say, "Why is this university being so stingy when the endowment is doing so well?"

We made those cuts through the usual budget process. The way the general budget process works at the university is that every single unit comes and presents its budget requests, and then the Budget Group makes the final decisions about what they should get or what they should cut.[14] In this case, since we were cutting and we were not allocating incremental funds, each individual dean or vice provost or vice president (that is, from the nonacademic units) came in and said, "Here's how we're going to take a 5 percent or 10 percent or 15 percent cut." And then the Budget Group decided. We actually made them present those alternatives and then decided, "This unit can take a 15 percent cut," or "This unit can't take a 15 percent cut, we're going to give it a 5 percent cut."

Financial Aid and the Student Body

Around the same time, in 2008, just before the global financial crisis, we had changed our financial aid program at Stanford. We made it much more generous, and so that made the cuts even more difficult because we had just incurred this much larger financial obligation. However, early on we made the decision not to reduce that commitment. We held fixed our promises on our financial aid. That was during the financial crisis.

More broadly, John and I did think long and hard about the fact that Stanford had such an incredible undergraduate education program, and yet we were turning down such vast numbers of really highly qualified people. We decided that we would try to the extent possible to increase the size of the undergraduate class slowly so that we could provide a Stanford education to a broader group of students.

That goal was constrained, first of all, by available housing. We needed to build additional housing. It was also constrained by the need to maintain the feel of the undergraduate experience. My view is that there are different sizes of student body and that you get different kinds of "feel." In a small liberal arts college, every undergraduate knows everyone in their given class. So that's one feel.

We don't have that at Stanford. We're too big for that. But another increment is where you still feel like you're in a community and you may not know everybody in your class, but you recognize them. You see them in classes and when you walk around campus. You see a lot of people that you know or recognize, and that has a particular feel.

By contrast, you can also get somewhat bigger, like maybe UC Berkeley. That has a very different feel. It feels more like a city where you might walk around for a large portion of the day and not see anybody you know. Then, every once in a while, you run into somebody that you do know.

Each of these sizes has a kind of different character, and the education that you can provide will be different depending on the size of the student body. We did not want to change the character of the undergraduate experience, so then the question was: How big can it be and still have that same feel? How big can it be so that you still feel like it's a community and you know most of the people in your undergraduate class?

When we started, Stanford was about 6,500 undergraduates. We thought that we could probably push it to around 8,000 and still have that feel, and so our goal was to move it in that direction towards 8,000. I don't think it is at 8,000 now, but that was the thought.

Thoughts on Press Coverage of Campus Sexual Assaults

There were a lot of changes in higher education during my time as provost. One that might be worth pointing out was a set of very significant changes on the Title IX front.[15] In 2013, the Department of Education's Office of Civil Rights issued what is known as a "Dear Colleague" letter in which they set out their expectations for how college campuses should be adjudicating sexual assault cases. This letter required every college in the country to completely revise its disciplinary process. It effectively required universities to be investigator, prosecutor, and judge on assault cases, but without giving us the requisite legal power, such as the ability to subpoena witnesses, to do this effectively.

That led to a very difficult time for universities across the country, and it was very difficult for, I think, reasons that people did not really understand. A lot of people, students, parents, and the press, felt that universities were trying to hide the presence of sexual assault to protect their reputations. That's absolute nonsense. Everybody knows that sexual assault happens, and it happens at every university. It happens because of the age of the students; it happens because they're away from their parents for the first time; it happens because of the residential character of many campuses. You have to figure out ways to decrease the incidence of it—to teach your students about affirmative consent and the importance of communicating clearly your wishes and intentions. But the idea that, say, a Stanford or Harvard or any other university would want to hide the fact that sexual assaults happen is crazy.

What is true is the following: The vast majority of assault cases on campuses are not clear-cut. It's not a stranger coming on campus and raping somebody in a dark alley. These are usually cases where the students know each other, they may even have dated or been intimate before, and there are often very different perceptions about whether anything unconsensual occurred. This is why educating students about affirmative consent is so important. But the university is required to adjudicate these cases and to decide between the accuser and the accused.

So some decision is made: either the accused is found to be responsible for sexual assault or is found not to be responsible. Invariably, one or the other party comes away from the process very unhappy. It can be either one: the person who was allegedly assaulted because the process didn't find that it was an assault, so "the university didn't believe me." Or it can be the person who allegedly committed the assault, who feels that "this was clearly consensual" and "I am being unfairly punished and my reputation is destroyed." One party or the other is always unhappy and generally blames it on the process itself.

Next comes the press—the *New York Times, Washington Post,* CBS News, CNN—who love to write a story when a student says, "I was assaulted, and the university didn't believe me. My assailant went free." Or a student says, "I was accused of sexual assault, and I was railroaded. I was not given due process. It was a horrible experience and very unfair." The reporter loves this and gets a lot of input about one side of the story. But the other party won't talk to them because they don't want the publicity. Then the press comes to the university and asks questions about the case. And the university by law—by FERPA, by the student privacy law—cannot say a single thing about the details of the case or the details of the adjudication.[16] So the one-sided story is published, and the university inevitably looks like it is doing a terrible job or hiding something.

And so, through that whole period, you will notice that every major university in the country was tarred and feathered by the press on this issue. The explanation was, "That's because they're all trying to hide this. They're all worried about their reputation, so they're trying to hide the fact that there is sexual assault on campus." And that is just not true. What's true is that the Office of Civil Rights has given universities a task that the U.S. judicial system, with all its resources and power, cannot or will not handle.

REFLECTIONS ON WORKING WITH
JOHN HENNESSY

I can't imagine a better working relationship than we had. This must have happened over the course of time. It didn't start that way. We did know each other as faculty members—not well, but we knew each other, so that probably helped. But over the course of time, we had complete respect for each other and each other's judgment. What that meant was that in some ways, it didn't matter who was making a decision on a particular thing. So sometimes something would come up—maybe a faculty member was being recruited and wanted a particular kind of retention package. Depending on the area, depending on who had the most work at the particular time, I might handle that, or John might handle that—"You've got that, John, you can take care of it," or "I'll take care of it"—and we just trusted each other to do what was right. We communicated an awful lot. Our offices were down the hall from one another. He and I met one-on-one officially every week. In addition, every week, we would have a meeting of the administrative leadership plus us, and we would a have meeting of the academic leadership plus us. So, we were seeing each other many hours each week, and we got a lot of work done that way.

President John Hennessy and Provost John Etchemendy at work in the President's Office in Building 10.

We also shared the responsibility. For example, I had a set of direct reports, and John had a set of direct reports. The vice presidents reported to him; the vice provosts and deans reported to me. But when it came to time for salary setting, we would do it together for the whole group. So, it really was a partnership. John is an incredibly talented guy, and I just enjoyed working with him the entire time.

Finishing as Provost

I really thought that I had the best job in higher education, and I still think that. The best job in U.S. higher education, at least, is the provost position at Stanford—not the president position, but the provost position. That's because you get to see the entirety of the university and at a depth and detail that even the president does not see. That is because you are reading every appointment file and every promotion file. You are understanding all the goals and aims of all the deans because they're coming through the budget process. And similarly with the administrative side—you know what the Alumni Association is doing, what the Development Office is doing. It's an amazing perspective that you get on the university. You realize what remarkable things are being done across the university, in teaching and in research, and are trying to make things better for all of those people and trying to bring up the quality of the entire institution. I can't imagine a more meaningful job.

Having said what a wonderful job it was, and how meaningful it was, and the best job in higher education, I have not for one single instant wished that I still had it. That may seem inconsistent, but there's a way in which it gets harder after a while. It starts off very hard because you don't know what you're doing—you're learning and so forth. And then you feel on top of things, and you can make strategic decisions. You understand the university and know what levers there are. But then it gets harder again. Partly it gets harder because you are seeing things you have seen before and you sometimes know the right answer to it quickly, so rather than bring the faculty along, you think you know what the right answer is, and so you become impatient. You've seen this kind of case over and over again, and you know how it's going to turn out, and you know what the right thing to do is. So, you are impatient with people who have not seen it before and don't know what the right answer is. There's a way in which that gets harder as you become more and more capable, and that's dangerous. It's dangerous to be in that position because you have a tendency to make decisions too fast, to consult people less, and that's not a good thing. It's harder to do the job, and at a certain point, it's time for a new group of leaders.

CHAPTER 3

JEFF WACHTEL

Special Assistant to President John Hennessy
(2000–2016)

Executive Director, Knight-Hennessy
Scholars Program (2016–2019)

Jeff Wachtel received his undergraduate degree from Stanford in 1979. He returned to Stanford as a staff member in 1985, serving in various administrative roles over a period of thirty-five years, including as chief of staff to John Hennessy during his years as provost and president. In 2017, Wachtel received the Cuthbertson Award for exceptional service to the university. The award citation acknowledged his "deep humanism and problem-solving skills."

Coming to Stanford as an Undergraduate

I was born and raised in New York City. I spent a year at a Greek high school as an exchange student. There was a terrific group of college students who came over to do an archaeological expedition. It was led by a professor in classics from Stanford, Isabelle Raubitschek.[17] I think I would have been excited and enthralled with any college students I met at that point in my life, but since they were all from Stanford, I thought, "This is the place for me." I decided that if I could be accepted to Stanford, that's where I wanted to go. The only real recruitment was when I got my letter of admission that had a nice little handwritten note on the bottom. I learned a lot from that. I learned about personalizing things that were otherwise impersonal. When I received the envelope from Stanford, it was done with such flair. It was an easy decision for me.

I had a remarkable experience my first quarter. It was a class taught by Phil Zimbardo on the psychology of shyness.[18] We developed a shyness clinic, and we did a lot of work in the dorms to get people to feel more comfortable with who they were. So at the very beginning of my undergraduate career, I was introduced to research. I thought that was absolutely a normal thing at Stanford.

I had this idea of combining psychology and urban planning, because psychology seemed important in the development of cities—how people live with each other and how they interact with each other. Before it was in vogue, I was doing multidisciplinary work. I thought I'd go on to be an urban planner, but I was also interested in law school. It turns out planning school wasn't quite as exciting as I thought it would be, but I loved law school. It trained me to get to the essence of what's important.

Forging Connections at the University as a Staff Member

I practiced law for a couple of years with a small firm in Palo Alto. It was litigation, and I was doing things that weren't all that rewarding or fulfilling. I was looking at jobs just to see what else was out there, and I saw this position at Stanford. It was for a city manager–type role in the Faculty Staff Housing Office. I thought, "Well, what do I have to lose?" So I applied, and the person who interviewed me was Robin Hamill—who later became Robin Kennedy—who also had a background in law and city planning.[19] She thought it was an interesting combination of skills and that I was just right. So, I made the move back to Stanford. I was happy to be back.

On the main Stanford campus, there are over 600 single-family homes. The people who live on campus pay ground rent to the university, and Stanford provides the services. My office was also a quasi-building department. If residents wanted to remodel, they would come to us for approval. When faculty wanted to buy a home, they would come through us. We got to know the residents pretty well, and people would call us about virtually anything. It was a sort of personalized small-town environment on the good days, and on the bad days, we were a complaint department. When the university decided to prohibit dog walking at the Dish, a popular open space in the foothills, people came to my home with their dogs, knocked on the door, and said, "How could you keep this beautiful, friendly dog from walking in the Dish?"

Before I even started the job, I attended a homeowners' meeting about the eucalyptus trees that were in the faculty subdivision. The Grounds Department had determined that they might fall, and Robin thought that we should remove them. When I arrived at the meeting, Robin said, "Here is the person who will be handling this going forward." And then everything erupted. Maybe more than half the people didn't want the trees removed. "We love these trees." And there was a professor there who knew everything about the eucalyptus trees. He said, "You can't take them down. They're not dangerous." And he went through each species. We ended up having impartial experts evaluate each tree to determine which trees were dangerous and which were not. That was the beginning of my education that there wasn't an issue that there wasn't an expert on at Stanford. So, it was tough to go toe to toe on virtually any issue.

I can't say that I wasn't frustrated at the time or that I didn't lose sleep, but there was great satisfaction in resolving those kinds of conflicts. Just meeting the people and getting to know them better outside of the issue made it all worthwhile. In almost every case, the people that I encountered in these difficult situations, I encountered again in a happier, more pleasant situation, and it really opened the door. I think there was a mutual trust and respect that developed, and it helped me to take on other responsibilities as I went forward.

One of the best parts of the Faculty Staff Housing Office was meeting with faculty during the recruitment process. How do you get people to move to a place where they're going to have to reduce the size of their home or spend so much of their income on housing? That was where the art came in. We had a number of loan programs, and I would explain the tax advantages to people and talk about the intellectual community here and the wonderful outdoor living space on the campus. I knew that when somebody came to the office, that was somebody the university wanted. If I could play a role in getting them to come to Stanford, then I'd done something to support the academic enterprise.

After a few years, I was ready to try something new. I played with undergraduates on an intramural basketball team. One of the students told me about this new adult education program that his father, Marsh McCall, was going to be heading up.[20] I met Marsh and liked him, and we started the Continuing Studies Program. We put together a very small offering of courses. I knew all the faculty that we invited to teach. It took a while to get it going. It was like a start-up business, and we were living on the edge whether we were going to make it financially. We had a deficit, which was funded from the Provost's Office. We eliminated that fairly soon though because we did a takeover—it wasn't a hostile takeover—of the summer session. That allowed us to spread out our administrative costs. We managed the summer school also, and then we no longer needed the subsidy.

MOVING FROM THE PROVOST'S OFFICE TO THE PRESIDENT'S OFFICE

I met John Hennessy in the interview for the position to be his sort of chief of staff when he was appointed provost in 1999.

I didn't really know anything about him other than he'd been dean of the School of Engineering. I had worked with Condi Rice quite a bit when she was provost, so I knew something about the office, but did not know John. I remember he was quite late for the interview, and I was sitting in Building 10—the President's and Provost's Offices—waiting and actually getting a little frustrated, waiting for so long and thinking, "Do I really want to work here?" And then he came in with a lot of energy, and I understood why he was late, and we seemed to hit it off right away. He was able to help me shed some of those moments of frustration pretty quickly.

I started with him in the Provost's Office. My sense was that he wanted somebody who knew the university, who had a lot of experience at the university and could step right in and figure things out—not with any specific tasks in mind, but just somebody who could be there to help out on just about anything that came up. Given how well I knew so many of the faculty and students, and I had been a student and had worked on the academic side of things, I think that seemed appealing to him.

I worked on a few searches for deans during that period of time. That seemed to take up a lot of our energy. We did not use a professional search firm. First, we pulled together a committee of people representing different areas of the school and people who had the respect of their colleagues, so when a decision was made, people would have confidence in that decision. It was very clear, though, that the committee wasn't there to choose a dean. The committee was there to make recommendations. The assignment was to give two or three acceptable candidates for the position—giving the provost the flexibility to make the final decision. So, it was really set up as an advisory committee.

There are different ways to source candidates. We first looked at whether there was anything special in terms of responsibilities that we wanted to describe or a particular focus. For the search for the dean of the School of Medicine, for example, we needed somebody who could bring the basic science people and the clinical people together. We tried to surface names of people that were worth considering, and we called people to get suggestions. Then we started to discuss names as a committee.

It was highly confidential. People sometimes wanted to see a search be more public and have candidates give presentations and talk to the community. Well, that would have eliminated a number of people who didn't want to be seen as looking for another position. So, confidentiality was a really key point in those searches.

When John made the move to the President's Office in 2000, it wasn't a complete surprise. When we learned that Gerhard Casper was stepping down, a lot of people thought John might be in line for the presidency, although he had only been doing the provost's job for a relatively short time. But he didn't signal that in any way. In fact, he was very good about keeping things close to the vest—not sharing too much—so it was a bit of a surprise when it actually all happened.

I was pretty good friends with Don Kennedy, a former president of Stanford.[21] He gave me a lot of advice when I moved along with John to the President's Office. He said, "First of all, always thank the president's spouse. The spouse doesn't typically get enough recognition or appreciation for what they do." And he said that it was important that people have a sense of how much the president is enjoying the role and how much the president cares about the university. Because oftentimes that doesn't come through. The president can't be everywhere all the time. He said, "You're the spokesperson. You're the person who can get out there and make sure that people know who John is as a person and the joy that he gets from doing the job even during the tough times." So, he really stressed the ambassadorial piece of my job, and how it was my obligation to represent John and to make him available to the public through me. It was great advice, and I followed it.

Approving New Initiatives with Presidential Discretionary Funds

One of the things that we implemented was a very different way of approaching funding for new initiatives. John was great at this; we were very nimble. We knew we had a large pot of money to work with, and so if a good idea came along, he wanted to approve things quickly to send the signal that he was excited about it and there was a sense of urgency. "Let's get going. This is a good thing to do." So, being able to communicate that to people—you have a great idea, we're willing to put money behind you, and let's get going—that made people feel really good about their projects. It wasn't a battle to get funding the way it typically is in most bureaucracies.

Dealing with these new funding initiatives was one of my major responsibilities. I believe the president has always had some discretionary funds to use. It's sort of a complicated form of budgeting exercise involving overflow. Once a certain fund was filled up with revenue from investments, the excess would go into a pool for the president's discretion. That built up quite a bit over time. When previous presidents had discretionary funds, they would get proposals, they would review the proposals, compare them against each other, and then decide which ones to fund. We were more fluid when it came to funding. We wanted to create this energy around these ideas and these proposals. So, it could come in on Monday, and if it met all the requirements, we could have an answer by Tuesday to fund it. That sends a really great message. Or, if we didn't fund it, we would say, "This is what you need to do to get funding."

There were a few things we looked for. One was some sharing in the funding—not because we didn't have the money to do it by ourselves, but things should ideally come from the bottom up at a university. We didn't want projects to be presidential initiatives. We wanted proposals to come from departments and from the faculty. So, we would say, "Look, we're happy to fund this, but we want to see some commitment from your department or from some other faculty research accounts." That would show that there was support beyond that of the President's Office. Otherwise, if it failed, it would be the president's failure. We wanted to see a sharing of responsibility.

The amount we expected others to contribute really varied. Often, we would fund half of a proposal, and they'd get 25 percent from one place and 25 percent from another place. We didn't want people to spend too much time running around chasing funds. The idea was to streamline the process, but we wanted to have meaningful buy-in. And it put the incentive in the right place for people to make progress on what they were trying to do.

The second thing we wanted to know, assuming a proposal succeeded, was how would the project be funded long term? Our funding was just interim funding. We wanted to see a plan for reducing the dependence on presidential funding. Then third was the time horizon for the project. If the proposal was only for one year, we would often send it back and say, "If you think this is such a good idea, don't you expect it will last more than one year? We want to see a three-to-five year proposal. We're happy to fund it for a longer period of time."

We didn't look over their shoulders while they were doing it. Previously, the person in my role looked over the numbers very closely and didn't fund things until they got the receipts to show how much had been spent. We started with the presumption that we had faith in everything that was being done by our faculty. We weren't always right, but we did that. We just gave the money that was asked for and sort of used the honor system. It became a less burdensome thing for people to get their ideas funded. The trust that we showed and the sense of excitement that we could convey around these proposals had people reporting back to us on a regular basis. It worked pretty well. It took a while to take hold, but the word got out. It was almost a venture philanthropy, venture funding approach.

We funded so many interesting things. Initially, we did some things supporting student initiatives. Eventually, we were getting lots of proposals from students, and we couldn't really make the decisions on those. So, we ended up giving block grants to the dean of students and let the dean of students make those decisions. But I do recall that there was a student who came to us to fund a project to bring Iraqi college students to Stanford for an exchange. It grew out of a seminar he took with Professor

Bill Perry, who had been secretary of defense.[22] It was focused on one-to-one diplomacy, and the student wanted to put this into action. Initially, I put up all these objections. I said, "How could you possibly do this? How could they get visas? Who's going to fund this? What if somebody defects?" I just saw so many problems.

He said, "Mr. Wachtel, if you fund this, we'll take care of all that. We've already been thinking about it." And they did. That was the last time I ever doubted the ability of a Stanford student to accomplish something. It was an incredibly successful program. Although it was a relatively small amount of money, it set an example for future cooperative programs of this kind—in the Middle East, in Asia, in Mexico. So, funding one thing early on helped start a whole bunch of other impactful programs. I have great memories of that.

Discretionary funds provided the impetus for interdisciplinary work—that was a big point of emphasis for John. We made it clear that we would support initiatives where there was cooperation across different schools. Bio-X received a lot of money from us in the early years. We put a lot of money into big neuroscience projects. We funded some of Karl Deisseroth's work early on. We helped fund the lab for a great young scientist named Marc Tessier-Lavigne with president's funds. He needed quite a substantial lab, so we helped with that. We would help with some key recruitments like that here and there.[23]

There were some examples of interdisciplinary work that were particularly appealing to me—maybe not as important for the university, but things that we funded that you would only see at Stanford. We funded a seminar with the St. Lawrence String

Quartet and constitutional scholars to talk about interpretation. The scholars debated whether you should be a strict constructionist or interpret the Constitution, and the St. Lawrence String Quartet did a comparative analysis interpreting Mozart and whether you should play Mozart as written on the page or interpret the music. It was typical that you'd see Biology and Computer Science and Engineering working together, but to get the Humanities working with the Law School, that was something that was a little different. We would support projects like that when there was interest from the faculty.

There wasn't a formal call for proposals. That may have been, in part, because the amount of money we had was so large that we weren't worried about running out. It was in excess of $100 million, although a big chunk of that did go by agreement with the provost to support financial aid for undergraduates. We also had additional funds from the sale of the Google stock. Those proceeds were used, I think, towards graduate student and faculty support. That was a substantial amount of money. It was $300 million, I believe, at the time. There were also individual funds where people had donated money for a particular purpose under trust agreements. The president had some discretion over how they were spent, given the restrictions within the documents.[24]

MEMORABLE MOMENTS AS THE PRESIDENT'S "AMBASSADOR"

In the President's Office, I felt like we were always on. I was often speaking with people, particularly from the Office of

Communications, well into the evening to get things done. And there were always weekend activities. There were a lot of evening events. I went to an incredible number of events either staffing John or representing John. It was fun. There was a lot of good stuff, but it was busy.

I often served as an ambassador for the president, and there were several memorable moments. I would meet with important people if John was away, like President Dmitry Medvedev, for example. I also met a lot of royalty. John said he was more interested in people who had earned their way to the top rather than who were born into their positions. I was out front, greeting people as they would come to the campus and working with the police and the FBI and sometimes the CIA and getting that all straightened out. I remember when David Miliband, who was the equivalent of the secretary of state for England, came. He is a big sports fan, and we took him to Stanford Stadium. Condi was there, and we were throwing a football around. I was thinking how incredible to see Condi and this other important figure throwing a football at Stanford Stadium. And he was trying to kick a field goal. That was really something.[25]

Commencement was another ambassadorial opportunity, working with the staff of the speaker and getting things just right for this important event. I suppose Steve Jobs's commencement speech in 2005 was the most memorable.[26] I think that speech set the tone for a lot of things at the university going forward. It was the basis for some of what we did at the Knight-Hennessy Scholars program. It was a great speech, and I'll never forget at the conclusion his kids came out to meet him and he said, "What did you think of the speech?" They said, "It was great!"

And he said, "Really?" He seemed kind of surprised that it was so well received. We told him he could keep the cap and gown. He hadn't graduated from college. So that was a good moment.

Steve Jobs, cofounder of Apple Computer, Inc., gave a memorable commencement address at Stanford in 2005. Front row from left, Provost John Etchemendy, Steve Jobs, and President John Hennessy.

When I say ambassadorial, it was also representing the president in situations where diplomacy was needed. So, I was known as the chief greeter for protesters. Whenever we had word of a protest coming to the President's Office, I would be the person who would be the spokesperson for the university and would get out there and represent John. That happened quite a bit, actually. We got better at it over time.

In the beginning, I was very nervous—in the middle of a crowd of people chanting at me. But I got used to it. I would ask who the spokesperson was and listen to them. And I tried to show respect. We tried to make sure that John wasn't in the building when they came so that I could honestly say, "He's not here to meet with you. And we usually schedule appointments, so let me know if you'd like to meet with him." I had respect and an appreciation for what the students were doing. I really, for the most part, liked that there was an interest in taking a stand on something.

I usually talked about the presumption of good intentions. I said, "You know, we don't get up in the morning every day and think how can we screw the students? I want you to know that if we make a mistake or if we do the wrong thing, we're not doing that intentionally. We make decisions that we think are the right decisions, and it's because we think it's in the best interest of the university." Sometimes that would be useful and sometimes it wouldn't. But I tried to get that idea across. We had to make what was the best decision for the university, not what was the most politically expedient.

Dealing with difficult correspondence was another aspect of my job. There were always questions around free speech and appointments of people who had controversial things to say or did controversial things, so I needed to respond to those. When the Hoover Institution appointed Donald Rumsfeld as a distinguished visiting fellow, there was great objection to that.[27] Then there was the Stanford Band. I mean, after every game, we'd get a whole series of letters regarding the halftime shows at the football games. Some positive, some negative. I had a fairly standard response on the Band: "You might be surprised to learn that the Band has some very talented musicians." One person I responded to wrote back to John and said, "I got a letter from your assistant, Jeff Wachtel, and he's not qualified to be the assistant dog catcher. He thinks the Band has some qualified musicians." So, when people would ask what my job was, John would tell them I was the dog catcher.

But I had some strange ones. I had a woman write that her cat had cancer, and she was having trouble getting treatment. What could we do to help with the cat? Typically, I think most people would say, "Well, we're not going to respond to that. It has nothing to do with the university." But I always wrote. That was the kind of ambassadorial work where it's the right thing to do, and you just never know how it would be of benefit in the future. We responded to every letter. Every Boy Scout who wanted to become an Eagle Scout would receive a letter for his scrapbook. We responded to all school kids with a personal letter.

But the difficult ones were mostly around free speech issues. On speech issues, John was very clear. He said, "We would rather shine a light on difficult speech rather than let it go underground. Expose it and respond to it. That is what you do at a university." That was very wise; I thought that was exactly the right way to handle it.

THOUGHTS ON THE NEW YORK CAMPUS AND THE ARTS INITIATIVE

In terms of special projects or initiatives, there was a flurry of activity around the New York campus. My main role was to co-chair a committee that was going to select the leadership for that campus. Things moved very quickly. There was a decision made to go forward because of the timing of the proposal. But then we had to do a lot of consultation sort of after the fact, talking to a lot of different people around campus. It was a difficult period because I think ultimately John's view was that the New York people wanted us to achieve certain milestones, and that's just not the way the university works. We couldn't get things done in the time that they wanted. It was just not possible to predict what was going to happen in the future with this, as with a start-up venture. I think that was the driving force for deciding to withdraw our application. I think there was a real problem with the whole thing because we did it a little backwards. We had preached this idea of things bubbling up from the bottom. And here was a top-down initiative, which doesn't work quite as well at a place like Stanford. We didn't have faculty clamoring for this, and a lot of them thought it was a real distraction and that it wouldn't be the real Stanford if we went someplace else. So, there was resistance. I don't know what role that played ultimately in John's decision, but certainly John thought that we couldn't achieve the milestones that New York had set for Stanford.

In terms of the arts initiative, John's biggest interest in the arts was in the fine arts and the museum. His mother-in-law is a great painter, and many of the works that were in the president's house and now in his own home were done by her—a professional, serious artist. John and his wife were very passionate about the arts. And people didn't expect that coming from a computer scientist, I think. But it seemed to be something he cared about. John made the Anderson gift a reality and was able to raise the money for the building for the Anderson Collection. John also was able to close the gap on fundraising for the Bing Concert Hall, although Gerhard Casper deserves the credit for getting that moving. So, John was a big supporter of the arts and made it possible for the arts to flourish through his fundraising.[28]

Leadership Team

The leadership team was different under John than it was under Gerhard Casper or under Don Kennedy. There were different people sitting at the table. John has a loud voice, as do some of the other members of the leadership team, so we wouldn't meet in Building 10. We'd have our staff meetings up at John's house. There's a conference room downstairs, and meetings could be more confidential up there. We would meet every Tuesday morning, and we usually sat in the same spots. Going around the table, it was Howard Wolf, the president of the Alumni Association; Stephanie Kalfayan, who was the vice provost for academic affairs under John Etchemendy, sort of my equivalent role; Randy Livingston, the CFO; Debra Zumwalt, general counsel; Bob Reidy, the director of Land and Buildings; Martin Shell, vice president for development; and then the head of the Stanford Management Company; and then the vice president for communications. The provost was at that meeting, too. That was the president's cabinet. There was a separate meeting that he and the provost had with the deans.

Typically, we just went around the room and talked about the most pressing issues or an issue that needed consultation. It was a two-hour session—you know, going around the room and just talking about things. There was no agenda set. People would just say what they were up to and keep everybody else informed of what was going on. John also had regular meetings with each of the people in that group.

John was always calculating things. He was certainly paying attention to the endowment and reports from the CFO. Fundraising numbers—that was always a big thing. There would be sort of a running joke: no matter how much money was raised, couldn't they raise a little bit more? There were some remarkable fundraising results during John's presidency.

As a leader, John is very confident and quick, and strongly opinionated. He knows so much. He is one of the most well-read people I've come across, and he could talk about any subject. He was really an expert on just about everything, and if he wasn't an expert, he could bluff his way through it. So, he would often come out with a pretty strong opinion on things and state that right up front. And very firm. He had very high expectations for people's performance. He talked about what it was like in the Valley and how quickly things moved there because he had worked in a lot of companies. He said something like, "You know, they cut ten percent of the people who are not performing well. Everybody isn't doing great all the time. We need to be more discerning. I expect people to get things right." I don't think he had a lot of patience for subpar performance.

I think there's a great appetite for risk-taking at Stanford. That was evidenced in how we used the discretionary funds. I think that there were some ideas put forward that he didn't think were going to succeed, but you need to just try things out. You can expect a certain amount of failure. In that sense, his expectation wasn't that everybody would succeed, but they would be highly competent in what they did and work hard and do their best. He wanted people who were highly capable around. Now, they could make mistakes—I guess, it was okay to make some mistakes. But I think it was on the student and faculty side that he was maybe a little more forgiving. He expected a little more risk-taking when it came to new ideas that students might put forward or getting students to take things that were out of their comfort zone or for faculty to push the envelope a little bit. I don't think he was as forgiving with the staff.

Sometimes he could be misinterpreted because he was so quick. You might think that he was dismissive when it was just that he was already thinking about the next thing. He was moving on. But people loved John. The trustees really felt like he was a great president, that he connected with them well and that he was a thoughtful leader and took the university to a great place. And the faculty thought that he was a real champion for their causes and was very supportive of them. I don't think the students had the same strong sense of him that, for example, they had of Don Kennedy, who would go out and run with the students in the foothills. John wasn't that kind of person. He did connect well with the students when he had time, but I don't think the students really knew him all that well.

I don't think the relationship between John Hennessy and John Etchemendy was unusual in that they got along really well. They both had great respect for each other and for their different roles. They could disagree, although they didn't often disagree. They worked incredibly well together. I saw that was true with Condi Rice and Gerhard Casper; I thought they worked well together. And Jim Rosse and Don Kennedy worked well together.[29] So I think that there's a tradition of that—picking the right person and that things work out. They're very different people; John Etchemendy and John Hennessy are very different personalities. John Etchemendy had more of the aura of a philosopher. He would sometimes pause and look out into the distance contemplating something. And John was interrupting. John Etchemendy hadn't finished his thought, and John Hennessy was kind of impatient and would keep talking. But they worked well together.

John Etchemendy worked incredibly hard. He was so meticulous in every little detail and could argue any point in a very calm, thoughtful manner. And John Hennessy had such respect for John Etchemendy. I know that he appreciated how hard he worked. He read every file for faculty appointments in incredible detail. He was very careful with that. And John Hennessy had great respect for how long he was willing to serve. He was the longest serving provost in the history of Stanford—a very tough job.

With the deans, there was some turnover over the long haul, but the ones who were there for the longest periods of time worked very well with both John Hennessy and John Etchemendy. I think there was a great sense of camaraderie and working together during this period. The deans all seemed to care about the whole university, not just their own schools.

LAUNCHING THE KNIGHT-HENNESSY SCHOLARS PROGRAM

Remarkably, John was energetic all the way through his presidency at a very high level. So, I think you couldn't have predicted when he would step down. He could have gone on for a long time in a lot of ways.

During that last year, there wasn't much in terms of transition because we didn't have a new president yet. We didn't ramp down towards the end. We just kept pushing forward. There was a lot of celebration. The campus, the trustees in particular, really were so grateful for John's leadership over the time, and they were very involved with planning all sorts of events for him at the end of his presidency. But John doesn't pause much to focus on himself, so the last year was just keep going and doing business.

I thought originally that I would step down from the university when John completed his presidency. But when I heard about the idea of the Knight-Hennessy program, the idea of a graduate fellowship program to attract future leaders, it seemed like something exciting, and I said to John, "I'd like to be involved in this and work on planning and getting it going." It started in the last year of John's presidency, and I spent a fair amount of time on that. It was just John and me in the beginning, and we were working on a lot of things at once.

I was involved in planning Denning House, the building for the Knight-Hennessy program. We had to get going right away because we wanted it to be there for our first class of scholars. We had a very compressed timeline from the time we started working on it. John raised the money, and then we had to get going. We had to build a building before we knew exactly what the program was going to be. So, we had to sketch out a program to figure out what kind of spaces we needed. It was a little backwards, but we started the planning. It was the Dennings, Maggie Burchat in Land and Buildings, and me. John sort of came in and out on some of that. We had regular meetings, and the Dennings were terrific. You don't often have the donors being so involved, but they were great to work with and really knew a lot about architecture. So, it was a great experience. We had a design competition among architectural firms and went through proposals. We selected a firm and then started designing.[30]

At the same time, we started to develop the program. We also were traveling around. I was doing recruiting worldwide to promote the program. I was in India. I was in China. John went to England and France. I had a great time traveling through the Deep South. I went to some of the historically Black colleges and universities because we wanted to find scholars who might not know about Stanford or know about the program. We were looking for those diamonds in the rough.

My favorite feature of Denning House is sort of a lounge area that has a piano, some high tables where people can sit and hang out, and a refrigerator and lots of places for snacks. I suggested that we have a piano prominent in the lounge area—and not just a regular piano. It had to be a beautiful full grand piano because I knew that that would be a place where students would gather. It would be a way of creating a community. As it turns out, we have so many great musicians in the program that it gets used; people play and they sing. It's really a convening spot for the students. Maybe it's because of my love of music that it just represents to me a place that you can build community around music and the arts.

Getting to know people in a meaningful way and getting them to connect with each other was the most rewarding part of my career. Like meeting somebody during a difficult home-owners' meeting and then being able to call on him later to be the convener for a course in Continuing Studies. Or just seeing how things sort of pieced together without any logic behind it. I became attracted to Stanford because of this wonderful professor and her students whom I met when I was a high school exchange student in Greece. So, throughout my career, what I reflect on is the meaningful connections that I made to people and that I helped make between people and among people.

PART TWO

CHAIRS OF THE BOARD OF TRUSTEES

CHAPTER 4

ISAAC STEIN

Member (1994–2004, 2006–2016) and Chair
of Stanford's Board of Trustees (2000–2004)

Isaac Stein graduated from Stanford with a JD/MBA in 1972. He has served on numerous public and private corporate boards as well as nonprofit boards. He served as chair of Stanford Health Services and UCSF/Stanford Health Care, a member of the search committee that selected John Hennessy as president, and the convening co-chair of the Stanford Challenge Campaign. He chaired the search for John Hennessy's successor and continues to serve on many advisory boards and committees at Stanford.

EARLY INVOLVEMENT WITH STANFORD

I came to Stanford in 1968 to go to Stanford Business School. To be honest, until I applied, I had virtually never heard of Stanford. There are no people quite as provincial as New Yorkers, who believe the world ends at best at the Mississippi River, and really the Hudson is more what they have in mind. I had met a man in London when I was on a junior semester abroad who was a graduate student at Stanford. He had pictures, and the pictures had palm trees, and that was looking pretty good to me. My wife and I got married directly out of college, and drove across the country on our honeymoon and showed up at Stanford. It was love at first sight. It was a stunningly beautiful campus.

I did a JD/MBA, so I did both a law degree and a business degree over a four-year period. Then I had a strange career that isn't worth going into, but suffice to say that I did a lot of different things in a way that if it works, you're a renaissance man and if it doesn't work, you're a dilettante, and the only difference is how it turned out. Fortunately, it did turn out well.

My first serious involvement with the university was in the late 1980s, when I joined the hospital board. At the time, Don Kennedy was president. Don had to resign his office in the early 1990s due to a whole set of issues involving indirect cost recovery with the federal government. Gerhard Casper became president, and it happened that he joined around a moment in time where I made a too early try at retirement. Gerhard wanted to look in-depth at the medical center and the way it was organized. Having heard that I was "retiring" and knowing that I was quite young, he said, "Why don't you work for me as a special advisor, and we'll have a commission on the medical center." We did, and we proposed a variety of structural changes that were going to take place.

Coming out of that, we restructured the governance of the medical center, and I was asked to become chair of the hospital board as well as a trustee of the university. By tradition, most of the people who served as chair of the hospital board were trustees because of the significance of the medical center to the university. At that point, I got so deeply involved that I just fell in love with being able to make a difference at something like Stanford, and I began spending a great deal of my time on different aspects of the Board of Trustees, the medical center, and other projects, including the presidential search committee that selected John Hennessy.

In the late 1990s, when I was chair of the Stanford Hospital board, I became involved in an effort to merge the hospitals of Stanford and UCSF. The merger involved only the hospitals and not the academic side of the two medical schools, which made it even more difficult to negotiate and run. Keep in mind that UCSF was a public institution; Stanford, of course, was a private institution. I was asked to become the chair of that board, of the joint enterprise. It was probably the most annoying and painful work of the many things I'd been involved in at Stanford. It was a very difficult merger. Cutting a long story short, when Gerhard decided to step down as president, I and others convinced him that if we couldn't make this merger work, we should not leave it for his successor to deal with. We executed our rights and dissolved it.

John Hennessy's Ascent to the Presidency

John Hennessy was, in reasonably fast succession, the chair of the Computer Science Department and the dean of the School of Engineering; and then, when Condi Rice stepped down, Gerhard asked John to become his provost. Gerhard did that, I think, in a pretty clear-eyed way. As he looked around the possible internal candidates at the university, he saw this as the best option. John was a solid internal candidate.

Our custom is very clear—although the provost appointment is up to the president, the presidency is something that is really a decision of the board. We choose to execute it through a somewhat elaborate search committee process. I was not the chair of John Hennessy's search committee, but I was a member. Obviously, it was pretty clear from the beginning that John was an excellent candidate. He's a very smart person; he's a very nice person; he's a person who embodies a lot of what people think of when they think of Stanford. He was an academic for sure to his core, but he also went off and started a company based on technology that he invented. He then came back to the university, but he continued to be involved with a number of other companies as a board member. He clearly loved not only the science, but also the translation of that science into productive use.

The way that we normally do such a presidential search, though, is that we treat a person who we think is a leading internal candidate simply as one of the candidates. We go to great effort to search the country. In this case, we actually looked at people outside of the United States as well. That's really important, and so is the way we structure the search committee. Obviously, the board could simply have said, "John is a wonderful leader and we all like him, let's just make him president." That would be a great way to set John up for failure because the faculty would believe that they had played no role in his selection, and they would surely find some things not to like about him.

Presidential Search Committee

Our presidential search process requires a reasonably large committee. For John's search, we had seven trustees, six faculty members, one undergraduate student, one graduate student, one staff member, and an alum who was active in alumni affairs but not a trustee.[31] It's very important that a committee like that be unanimous in their ultimate conclusion. Going into the search, it's typical that most of the members do not actually know each other. The seven trustees know each other, but the faculty members often don't know each other. They certainly don't know the trustees. The students, of course, have a whole different perspective. A big part of the process is to build up trust so that people will listen to each other's views and try to agree on the best answer for the university. One thing we have always made clear is that although the faculty members come from different schools and different parts of the university, they're not there as representatives of their school, nor is the under-graduate student the spokesperson for the student government. We tried to carefully select people who understand that they bring different experiences to the process, but they are all making decisions about what is best for the university, not what may be the will of their particular constituency.

We all come in with opinions, but we have to be able to spend, as we did, hours debating the finalists and come up with one name. One of the reasons we take so much time up front before we look at candidates is we want to learn more about each other so that when we get into the more detailed review of candidates, we understand where people are coming from. By definition, every candidate has different strengths and different risks associated with them. I need to be able to get committee members to understand my perspective. I have the perspective of a board member, and other people have the experience of being faculty members from different schools. We are going to worry about different things.

The chair of the search committee is always a trustee because, ultimately, it's only the Board of Trustees who have the final vote. But if a unanimous recommendation from a committee of such disparate people comes forward, our board culture is very clear that nobody is going to say, "Well, I might have a different view. I'd like you to bring in the finalists."

On that committee we learned that every member brought something to the party. It's diversity in the broader sense of the term, in that everybody had a different perspective, with the experience of being a student, faculty member, or trustee. For example, when we needed to see how candidates were perceived, our faculty members were able to call their friends at a given school and get a reading on the candidate's reputation with the faculty there.

Harvard, for example, still uses only trustees to do their presidential searches, and then they have an advisory committee of faculty. But they won't discuss candidates with the faculty because they think it threatens confidentiality. We have never had a breach of confidentiality, and that's exactly because we tell only a hand-selected group of people on the committee who all have a deep commitment to the process.

In the early phases of the search process, we ask ourselves essentially three questions. What are the big opportunities and risks for Stanford in roughly the next decade—because we are going to be picking a leader, so what are we picking a leader for? Do we think we're going to try to change the institution, and what external forces do we see at work? For example, we have a huge medical center that is larger than everything else in the university combined. At the time that John took over, there was a lot of turmoil in healthcare and our medical center, so how is that going to be an issue going forward? What are the risks associated with the medical center and the opportunities? Some of the world's most important medical innovations have come out of our medical center, so people really wanted to understand that.

The second thing we talk about is how those risks and opportunities translate into the characteristics we should search for. As we debate these things, that's where you really learn to trust each other, because people will make good points that give you a better understanding of the university as a whole. That includes the students. They know what kinds of things in general students are concerned about, like the economics of going to a place like Stanford, which is unbelievably expensive, but fortunately has very strong financial aid.

How important is it for the president to be an academic leader? At Stanford, it's very important. After World War II, Dwight Eisenhower came back from the war and became president of Columbia University.[32] I always like to say that may be true, but he could not be the president of Stanford. He might be a fabulous manager, and he may have won the war, but he doesn't understand the way research is conducted at a large research university and would never be accepted by the faculty.

Candidate Selection

In the case of John's search committee, we went on for about four months; we met roughly every week for the better part of a day, mostly on weekends. We had a secret location where we met, and we put a great deal of time into it. We met with many people who were thought leaders in higher education, and some of them could be possible candidates themselves. We made road trips around the country. We visited all of the obvious peer institutions—the Ivies, Duke, MIT—and we met with some former presidents of those institutions who had a broad perspective.

That process ultimately yielded a group of finalists. We then put each of them through a very intense day of interviews, doing everything from role-playing to questioning them on their philosophies on different issues. We were looking for how articulate they were in describing their views. John performed quite well. He obviously had a great amount of knowledge of the university, and he, of course, had been provost. But even allowing for that, he was very thoughtful and very articulate. I think we all recognized that John had the potential to be a great president, but he was young as presidents go, and that was a risk to some people. I looked at it as an opportunity because you rarely get a president who can stay for a long period of time, as ultimately John did. If they can, I think they have the potential to accomplish even more.

Everyone understands you cannot be the president of Stanford and not be a serious academic. We knew we needed somebody whose academic achievements would command respect. John was a full professor, a former dean, and the provost. If he didn't have the academic chops, who would? So that box was easy to check.

But there also had to be confidence that the candidate would be a good manager. In a university, particularly this university, the president has to deal with the fact that much of the university planning develops from the ground up—that is, the faculty—but it has to be steered by the president. I sometimes use this analogy: if you've got water coming downhill, you can try to stop it with a dam, or you can try to channel the energy by building some tributaries that absorb the flow and move it in the direction you're trying to take it. That requires someone who is a good manager, someone who is savvy.

Of course, we knew John. We had watched him perform some difficult tasks as both provost and dean of Engineering and do so in ways that the faculty respected and that got the right result. For example, when John was dean, there were two departments in Engineering. Both were suboptimal and increasingly looking a lot like each other. Rather than saying one would take over the other, John told them that he wanted to create a new department that had a different name and that he wanted these two departments to become that department. It worked very well. To this day, the guy who was chair of one of the departments says it was genius. He said it felt like, "We're all getting a promotion to this big new department." But John was really getting rid of two suboptimal ones. That's just a human skill that we thought was very important.

The next criterion is the X factor. It has to be somebody who you think can take one and one and make three, because Stanford is more nimble than most universities, but that's damning with faint praise. It's not as nimble as most businesses that I'm involved with. Considering the constraints on it, it requires somebody who has vision and can hold the vision. I think John had that X factor.

Then, it requires a personality that would work well in the role. Who does the president have to work with? Pretty much everybody. A president has to be successful in finding resources—what we call development—and that requires a specific personality. People must be able to relate to the person and be inspired by the person. It has to be a person who's willing to say, "This would be an incredible opportunity, and if you could make the core gift here, I can go out and raise the rest of the money." A lot of people find that difficult. John does not.

They also have to be able to relate to the surrounding community, because we have a lot of issues with our neighbors. I would describe John as having authenticity. There is an expression in the computer industry, WYSIWYG—what you see is what you get. That's John. He is exactly what he seems to be. He's the same whether he's talking to a student or his board chair, or out at dinner with his wife.

When you're doing a search—this is true in a corporate search, too—you're either looking for a change agent because you're unhappy with the status quo, or you're looking for someone where you can take some risk. We were clearly in the latter situation. We did not need John to turn around Stanford. Stanford was seen as one of the world's great universities, and it was going to be a great university pretty much whatever

John did. It would be hard to destroy it that quickly. We were willing to take risk for upside. The risk was the fact that John was young.

We did select John, and I was asked to become board chair as he began his tenure. I succeeded Bob Bass who was on the search committee as well, but his term was up.[33] I had four more years remaining, and that's exactly the term we use for a board chair. So that was an advantage, that John started with someone who knew him before his tenure began.

STRATEGIC PLANNING DURING JOHN HENNESSY'S PRESIDENCY

We had something that was called a needs assessment process that was led by John Etchemendy, and I attended many of the meetings. The first attempt to do that involved essentially going around and asking everybody, "Over the next five to ten years, what do you think your school needs?" The schools would then talk with their departments, and come back with their ideas. Their ideas added up to a lot. As I recall, we would have gone through about half of the endowment if we did them all. It was a ridiculous wish list of things. But it met the test of, again, getting the faculty engaged and stretching people's minds to think about not what do I need this year, but where am I heading ten years from now?

John Etchemendy was by then John Hennessy's choice as provost, and that was a good choice for lots of reasons. John Etchemendy is a phenomenally thoughtful and capable person. He is literally a philosopher and is an expert in logic and symbolic systems, so they were a good fit together. They had a lot of trust between them, and that helped a lot. It's a little bit like being good parents. The parents can't let themselves get "mommied-and-daddied" on issues, where kids ask one parent for permission using partial information and then tell the other parent that the first parent agreed. Similarly, there can't be any space between the president and provost. They have to think about how to make that relationship seamless so that they don't say something that contradicts the other. They did a really good job of that.

Looking at the needs assessment, they identified two core issues. The first was that when they looked at all the proposals, the most interesting and exciting ideas were at the intersections of schools and departments; that registered as something that was interesting and unique. The second was that there was a lot of appetite to turn this powerful intellectual engine towards issues in the real world—the environment, K–12 education, human health more broadly. Of course, the university is not organized that way. The university is built around disciplines in the same way that universities have been organized since the Middle Ages. They put those two things together, and that became the first leg—interdisciplinary solutions to real-world problems.

The second was a recognition that education is still at the core of much of what we do at every level, and we needed to rethink what needed to change in our education model. When you're in a place where there are some faculty who have very little contact with undergraduate students, and there are under-graduates who are incredibly talented people, it would enrich everyone's experience to strengthen those connections. So, we focused on coming up with ways to do that. Some things had been done on that already. Gerhard Casper had done quite a bit of work on something called the Campaign for Undergraduate Education, which implemented programs like freshman and sophomore seminars. John inherited the last stages of that CUE Campaign and so was ready to move forward.

Finally, there needed to be continued investment in the foundation of the university. It is sexy to go out and buy very costly supercomputers, but it's difficult for any one researcher to justify the cost of doing so. We were almost an early version of the cloud, in the sense that we were determined to get some major computational power and then make it available around the university. If you're building a house, it may not be sexy, but if you don't build a good foundation, the house is not going to last very long. So, we needed that investment.

Inevitably, a president eventually goes out and does a fund-raising campaign. Those three legs I just described became the basis for a campaign that we called the Stanford Challenge. I stepped down as board chair and as a member of the board in 2004, and John immediately asked me if I would take a major leadership role in the campaign. We spent two years raising the nucleus fund for that and then five years doing the campaign itself. We completed it in 2011–2012. In our terminology, the president is always the chair of the campaign, and the leadership are called co-chairs, one of whom is called the convening co-chair. As we finished raising the nucleus fund and went to launch the campaign, I was asked to take on the role as the convening co-chair. I was the one mobilizing the co-chairs and leading the meetings and so on. Simultaneously, I was asked to go back on the board for another ten-year term. So, I started

John's term and I ended John's term on the board, continuing in many roles.

Fundraising and Financial Stewardship

John and I obviously spent a lot of time together on the campaign—an enormous amount of time—and it was great. John was an excellent fundraiser. I don't think there's ever been a president of Stanford or any other university with a better fundraising record than John.

First of all, John is authentic. I've never met anyone who didn't like John. I'm sure there are people, but I haven't met them. He's just a nice person. He is what he is, and people like that; they understand that. The second is, he is a polymath who has such a broad range of knowledge on so many strange subjects. His wife got him really interested in the arts, so I have heard John talk about art at length. He reads widely and can discuss those things, and he has an encyclopedic knowledge of things related to Stanford. I think those things all contributed. He had a way of describing his vision in a clear way, of what the university could become with this external focus and mixing the pieces together.

Something emerged during the campaign that I think was a critical factor in John's success, but probably rarely gets mentioned. When the financial crisis of 2008–2009 came along, Stanford, like most universities, had a smoothing process for the endowment payout that was designed to mitigate the impact of market downturns on the university's operating budget. In effect, it increases the payout percentage if the endowment value drops, and you make up that incremental cost when the market recovers.

John and John decided not to do that. They decided to take the hit over a shorter period of time because if you do the smoothing formula, when the world recovers—and it always does—you're going to have to reduce your payout because you still have to pay back the money you took forward.

John and John went very clearly in the direction of acting the way responsible businesspeople would. They said: "We are going to tell you now that you're going to need to come up with X dollars in savings in your budget, and we would encourage you to make the changes now, as much as you can. Some things are off limits: we're not changing financial aid and we're not firing faculty. Anything else is open." They did this in a disciplined way. It wasn't done by dictum or fiat; it was done by having groups. There was a budget group that met with the different schools. They came up with ideas, but they left a lot of flexibility to the schools.

There's a famous saying in American politics, "Never waste a crisis." They viewed the financial crisis that way, that if we're going to have this problem, let's at least try to do something. They led by example. They took cuts to their own salaries that were larger than anybody else's, and they asked each of the deans to take modest cuts. There were no faculty salary cuts, but there were no raises either. There were no hires without the express approval of the provost. It wasn't the most popular thing.

Just because we have a large endowment, it does not mean that the money in it is interchangeable. Very few people, even within the university, understand that. If you gave us $10 million to fund research on glioblastoma, we can't take that money and put it into the English Department. It's a restricted fund. Most of our endowment is restricted endowment that is not usable wherever people want it to go, or even where the president wants it to go. So, this accelerated budget cutting worked effectively, and it changed some of our priorities during the fundraising.

John was also a hard worker in the literal sense. Nearly every day he was meeting with some donor or group. Those people evaluate the university on how the president impressed them that day. It's not fair, but it's the way the world actually works. So, you may have a headache, but you better keep your act together and look happy to see whoever it is and have a nice meeting to get them excited about the project you want them to give money towards. We did a lot of trips around the country. We did these big events. It's quite an elaborate process that we go through in a university-wide campaign. On the other hand, we raised $6.3 billion in the campaign, so it's worth a lot of work.

John has a unique set of experiences that I think lets him bridge academia with the corporate environment. Condi Rice used to have a great expression that, in a university, when you ask someone what time it is, they look at their watch and say, "It's quarter to spring." I always loved that. It's true. Academics think in longer time periods. Businesses obviously operate in a different time frame. John was not asked to become the chairman of the board of Alphabet because he was incapable of understanding the timing of corporate decision making. I think that's just a set of experiences and skills he developed. Donors trusted John to be a good steward of the money.

Challenges

The Medical Center after the Dissolution of the UCSF Merger

When we dissolved the merger, there's no question that it set back both institutions. We were financially stronger than UCSF, but we had clearly been hurt by the net flow of funds, which went effectively from Stanford to UCSF. Money from the combined enterprise had to go up there to pay for some problems that they could have taken care of earlier but hadn't because they were owned by the government. In a government entity, the way you get money from the government is to have a crisis.

We came back, happy to be out of it, but John clearly needed to continue being very engaged with the hospital. Very few presidents want to be deeply engaged with their medical centers because they involve a lot of financial risk. You have to be involved, but you don't wake up and think, "Boy, another exciting hospital board meeting! This will be fun!" I think John did a good job of rising to the occasion. He spent more of his time than I think he wanted to in the early years of his presidency dealing with those kinds of issues, but I think it was good for him because it gave him a grounding in those areas. In the later years of his presidency, when things were stronger at the medical center, he was much more knowledgeable about the issues that could go wrong or could go right, and he was willing to make investments to stay strong. I think he did a great job with respect to that.

Negotiating the General Use Permit

One other challenge worth touching on is the GUP, the general use permit. Stanford is located in a variety of political jurisdictions: part of our land is in the City of Palo Alto, part is in the City of Menlo Park, part is in Portola Valley. The largest area is in unincorporated Santa Clara County, and, for that land, that means rather than negotiating with a town, we negotiate with the county supervisors. There's no entity remotely comparable to Stanford in the county.

The GUP was an arrangement where instead of going to them for every building we put up, we would get blanket approval from them to build, over the next ten to fifteen years, a couple of million square feet of academic space, a couple of million square feet of housing, and we would agree to give certain things as mitigation of the environmental costs of doing that. The first negotiation process was pretty easy. It began as a simple document in the late 1980s

The second time began before John came into office, but he was involved as provost. We had one supervisor who saw this as his opportunity to get a lot of money from Stanford. As somebody once said to me, we were viewed as rich Uncle Leland who lived up on the hill. We had land and we had money, and they needed both. We had a long, multiyear negotiation with the county. I was involved both as board chair and on a separate committee that we had advising the team at the university. John had to play a big role in that he had to meet with each of the different supervisors, and we had to decide whether we were willing to pay what they wanted. It was a bloody process, but we received our entitlement in the end, although at a significant cost.

Over the last five years, we had been doing the same thing, trying to negotiate a new GUP. But, this time, we just couldn't reach an agreement. In late 2019, the university walked away from the discussions. And that's a shame, because we were going to build a lot of affordable housing that would have been great for our neighbors. It would have pulled back onto the Stanford campus a lot of our people—graduate students and staff—who commute or live in surrounding communities and now would be able to live on the campus. So, land use disputes will clearly be an ongoing issue for Stanford in the decades ahead.

One good thing about a university is that we have a long-term perspective. Long after this county supervisor is gone, there will still be a Stanford. We can outlast people who create the kind of problems that this guy has created. You know the expression NIMBYism? Not in my backyard? They have one around here which we call BANANA: build absolutely nothing anywhere near anybody.

New York Campus

The New York campus was interesting, and it actually relates to the GUP in a way. If you were looking at the big issues going forward for Stanford, one of them is going to be that we cannot expand the core campus forever. Even though we have 8,400 acres of land, much of that will never be built on, and there's a limit to the densification that you can create on the campus.

Realistically, the idea that the university might grow in a different way—be it globally by building a campus in Abu Dhabi or China, or domestically with satellite campuses—sounds reasonable at first pass. But expanding elsewhere is really complicated because of the residential nature of Stanford and the interdisciplinary nature of much of our research.

One day, John got a call from New York City, from Mike Bloomberg, who was then the mayor, about Roosevelt Island.[34] It is right by the 59th Street Bridge going over to Queens, and it's literally an island connected to Manhattan by a gondola. It was mostly used by the government, although there's some housing on it, apartments. Otherwise, there was a mental institution that had shut down years before. Bloomberg had this idea: Why not make a technology university there, and who better than Stanford to be a partner for that?

John thought this could really be an amazing thing, and he wanted to do it. He was perhaps startled that there was not universal acclaim for the idea, but he wanted to go ahead and do it. The board discussed it, and I think the view that many of us had was the amount of risk to explore the idea, given the scale of Stanford, was not overwhelming. So, we decided to pursue looking at it and planning. We'd have to invest a couple of million dollars to investigate the opportunity, but it wasn't tens of millions of dollars.

My belief as a businessperson is that the CEO of a successful enterprise has to be given the right to take a flier on something. This was something John really believed in, and he was happy to listen to those of us who had concerns. But, in turn, I was happy to say this is his call to explore it. It would obviously be different if we were talking about making major commitments to it; that would require a lot more information for the board because that's a really major decision. John pursued it. Many of us went back to New York and helped in that process.

In the end, John discovered that the city—shockingly or not shockingly to those of us from New York—started changing the deal. John came to us and said, "I don't believe we should proceed with this." I was happy that he tried, and I was happy that he didn't fall so in love with it that he would blind himself to the problems that developed. I think it reflects well on John that he took the risk and reflects well on him that he knew a losing hand.

Final Reflections

When I stepped away from the role on the campaign, I continued on the board. Then as John realized that he was ready to move on, I took over the search process for his successor. I have enormous respect for John as I did for Gerhard before him. So, we began again with a search committee process much like that which selected John.

Since John Etchemendy, our provost and John's partner for his entire presidency, told us that he did not want to be considered for the role, our focus was on external and a few internal candidates. This process resulted in the selection of Marc Tessier-Lavigne. Like John, Marc was a distinguished academic and a former professor at Stanford. Marc, like John, is also a former business leader and co-founder of several companies. And so, another great leader has taken the helm at Stanford and will shape the university's future direction as John has done.

One of our enduring strengths is that Stanford is more flexible than most institutions. Most of our peers have deep, hidebound traditions. At the first opening of the university, David Starr Jordan, who was the first president of Stanford, said something like, "Our signposts all point forward here. We are hindered by no traditions and no customs." It was true then, and it's still true today that people are willing to experiment with new ideas at Stanford that people at places like Harvard and Yale struggle to do within their frameworks.

The Board of Trustees of Stanford University, October 2006. John Hennessy (front row, center left) stands next to Burton McMurtry, who chaired the board from 2004 to 2008. Steve Denning, Leslie Hume, and Isaac Stein—all chairs during Hennessy's presidency—are also part of the group.

CHAPTER 5

LESLIE HUME

Member (2000–2012) and Chair (2008–2012)
of Stanford's Board of Trustees

Leslie Hume is a historian and philanthropist who earned her PhD from Stanford. She has devoted much of her career to supporting the university.

History with Stanford

My first encounter with Stanford was as a graduate student in the History Department. I came out to do a PhD in history with the support of the Ford Foundation and Stanford. It was a wonderful experience, a terrific department. I had a great mentor and advisor in Peter Stansky.[35] I did my graduate work, then had what would be called a postdoc now—essentially, teaching in conjunction with a senior faculty member. I was teaching a course with three of the greats of the History Department in Modern European History.

After that, I went to work for an organization called the Research Libraries Group, which was a consortium of universities that was based at Stanford. For all intents and purposes, on paper I looked like a Stanford employee and worked in that capacity for ten or eleven years. I got to know the university and a number of universities fairly well.

My first volunteer job for Stanford was on the advisory council for what was then the Center for Research on Women, which is now called the Clayman Institute.[36] Then I served on the Dean's Advisory Council for the School of Humanities and Sciences. In 2000, I was asked to join the board of the university. From 1969 until 2000, I'd never left the university.

Joining the Board of Trustees

Isaac Stein was the person who called me and asked me to serve on the board. I was astounded and thrilled. It was a great honor to be asked to serve on the board for an institution that had made such a difference in my life and that I loved. The idea of being able to serve this institution in any way was something I considered a great privilege.

I felt that I had a good understanding of the academic side of the university, at least as reflected through the School of Humanities and Sciences. I knew a number of faculty and had worked with them, and I had some experiences on the development side. My husband and I had been involved as the parent co-chairs of the Campaign for Undergraduate Education, so I was very comfortable on the fundraising side of the university.

There are aspects of the university which I knew nothing about—the medical center, the hospitals. My husband was a graduate of both the Law and Business Schools, so I had secondary exposure to those; Engineering, no exposure at all; and the finances of the university, the Stanford Management Company, completely new territory to me. There was no mystery about my background. Everybody on the board was aware that that side of the university was really something I knew nothing about.

December 2000 was my first meeting. John Hennessy and John Etchemendy had become president and provost of the university in October. The trustees do an annual retreat, which in my case was held in April 2001. That retreat was focused on the hospitals, which at that time were a real cause of concern, because they were a big financial drain on the university. I recognized very quickly that the hospitals and medical center were in many cases the elephant in the room, and an elephant about which I knew very little. So, that retreat was an eye-opener in that respect.

The next meeting, the June meeting, was when the university budget was established. I began to get an initiation into university budgeting, into the role of the Stanford Management Company. I think in September of that year, in 2001, I was asked to chair the Academic Affairs Committee, which I was perfectly comfortable doing. That was my first experience at chairing a board committee for Stanford.

Stanford has a thirty-five-person board, which poses its own challenges in terms of the dynamics of meetings. How do you set a table in the boardroom where trustees can really have a conversation with management about the university? That was a completely different experience. But I was also struck that although the scale and complexity of Stanford were exponentially different from those of other institutions with which I'd been involved before, the tenor of the atmosphere in the board meetings was one of respect and collegiality and inclusion.

One of the things that the Stanford board has prided itself on is the attendance record of the trustees. One of the conversations you have with prospective board members is that attendance at the board meetings is taken very seriously. It is made very clear that if you do not have the time that this commitment involves, you should not accept the invitation to serve on the board.

As a very junior board member, I was certainly struck by what an adept and thoughtful and wise board chair we had in Isaac Stein. Isaac is extremely measured. He is thoughtful, and there is never a rush to judgment. He listens really well. It was very clear that he was respectful of the leadership of the university and really understood that the role of the trustees was not to involve itself in the day-to-day management of the university. It was to provide guidance and counsel and support for the president and his team. I think you also got a sense that if you had a question or a thought, you could always go to Isaac and have an honest, open conversation. There was nothing that he was unwilling to talk about.

It was clear that he had a superb working relationship with John Hennessy, and it was also very clear that the partnership between John Etchemendy and John Hennessy was exceptional. They really were a team in the best sense of the word. You can tell when there is an openness and an integrity to a relationship and when people really trust each other and work well together. It's apparent.

COMMITTEE ROLES

I think the Board of Trustees has a fairly typical committee structure. The two committees that I served on were Academic Affairs and Development, and those were both areas with which I was very comfortable. The purview of the Academic Affairs Committee is the entire academic enterprise of the university. It would review everything from the opening and the closing of departments, to periodic reports from the deans of the schools. It reviews admissions, student affairs—every aspect associated with the academic side of the university. Financial aid was another topic that was discussed. In 2007, the university introduced a major change to its financial aid package for undergraduates that had been discussed at the committee beforehand.

I brought the experience of a graduate student to that committee. I think at the time I was one of two people with PhDs on the board. That experience and the experience of actually having taught at the university were valuable. Because I had been a graduate student, I understood how departments operated and the relationship of a department to the dean's office. So, the dynamics of how the academic enterprise worked were something that I just understood. If you come from one of the professional schools, I think your experience is very different.

The chair of the committee works very closely with the provost, who is the member of the administration who leads that committee, and, together with the provost and vice provost, sets the committee's agenda—what are the issues the trustees want to talk about and who are the faculty who are going to be asked to come and meet with the committee. I think I chaired Academic Affairs for either three or four years and then moved to chairing the Development Committee.

On the Development Committee, the trustee chair works very closely with the vice president for development and sets the agenda for the committee for the year, covering all aspects related to development. Development had been part of my Stanford DNA. My husband, George, and I co-chaired the parents part of the Campaign for Undergraduate Education. We worked very closely with the vice provost for undergraduate education at the time. We held a lot of meetings around the country with Stanford volunteers, with Stanford parents, talking about building a parent effort to support the university. I'd done some fundraising for the Center for Research on Women. I'd been involved in a bit of fundraising for the School of Humanities and Sciences, so this was not something that was new to me. And I'd also fundraised outside of Stanford for various organizations in San Francisco.

The Stanford Challenge

During the whole time I was on the Board of Trustees, we were engaged in a capital campaign. The Campaign for Undergraduate Education was launched under Gerhard Casper; I think it wound down in about 2003/2004. The planning for the next campaign, the Stanford Challenge, which was a $6 billion campaign, began in 2004, and I think the public launch was in 2007. It ended in 2012.

The first meetings around the Stanford Challenge were in 2004, and a campaign cabinet was formed. Isaac Stein, after he stepped down as chair of the board, chaired this campaign cabinet. It met initially weekly, and then monthly for the duration of the Stanford Challenge campaign, and I was part of that group.

That group was very much involved in shaping the messaging for the campaign, shaping the outreach effort, traveling all over the world to connect with the Stanford community. In some ways, the Stanford Challenge provided an organizing principle for the university. It was a story that was told in every single part of the campus.

It began with John's seeking the ideas of the faculty and the schools: "What are your ideas about what Stanford could and should be doing?" What John was brilliant at was taking what were very inchoate ideas, and with help and advice from the administration and the volunteers, really shaping them into a compelling whole. It took what were assets of Stanford—the uniform excellence of schools and departments, an "unsiloed" interdisciplinary approach to teaching and research, and the geographic proximity of schools—and married these with the bold, entrepreneurial, innovative culture of Stanford, the university's DNA. That became the Stanford Challenge.

In my experience, this was unique. In some cases, you have a much more top-down approach—the leadership sets the direction. This really bubbled up from the faculty and the schools. It was the ability of John to take these disparate parts and separate the wheat from the chaff and forge it into a compelling whole. That was his genius.

Campaigns have their own rhythm and time frame. It begins with intensive planning, and then you have a period in which you're really testing your campaign statement with small groups of volunteers, and you're getting feedback which makes you alter your campaign plan. Some of the feedback that came back very early on from these lunches and dinners that we were doing to test the campaign was: Where is the focus on education and how does the School of Education fit into this? And so that became a much more prominent piece of the campaign that wasn't there to begin with. That test driving of the case really is very important, and that overlaps with the quiet fundraising stage. Usually you have raised about half of the dollars that you intend to raise prior to the public launch. The response and the magnitude of some of the donations we got was just a huge yes to Stanford and to John Hennessy's vision for the campaign. But the messaging was that this was not a campaign about dollars. It was a campaign about ideas.

Once the public launch was official, we traveled to different cities and experienced how proud people were to be affiliated with Stanford and what it was trying to do through this campaign—the vote of confidence in John's leadership, the pride of association with the university, and what a really exceptionally devoted group of alumni and volunteers Stanford has.

The president went to absolutely every single event. I don't know whether there were twenty different stops, from Beijing to Taipei to Singapore to Paris to London, you name it. Different members of the campaign cabinet went, too. There's no question that the president of the university was the star attraction, but it was important to have some members of the supporting cast along. We joked that there should be a T-shirt—that I think I was actually given—saying, "I survived the Stanford Challenge!"

Stanford Board of Trustees Chair Leslie Hume addresses the audience at a Leading Matters event at Maples Pavilion on the Stanford campus in October 2011. As part of the Stanford Challenge fundraising campaign, Leading Matters presentations—designed to engage alumni with how the university was addressing the challenges of the twenty-first century—were held in nineteen cities throughout the world.

When you'd go on the road with John Hennessy, as part of this Stanford Challenge, there was always a student panel. John Hennessy would interview the students. The way in which John engaged with these students, you couldn't fake that if you wanted to. You could tell that this is a man who really loves this interaction and the student engagement.

One of the things I should say—and I experienced both in chairing the Development Committee and working on the campaign—the professional development team at Stanford is the best in class. The way in which development works with the volunteers— they are just really good at making volunteers feel as if they are partners in the enterprise. Some development teams have a much more what I would call distant relationship with their volunteers. I think people volunteer for Stanford because they really feel as if their ideas, their input, their participation matters, and there is a true partnership.

TENURE AS CHAIR OF THE BOARD OF TRUSTEES

I think the first conversations I had about chairing the board were in November or December 2007. This was not anything that I had ever anticipated or considered, and my first reaction was, I do not know anything about finances. Finances are not my first language or my second language. I wanted to make sure that what the board thought it was getting in my leadership was what it was going to get. I felt comfortable on the academic front. I felt comfortable on the development front. But the audit committee, finance committee—or for that matter, the medical school and hospitals—were not anything that played to my skill set at all. I was told that wasn't a problem. There were fifteen people on the board who had those skill sets. I was assured that finances were not an issue.

You ask yourself, first of all, "Do I have the passion for and the commitment to the institution? Do I want to dedicate my time to this?" It sounds really trite. I love Stanford, and I have tremendous gratitude for the education it gave me. It's hard to imagine all of the things that it has done for me, and for my husband, and for our children. I had the time to do this. I did not have a day job, so I could devote the kind of time that I thought it was going to take to do this. I talked to my family and got input from them. The consensus was, "If you are asked to do this, you should do this. You can do this."

The process is, by the time you are asked to chair the board, the president is comfortable with the idea because you would not name someone chair of the board whom the president did not think he or she could work with. Long story short, I was named the chair-elect in April 2008.

THE GLOBAL FINANCIAL CRISIS

Having said that my first language was not finance and having been assured that the university's finances were not a problem, my first board meeting was around October 10, 2008. The market had crashed the week before. It was the beginning of what we now call the financial crisis. Suddenly, the university's finances were a problem, and what was not my language, was the language of the day.

What was very clear to the board and to me in that first October meeting, was that this was going to be John and John's focus and that they were under no illusions that there was any quick fix here. They were prepared to be decisive and bold in dealing with this crisis. In what were very frightening, uncertain times, they had the confidence and the support of the board, because of the way in which they navigated through the crisis and the consistency, clarity, and frequency of their communications. And I think they had the confidence of the rest of the university.

A very expensive new financial aid program went into effect, ironically, for incoming students who matriculated in September 2008. One of the things that the university did was make very clear to the students that our financial aid commitments were going to stay in place, irrespective of the 30 percent decline in the university's assets. I think the communications not only internally with staff and faculty, but externally with our alumni were also very important. There were town halls, there were weekly communications. There was no feeling that decisions were being made in a dark room where people didn't know what was going on. It was really full disclosure.

John and John had been in office for eight years when this hit, so I think the confidence in and respect for them was a huge asset to them in dealing with this crisis. They'd also been on the faculty since the 1980s, and that faculty trust is huge when you're asking departments to cut budgets 15 percent over three years. What John and John's stance was—and this was absolutely supported by the board—was that this is not going to be death by a thousand cuts. We're going to do this deeply, we're going to do it once, and then we're going to move ahead. And if we do this, we will come out a stronger university.

I will never forget one event in particular. Usually, the president of the university has an open meeting once a year for the whole university. He or she invites anybody who wants to come to hear a report on the state of the university. I would go to this, and usually, you'd get forty or fifty people. I think 600 people showed up in April 2009 and gave John Hennessy a standing ovation. That was year one of my chairing the board.

The irony is we had a campaign in full swing during the financial crisis. The Stanford Challenge was not put on a back burner. Actually, I think it ended up being an asset to have this going on, because you could tell people about the impact of the financial crisis and how the university was responding to it, but you could also tell the story of how Stanford was going to emerge as a stronger university post financial crisis. We were also fortunate that in the quiet phase of the campaign, we'd raised a lot of money.

THE NEW YORK CAMPUS AND THE REDWOOD CITY CAMPUS

The New York campus posed its own challenges. We were finishing the Stanford Challenge campaign. I think the trustees expected to have a little breathing room before doing something dramatic again. In December 2010, the City of New York announced it wanted to enter into a partnership with a research university—"enter a partnership" is probably not the right phrase. It was launching a competition for a research university to develop a campus on Roosevelt Island with the idea that there was going to be a close relationship between that entity and New York, and a strong focus was going to be on science and technology.

When this announcement was made, I think the assumption was that this was something that Cornell and maybe NYU and the institutions proximate to New York were going to fight over. In January 2011, John said to me, "I think Stanford should have that campus in New York." So, for the whole year of 2011, a lot of the board's discussion was around Stanford's undertaking this effort.

On the one hand, you had the president of the university who is a man of boldness, ideas, entrepreneurship, ingenuity—all the assets you want—and all the board members wanted to be supportive of John. On the other hand, I think it came sort of like a bolt of lightning from the sky. No one had anticipated this, and I think there were real questions: Was this the best use of Stanford's financial and academic assets? What were the strains that were going to be put on the main campus if you had this remote campus that you were going to be building and developing and operating? How was this relationship going to work to both the Roosevelt Island campus's and the Palo Alto campus's benefit? Did Stanford have the knowledge of and the relationships in New York to make this successful?

John's excitement was contagious on one level, but there were real hesitations about it. In December, when Stanford pulled the plug on this, I think there was also a sigh of relief on the part of a majority of board members.

The Redwood City Campus? There was a board member named John Scully—and I think this was probably done around 2004—who had the foresight to say, "Stanford should buy this land."[37] I think when we bought the land, we thought, "What are we going to do with this?" The Redwood City campus was

116

really mainly developed after I left the board. When we say it's our remote campus, it's what, a fifteen-minute drive? It's in a county in which we operate. We have relationships. We can move personnel back and forth—aside from traffic—reasonably easily. I think it's not comparable to the New York campus. The politics of New York City and the politics of New York State are also completely different from the politics of San Mateo County and Redwood City. Roosevelt Island was really an environment about which we knew little. Redwood City, completely different animal.

Focus on the Arts, the Humanities, and the Hospitals and Medical Center

As I was stepping down from the board, I could see the results of the university's focus on the arts—under Gerhard Casper first and stepped up under John Hennessy. Bing Concert Hall was built then, the McMurtry Building was built.[38] There were terrific faculty recruited into arts departments and new chairs funded. There were new graduate fellowships in the arts and humanities. There was a real recognition that Stanford had underinvested in the arts. If Stanford wanted to offer the best liberal arts education in the country, we really needed to build up our strength in the arts. Through Gerhard and through John Hennessy, this was accomplished.

I think though, by the time I left the board, there was a recognition that there was an imbalance between the sciences and engineering at Stanford and the humanities. We had the best-ranked humanities departments in the country, but humanities at Stanford were losing ground—they were losing ground all over the country. We needed to focus on what we at Stanford could do to reinvigorate and strengthen the humanities. This is still an issue for the university.

The hospitals and the medical center had a remarkable turnaround during the time I was on the board. My first retreat was in 2001. The hospitals were the focus because they were in such dire financial straits. By 2008, there was a major $2 billion plan for hospital renewal and replacement, and in May 2012, there was a campaign—I think it was $1 billion—launched for Stanford Medicine. Thanks to John and a few key people, the medical center and the hospitals were in a whole different place. The relationship with the university, in terms of development and governance was also in a much more constructive, much more integrated, much more positive place.

PROMOTING A POSITIVE BOARD CULTURE

One of the things that we instituted was a board orientation for new members. When I was given an orientation to the board, it was really on a one-on-one basis and spread out over a year, year and a half. We instituted a half-day orientation—a crash course in what you'd like board members to know about finances, about development, about university governance—even before their first formal board meeting, to try and get them up to speed. We gave them a board buddy, for lack of a better term, whom they could do check-ins with. The board buddy could also do check-ins with them to see if they had questions, if there were things they did not understand, if they needed help in navigating something. I made a point as board chair to have one-on-one conversations with all board members.

Another practice we instituted was that of exit interviews with board members who were leaving the board. This provided an opportunity to capture their reflections on their experience and ways in which it could be improved. We tried to incorporate the ideas from those exit interviews, both in structuring our board meetings, and also in our conversations with committee chairs about structuring agendas. We obtained feedback from board members, both through exit interviews and through a board self-evaluation that the Governance Committee Chair Jim Canales organized that looked at the functioning and the practice of the board as a whole. We took that feedback to try and build a stronger board, to make sure we were maximizing the participation and expertise of board members. I think these were efforts to make what was a well-governed institution even better governed.[39]

The Governance Committee is charged with the prospecting and nominating of trustees. We have a group of trustees who are nominated through that process, and then we have a group of trustees who come in through an open process that is run by the Alumni Association. This starts with a call for anybody who wants to be a trustee to submit an application, and then the applicant pool is culled and culled and culled. But one of the things that the Governance Committee is always looking at is: What is the diversity of our board? What is the diversity by every single measure: by expertise, by Stanford affiliation, by profession, by ethnicity, by geography, you name it? You want a board that is truly diverse in all of those ways. It gives you a better sounding board and a much broader set of skills and experiences to tap. Boy, are you happy when you have people who have operating experience and have run a company, like Mary Barra who is CEO of General Motors and is a trustee now. Then you want someone who has foundation expertise, like Jim Canales, or worked in finance, like Ruth Porat, or ran a major university, like Bill Brody, or founded a tech company, like Jerry Yang. But you also want people who've done none of those things. One of the things about a thirty-five-person board is you have a little more wiggle room in terms of the variety of experiences and expertise you can have. If you're a twelve-person board, that becomes even more challenging.

When I was board chair, we did our first field trip as a board to another institution. We went to Yale. Later, the board visited MIT and Harvard. I think getting outside your own culture once in a while is really important, because you have an opportunity to learn best practices from other institutions. But when you come back from that field trip, you also become much more attuned to and appreciative of your own culture.

There were two other governance practices we began when I was board chair. We began our board meetings with an executive session with John Hennessy, so that if he wanted to alert the board to anything before the board started meeting, the board would be given a heads up. We initiated an executive session with John Hennessy at the end of the meeting, so that the board had an opportunity to talk to John confidentially about an issue or a problem without other members of the staff or team there.

Final Reflections

I loved being on the board and chairing the board. Working with John Hennessy was both a great learning experience and a great privilege. All I can say is, I learned. I'd never worked with an engineer before. Engineers approach the world very differently than historians. Historians tend to look in the mirror and look backwards and see what has happened, and engineers just look forward.

I could not have had better leadership to work with. Both John Hennessy and John Etchemendy are inspiring in their own ways. John Etchemendy is thoughtful, measured, a great listener, and a patient problem solver. John Hennessy is bold, decisive, entrepreneurial, energetic, enthusiastic. John Hennessy is the consummate polymath. He will talk to you about a novel that he's just read, then the next day he'll give you a tutorial on China. He's got a voracious appetite for learning, and his curiosity is remarkable. Both he and John Etchemendy are also just natural teachers. When John Etchemendy would do his annual budget presentation to the board, it was a teaching exercise. They were masterful in their ability to teach the board about a problem, and I think that gift really enhanced their leadership.

My feeling is that when I left the board, Stanford's star had never been brighter. We had arguably the best leadership in higher education. We had completed an enormously successful capital campaign. The endowment was almost back to its high-water mark. The schools and the departments were ranked the highest in the country. Recruitment and retention of faculty were at an all-time high. We had a national reputation for being the pacesetter in interdisciplinary research and had as supportive an alumni body as any university in the country. I felt that as I was leaving Stanford, the university could not have been in a better place across the board.

As for the board itself, its members were committed, talented, and generous. The board culture was one of collaboration, respect, openness, and honesty. The board understood the boundaries between management and the board, and it really looked for ways to offer constructive advice and to be of help to John Hennessy and his team. That culture is something that you can never take as a given. It's something that Stanford needs to be vigilant about perpetuating, and it really needs to transmit that culture as it adds new members to the board.

If you think about things that really need a sharpened focus, they are the values of diversity and inclusion. The university needs to be extremely intentional about the recruitment of women and alums of color to the board, as well as to the administration and the faculty. This is an ongoing issue, and an opportunity for Stanford to be a university that is truly diverse and truly inclusive.

I talked a little bit about volunteers and their role in the university and what an exceptional job Stanford did in partnering with volunteers, and how the Stanford Challenge really gave us a common language and a common purpose. How do you continue to capitalize on that volunteer spirit and how do you keep volunteers engaged and involved with the university in a meaningful way?

CHAPTER 6

STEVE DENNING

Member (2004–2017) and Chair (2012–2017)
of Stanford's Board of Trustees

Steve Denning is chairman of General Atlantic, a global private equity firm with approximately $60 billion in capital under management. He previously served as chair of the Stanford Board of Trustees and the Stanford GSB Advisory Council, and currently serves as chair of the Global Advisory Council to the President, the Freeman Spogli Institute, and the Natural Capital Project Advisory Council at Stanford University. He also is a member of the Knight-Hennessy Scholars Program Advisory Board and the Stanford Distinguished Careers Institute Advisory Council. He earned an MBA from Stanford in 1978.

Serving on Stanford's Board
of Trustees

My Stanford degree is an MBA—that was in 1978. I joined the Stanford Board of Trustees in April of 2004. I'd previously been very involved in the Business School at Stanford, including chairing the Advisory Council. The whole notion of being a trustee was not something I aspired to do or thought about, so it was quite a shock when Isaac Stein asked me if I'd be interested. He and I stayed very close after that; we're very good friends.

The first meeting was a retreat at Fallen Leaf Lake up in Lake Tahoe. The board meets five times a year, four regular meetings, plus an off-site retreat where we deal with longer-term issues—opportunities, challenges, and so forth. My first impressions were very positive about the people who were involved, the other trustees. I was impressed with the collegiality of the group, even though it was a large group—thirty to thirty-five trustees and staff. Everyone was very intent on making Stanford an even better institution, despite how good Stanford was already. It was something that I identified with and really wanted to be a part of—making it more impactful, more purposeful in terms of its mission, its vision, and what it could accomplish in the world.

John was in the formative stages of putting together his longer-term vision and plans for the university. We were assessing a variety of different options, thoughts, and ideas that he had. We played a simulation that predicted various outcomes depending on how you put money into the endowment, how you spent money on the faculty, students, tuition. It was a computer game, but its real purpose was to begin to highlight some of the trade-offs in terms of how you spend the capital, how you budget, how you build the faculty, and the importance of the various attributes and characteristics of the university.

I think it began to reinforce John's vision and view that he was putting together a plan that was trying to look at the university as a whole and its various individual components to address some of the most significant challenges, opportunities, and issues in the world. It was very much a global outlook. When you considered individual components of the university, you were looking holistically at what it would mean for the university to address these. It became clear in the meeting that the real strength was the university as a whole, not as individual pieces. These discussions eventually led to the establishment of the Freeman Spogli Institute for International Studies, the Woods Institute for the Environment, the Precourt Institute for Energy, and some of the various interdisciplinary institutes and centers around the university.[40] Isaac was chair then, and then it was Leslie Hume, and then I became chair in 2012.

Navigating the Global Financial Crisis

The global financial crisis was one in which you saw the strength of the board come together to address something as a group and as a collegial body. Many of us felt like what we were witnessing was something we'd never experienced in our lives—that it was very significant and we should move on the basis that it was not easily going to correct itself. A number of us were quite adamant, with regard to advice and counsel to John Etchemendy as well as John Hennessy, that you needed to run this like you'd run a business. Go in there and figure out what kinds of cuts and adjustments and changes you need to make, do them rapidly, readjust the organization; don't incrementally cut.

John and John basically executed that to a T. Because of the rhythm of the endowment and how it works—smoothing formulas and so forth—you could still be making cuts two, three years out, and you wouldn't have the rationale at that particular point in time, because the global financial crisis would hopefully have faded by then. It was a very, very good example of the board circling the wagons and giving John and John the most candid and heartfelt advice and counsel we could. Those guys were really extraordinary in terms of their execution. They didn't just do what we said. They used our advice as input to their own perspectives and their own knowledge of the university to make the right kinds of adjustments and cuts and the reshaping that was required, not only to get us through the global financial crisis, but to come out stronger on the other end.

We had a policy that we didn't approve funding for construction of any new building or major renovation until it was fully financed. I remember calling John one time when I was up in the foothills looking back over Stanford, and I saw the cranes and all the activity. It was 2010–2011. I said, "John, you'd never know there was a financial crisis when I look at Stanford's campus." That was a tribute to the way that John and

John managed the institution and to the fact that we wouldn't start construction until a project was fully financed.

We definitely realized the global financial crisis could potentially alter the financial capacity of our students and our parent body. So, we analyzed that and assessed it, and we increased financial aid to accommodate that. We raised more money for financial aid. We put in place the parameters: if your total combined income was below X, you got the complete room, board, and tuition free, and if it was below Y then you got your tuition free.

We really felt like we needed to step up and address financial aid. As you can imagine, while the need was apparent, the ability to raise that kind of capital was less so, because we were in the middle of the global financial crisis. But we felt like it was something that we should do. It was the right thing to do, and so it was done. And again, John and John executed it superbly.

A HISTORIC FUNDRAISING CAMPAIGN

The trustees were, of course, involved with fundraising. The chair of the Stanford Challenge campaign was John Hennessy, and there were four co-chairs—Chris Hazy, Linda Meier, Isaac Stein, and myself.[41] We met almost weekly for five-plus years. The campaign started formally in October 2006 and ended in December 2011, but we were also involved during the quiet phase. So we were involved for six or seven years.

John had come to us with his ideas, his thoughts, his rationale, his visioning statement. We worked with him—again, on a very collaborative basis—to refine them, shape them, potentially change them, extend them, and so forth. These were very much working sessions. The planning process involved not only getting the substance right, but also getting the messaging and the communication right so that the campaign's goals were compelling to the entire Stanford community—not only the alums, but the faculty, the students, and the staff.

John and John had kicked off a number of fundraising groups and initiatives across campus, so they weren't done sequentially. They were done in a massive parallel fashion. We did basically a roadshow around the U.S. and then ultimately around other major cities in the world. Before we did that, we went out to a select number of cities to test out the ideas, to test out the initiatives, to get the reaction from our alumni body. If Stanford was pursuing an interdisciplinary initiative in the environment, here's why you would donate. Here's what we intend to do, here's what it might involve, and here's what it might cost. Those initiatives were very interactively discussed with alumni groups around the country. John and John were doing that with the faculty, so the faculty were very much an integral part of the operation. In December 2011, the campaign closed out at $6.3 billion.

THE NEW YORK CAMPUS

I chaired the New York campus committee. John Hennessy was very enthusiastic about the process and the potential of having a campus there. Frankly, I was too, but I think both of us had conditions. If we were going to New York, I didn't want to take

just a part of the university; I wanted to extend the university—
to have more of a one university holistic approach, more than
just ten or twelve acres. I wanted to have a long-term game plan.

I felt one of the huge advantages of Stanford being in New
York was it would introduce our faculty and students to the whole
notion of a complex urban environment, which is the way the
world's moving in terms of where we're going to live and work
and play. I thought it had that huge advantage, because you're
not going to have that here in the Bay Area for many, many years.
It also offered the opportunity to have true bidirectional interconnectivity, both technologically through telecommunications,
and with people. Our people tended to operate within their own
time zones. Having an ability to connect the two most entrepre-
neurially innovative areas in our country, Silicon Valley and New
York City, was a huge national benefit.

New York had a bunch of peculiar ideas about the rate at
which we built, the faculty involvement, what we had to have
going, how many students we had to have at each certain test
point each year. There were a lot of constraints and requirements that ultimately John and his team just weren't comfortable
with, and so we passed. And then Cornell University stepped
up—the next day, actually. Chuck Feeney put $350 million in.[42]

TENURE AS CHAIR OF THE
BOARD OF TRUSTEES

I became chair in 2012, and I was chair for five years: four
standard years and another one-year extension due to the

presidential change. It was a big responsibility and something that I really thought about in great depth. I had a lot of discussions with my wife, mainly because I was still active at this private equity firm, General Atlantic, and I was involved in other philanthropic activities, and it would require me to commit real time. The position requires roughly half your time, probably in reality it's closer to three-quarters of your time, so it was a real time commitment. We lived on the East Coast, in Greenwich, Connecticut. We realized that if I was really going to do this, we probably would have to get a place out here, in San Francisco, and spend real time out here, which we did.

But having said that, it was an enormous opportunity, and I felt quite humbled and challenged by the opportunity to do it. I didn't go on the board thinking, "One day I'm going to be chair." It was something that I really wanted to do. I wanted to make certain I could do it well.

We were past the global financial crisis by then, but other issues cropped up that we had to deal with, more operational. Online education was a big issue at the time. We had a big debate, because we thought it was going to radically change and reshape not only undergraduate education, but potentially graduate education. We had a group of trustees working with the faculty on that particular issue. We realized that it wasn't a standalone issue; it was something that would be integrated and baked into education in the twenty-first century. We went after it with a vengeance and really attempted to deal with it.

Financial aid access continued to be an issue. Then, we were in the execution phase of the capital campaign, so making the Freeman Spogli Institute for International Studies real—the same with the Woods Institute for the Environment, the Precourt Institute for Energy, and other institutes and centers around campus.

DEVELOPING THE KNIGHT-HENNESSY SCHOLARS PROGRAM

The notion of a highly selective graduate scholarship program at Stanford, something that was Rhodes-like, was something that John and I would talk about from time to time. It was something that confounded both of us, in that here we were with the best graduate programs in the world, yet many of the students with the most potential to be global leaders were going to Oxford and Cambridge to pursue graduate study. Why shouldn't they come to the United States? In particular, why shouldn't they come to Silicon Valley and Stanford University?

The idea really began to take shape with John during the latter part of his tenure. He really liked the idea of bringing scholars to Stanford University as well as to Silicon Valley, exposing them to both, having something that would be a little bit bigger scale than the Rhodes program, allowing them to study any graduate degree or combination of degrees that Stanford offered. As it began to take shape and come to fruition, it just became more and more exciting as to what that really meant and what that could be. We'll eventually have cohorts of 100 students each year who have a strong commitment and desire to improve their countries and are committed to making the world a better place—committed to building the right kind of foundation at Stanford through the degree offerings that we have.

John was extremely excited about it. He proposed the idea at one of our board retreats when we were down on the coast near Monterey. It was something that got the enthusiasm and support of the Board of Trustees. We raised $750 million in a very short period of time. I think we raised it for two reasons. First, it was a very compelling idea. People love that, and they love being able to attract that kind of talent to Stanford and to the Valley. Second, it was a way of honoring John Hennessy and his many, many contributions to Stanford and what he represented. He's a kind of renaissance man—an extraordinary, very capable, visionary, and inspirational leader, but also an esteemed faculty member.

What other individual can you name who won the Turing Award and played a major role in the development of Google? He's a very successful entrepreneur. He started two businesses of his own, and yet was one of the most respected university leaders in our country, if not the world. It was just an extraordinary combination of talents and capabilities. John is a really unique individual. That's one thing I learned to appreciate more and more, the more time I spent with him. So, I think it was those two things: it was a way of honoring John, and it was a way of meeting and responding to what we considered to be a huge need globally.

I contributed personally because it was an idea that I loved. We studied the Rhodes program to try and figure out what we could do to make the Knight-Hennessy program even better than what might exist at Oxford. One of the notions was not only to have three years fully financed plus a small stipend, but also to have a building that would allow a real sense of community to be developed, fostered, and maintained. Phil Knight obviously provided the lion's share of the capital to get the program underway. Bob King and his wife, Dottie, provided another $100 million. It was appropriate for me and my wife to do what we did, to play a role in defining Denning House as a meeting spot to foster community and community awareness.[43]

Denning House, the home of the Knight-Hennessy Scholars Program, at Stanford.

I'm very optimistic about the Knight-Hennessy program. We've got great classes today. We've slowly built up, and we've decided to take it even a little slower than we had initially planned. The number of applications is astounding. I think a lot of people respect going to Oxford, but if they could get something similar for three years and go to Stanford and the Silicon Valley in California, it's not a bad combination.

I find that some people want to do the shortest degree they can and still be declared a Knight-Hennessy scholar. They should be taking just the opposite perspective. If you're going to live to be over 100, build the strongest, best foundation you can. If you've got an extra year of funding, take an additional degree, like a master's in bioscience or environmental science or medical design.

THE WORKING RELATIONSHIP BETWEEN JOHN HENNESSY AND JOHN ETCHEMENDY

You see a lot of teams, but you see few teams that operated as effectively as those two individuals did. I think they both brought different attributes, strengths, weaknesses, and insights, and they learned to operate very effectively as a team. John Etchemendy was the chief operating officer, chief budgetary officer, chief academic officer, and so he had a huge responsibility. They worked very closely together. John Hennessy might have an issue that was more in the strategic domain, but he would always play it off John Etchemendy to see what the reaction was. They were seamless in terms of their ability to work effectively as a team, and they implicitly trusted each other, so there wasn't any second-guessing going on. They each had their domains, but it was a situation where the two individuals together were so much more than the two individuals alone. It was truly a symbiotic relationship, and it worked extraordinarily well.

We moved to having executive sessions after every board meeting without the staff who normally attend so we could get very candid feedback about issues and concerns and opportunities we might not be pursuing aggressively enough. The idea was we would start the executive session with John and the trustees, and then John would leave and it would just be the trustees. I said to John: "It's your call as to whether or not you want to do that first part of the executive session individually or with Etch." He said, "Clearly, with Etch." We loved that. I think they were extraordinarily successful because they were able to get so much more done through that team approach and that division of responsibilities.

I think John Hennessy is very entrepreneurial and spontaneous, and John Etchemendy is very thoughtful and introspective. It's not that John Etchemendy is not innovative and entrepreneurial, but he comes at it from a different perspective. The two in concert work extraordinarily well together. Even in the public domain, they were very much supportive of each other. You never saw any daylight between them.

The End of John Hennessy's Tenure and Finding a New President

John knew better than anybody that as you get through one capital campaign, you have a period of time when you execute that. Then you naturally want to modify that vision, adapt it, and have it reflect the world you live in today. That's roughly a ten-year cycle plus—the time it takes to assess what you need, formulate it into a plan and a series of programs and other elements that need to be changed, go out and raise the capital, and implement it. It was a natural thing for John to say, "Look, I've done it for fifteen years. I'll stay for another year. I probably don't have it in me to do it for another ten years."

It triggered the need for us to conduct a search, a need for us to understand where Etch was on the whole situation. We wanted to see if we could have some overlap with Etch so that he would get to spend some time with the new president. Other than selecting a new president, the Board of Trustees has derivative responsibility. We work in concert with the president, the provost, and the university staff. The board chair, in consultation with others, puts a search committee together and then manages that process in conjunction with the chair of the search committee. Isaac Stein was chair of the search committee. That was something that I thought was appropriate. He and I worked together to fill out the team, because it's important to get the right kind of representation from the trustees. We ended up having one more trustee than the last time they had a search committee, just to ensure the right composition. So, it ended up being a committee of nineteen members.

I can't get into a lot of detail because it is confidential, but we wanted a leader who was strategic in orientation, yet inclusive in terms of formulations and so forth, because developing the vision and the strategy for the university is something that's done in a very collaborative way with the faculty. You get student input, you get some staff input, but in particular, the faculty. John and John had a really magical ability to work with the faculty, to understand what were the areas we needed to build, and what were the areas we should maintain as they are, and what were some that potentially we should decrease somewhat.

Stanford being what we perceived to be one of the very best universities in the world, we wanted to get, in our terminology, a leader among leaders—someone who was not only able to be highly respected inside, but highly respected externally, and could take Stanford to the next level. So, you're really looking for someone who has that kind of capability, that kind of track record, that kind of desire, those aspirations, those ambitions to go out and do that. You go around and talk to people from most of the top 50 universities in the country. It's very time intensive. We had a tremendous search committee—a highly dedicated, really driven committee—and we came to the consensual decision to bring in the new president, Marc Tessier-Lavigne. I think the new president has come in and reaffirmed what we all wanted to do, which is we want it to be a purposeful university that's really oriented towards providing the means whereby we can make a positive impact in the world and improve the human condition.

After the search ended, I had another year as chair. They had the option to keep me on for another year, and they chose that option. Clearly you can't equate what the chair does to what the president does; the president is so much more important. But having us both leave at the same time didn't make sense. This gave me an opportunity to work with Marc for a year, and then we brought in a new chair, Jeff Raikes.

REFLECTIONS ON JOHN HENNESSY

The opportunity to work with John was one of the extraordinary experiences of my life. There aren't that many times when you're able to work with someone who has such distinctive capabilities in so many different areas. John was an esteemed academic, a successful entrepreneur, and a gifted, brilliant, visionary, inspirational leader. To have those things coming together in one package is phenomenal. He had an uncanny ability to work collaboratively, not only with his provost, but with the Executive Cabinet and the faculty, too. And he had an incredible relationship with his wife. They operated as a team. It was most evident in terms of the strengthening of the arts at Stanford. We did a lot in that area.

The other thing I found unique about John is his incredible breadth of knowledge. He is a prolific reader. We'd be in a casual conversation, and somehow the name of, say, Millard Fillmore would come up. I knew he had been a president, but I had no idea what number or what he stood for. John would start talking about him, "The thirteenth president of the United States. He's the guy that really provided the basis for the state of California to enter the union as a slave free state." He had an incredible curiosity and a deep drive to continue to educate himself.

He brought all that together in an incredible intuition as to what was right and best for the university, and how to make us an even more impactful university in the world. That was communicated to the various constituencies in the Stanford community, be they alumni, students, faculty, or staff. We raised probably in his full tenure $12 billion-plus. I think John was so successful as a fundraiser because people trusted him. They believed his vision, they believed in the plan that he put together, and they trusted him to be able to execute those things and deliver the results that he'd promised. A lot of people can tout things, but to have that ability to communicate a confidence in terms of being able to deliver the end result—and to have the tenure and the time to do it—I think is remarkable. To be an effective university president, you need to have the skills of a tenured scientist or researcher and the business acumen of some of our great strategists and great leaders in the business community. I think it's why John was selected to be the chairman of Alphabet.

The other guy that didn't get a lot of credit is Gerhard Casper, who was the president that preceded John. Gerhard selected him as provost, and he played a really significant role in identifying that talent, developing it, and nurturing it. Ultimately, it was not his decision who the next president would be, but he put John there so it became evident what the decision should be.

REFLECTIONS ON THE IMPORTANCE OF UNIVERSITIES

I think it's very important for the university president to be able to effectively communicate what the university does. A lot of it is self-evident, but a lot of it is less evident. There's a certain subtlety that might be unappreciated, forgotten, and not brought into the equation in the way that it ought to be. I think being a good university president is one of the harder jobs in the country, but one of the more important jobs. Universities provide, in essence, the economic underpinning for our economy and the richness of the fabric of our society. They play such a huge role in our lives, oftentimes in ways that might not be as fully appreciated by the general public as it ought to be in terms of what they provide—not only for the communities of which they are a part, but also the broader community, the state, and world.

In terms of federally funded research, I think what our universities are doing in the basic sciences, basic engineering, medicine, humanities, social sciences, is so critical. You want to, as loudly and as often as you can—not in a boastful way, but in a substantive way—communicate the benefits of these universities that sometimes get castigated and categorized as elite institutions that are detached from the real world. I think that is very unfair and untrue, and not representative of what they really do and the value they really add. People don't often think about it this way, but the higher education industry in the United States dominates probably more than any other industry, including high tech.

I think China certainly understands the benefits of our research universities. It's trying to replicate them to a degree, and you have some very good universities throughout Europe and other places in the world. But you want to make certain the appropriate resources are applied in areas where you can really work together. In our government there are areas like that. We have these national energy labs—seventeen of them—and we have one here at Stanford. They've taken a portion of the accelerator at SLAC and repurposed it to create the most capable X-ray laser in the world. It will take basically video pictures at the atomic level, and that has a huge impact on a variety of areas. It relates to materials, solar efficiency, battery efficiency, artificial photosynthesis, all kinds of things. That's obviously a collaborative relationship between the government and Stanford. You can take the appropriate long-term perspective and really build your scientific and your cultural and technical base. Research universities like Stanford are a key building block in our society, and I think that's what makes Western society so strong.[44]

The thing you realize through having the fortunate situation of being able to be around Stanford and what it represents is that the Stanford faculty are just extraordinary individuals. They are so capable. It's one of the reasons Stanford has the reputation it has—probably the principal reason why we have the reputation we have. Then, obviously, we attract very good students.

I think universities, if properly managed, provide an incredible benefit to the nation of which they're a part on the research and the education front. It's just a real pleasure and privilege to be able to be a small part of that and play your role in beginning to shape it. Stanford has had such a huge impact, but there are so many areas on the horizon—whether it's neuroscience, life sciences, lifelong learning, urbanization, artificial intelligence. In the digital era, there are so many areas to shape going forward.

PART THREE

ACADEMIC LEADERSHIP
AT THE SCHOOL LEVEL

CHAPTER 7

JIM PLUMMER

Dean of the School of Engineering (1999–2014)

James D. Plummer is an electrical engineer and the John M. Fluke Professor of Electrical Engineering at Stanford University. He joined Stanford's Department of Electrical Engineering in 1978 and served as Frederick Emmons Terman Dean of the School of Engineering from 1999 to 2014.

Becoming Dean of the School
of Engineering

I had been senior associate dean in the School of Engineering between 1993 and 1996 when Jim Gibbons was dean.[45] Then when John Hennessy became dean, I became the chair of the Department of Electrical Engineering, which was a job I liked a lot. Then when John was appointed provost, that opened up the dean's position yet again. There was a search, and Gerhard Casper asked me to consider it. After some thought, I went ahead and agreed to do it. We actually had two small kids at the time; our children were one and three, so I was a little unsure as to whether I should really do it or not. But I did, and it worked out. I became dean in 1999.

Up until that point, I had spent my whole career in the Engineering School, so I actually knew the school pretty well. Because I had been in the dean's office, I had interacted with all the departments and had a pretty good understanding of where the strengths and weaknesses were. At that time, the really strong departments were probably Mechanical Engineering and Electrical Engineering. The smaller departments were uniformly excellent, but many lacked critical mass. When we looked at Materials Science and Chemical Engineering, for example, and considered their national ranks, they were ranked in the high single digits, whereas Electrical Engineering and Mechanical Engineering were always competing for number one and number two in the country. So, I decided pretty early on to focus a lot of attention on some of the smaller departments and see what decisions we could make or what initiatives we could take that might make them more competitive nationally and get them up into the top five at least. That was one area I focused on as dean.

Another area that had been under consideration for a long time in the school was trying to sort out what in the world we should do about bioengineering, biomedical engineering, and those kinds of things. We had no such department, and almost all of our peer schools had formed such departments quite a long time before we did. So there had been ongoing discussions about what Stanford should do or shouldn't do with regard to bioengineering.

My style in approaching these issues was basically to have very open, frank discussions with however many people wanted to talk about a topic. If you want to develop a strategic plan in a university, you've really got to do it bottom-up and encourage people to be outspoken about ideas and not reject any ideas out of hand. So, we did a lot of that. Everything was on the table early on, from merging a couple of the small departments to give them the critical mass, to trying to potentially grow one or more of them and to try and get them interested in more futuristic research areas than they had perhaps done in the past.

We reviewed the whole portfolio of opportunities, and in the end we came to a consensus that especially with respect to those two small departments, Materials Science and Chemical Engineering, it didn't make sense to merge them. There really aren't any national examples of such merged departments being very successful, and their disciplines are so distinct that it didn't strike me as a viable thing to do other than getting the numbers up. So we decided to put a carrot out there and say, "Look, we're going to provide both of these departments the opportunity to grow by one or two faculty positions per year for five, six, seven, eight years, maybe longer. Whether or not the billets get allocated each year is going to depend upon the quality of people that get hired each year, and also the level of excitement in the strategic plans that the departments develop. So we put it out there as an opportunity, but let the departments try and figure out where their futures might lie. Both of them, to their credit, hired a bunch of exciting junior faculty in new areas for them. Both of them got to the point where they were ranked three, four, five in the country, sometimes even higher, after a period of five or ten years. And so, we really did get a critical mass.

I think that actually worked out pretty well. It didn't require massive resources. The school has 250 faculty, and those two departments were initially around ten to twelve faculty. We grew them to around twenty faculty. So, it wasn't a huge transfer of resources from larger departments to smaller departments.

DEVELOPING BIOENGINEERING
AT STANFORD

The interesting thing about bioengineering, or biomedical engineering as it's often called, is that the historically dominant departments in places like Georgia Tech and Johns Hopkins that were started literally decades ago in some cases, typically were founded around fairly traditional engineering applications:

everything from medical devices to biomechanical engineering and so on. The science base they used to work on those applications was the traditional engineering science base—mostly physics and math and a little bit of chemistry. So, there wasn't anything uniquely different about those biomedical engineering departments except that they were focused on a different set of application areas. For a very long time, the view at Stanford was, "We've got faculty in Electrical Engineering who are working on medical imaging. We've got faculty in Mechanical Engineering who are working on biomechanical things. What are we going to do that's different than that in a separate department?"

If you look historically at some of these other peer institutions, they actually formed their biomedical engineering departments by pulling faculty out of electrical engineering and mechanical engineering and putting them into new departments called biomechanical engineering. So there was a lot of resistance—I think rightly so—to doing that, because it didn't really create something new.

The thing that finally turned the conversation was the growing recognition around 2000/2001 that there's another science out there that historically had not been part of engineering: biology. The reason it had not been part of engineering is because it was very much a reductionist science. Biologists were still digging ever deeper into cellular structure, and that was the time when DNA discoveries were being made. So, the underlying science was not nearly as deep and as rich as you can find in physics, where a lot of stuff engineers use is 100 years old.

When we thought about this, the conclusion we came to was that if we wanted to create something that was uniquely different, then we had to think about a department whose foundation or science base was primarily biology rather than physics and chemistry and math, although it would certainly use elements of those well. That would be something that was actually very different than the kinds of applications-oriented research going on in Electrical Engineering and Mechanical Engineering. That thought process and discussion led to the creation of a Bioengineering Department, and the goal was to have a different science base than what we had in our other departments so that it would really add something new to the picture.

The second thing we did that was new and unprecedented with respect to our peer institutions was to set up the department so it was actually in two schools. It was equally managed by the School of Engineering and the School of Medicine. The reason we did that was that I'm a real believer in owners rather than renters: people that own something take care of it and watch out for it and invest in it and so on. Having a department that is in the Engineering School but that occasionally goes over to the Medical School and talks to the physicians or research staff scientists is very different than having the School of Medicine be a co-owner of the research portfolio of the department. So, we set it up as a joint department between the two schools, much to the chagrin of lots of people who thought that was a really bad idea. Their concerns were everything from, "one dean is bad enough, two would be a disaster," to "the Medical School is completely different in terms of what it does, and how it's managed, and its financial model." Also, the Medical School has little interaction with undergraduates. They do not do a lot of undergraduate teaching. Their PhD program is relatively small because they're so focused on medical students. They have a huge clinical program.

There was a whole list of reasons why you could argue this was a bad idea. But we pressed ahead anyway and tried to create something that would add to the pie in the sense that it would be biology based and jointly managed, and would hire a set of new faculty who would be very different from anything we currently had in the Engineering School. And that's how it's played out. They've hired a set of remarkable faculty who have launched the school into a whole bunch of new research areas compared to what was going on in EE and ME and ChemE and other departments that existed at the time.

EMERGENCE OF THE UNDERGRADUATE COMPUTER SCIENCE PROGRAM

By principle, Stanford wants to be a place where any undergraduate can pick any major he or she wants. So, you never know from one year to the next how many majors you're going to have in EE or History or whatever. These are choices that individual students make. You have to look at the emergence of Computer Science in retrospect and then ask what were the contributing factors that led to those choices.

It was probably around 2007, 2008, or 2009 when things began to change. As dean, I tracked undergraduate enrollments by department, major, and everything else. At first, the numbers had been pretty constant, bumping up and down in each department over long timescales, but averaging a pretty flat number. So, when we started seeing some of the student numbers going up, particularly in Computer Science in about 2007 or 2008, the first conclusion was, "Oh well, this is just a random variation. We'll see it bounce back down again in another year or two."

It didn't. As we plotted this trend year after year, there was a straight upward slope that was consistent over the next decade. It got to the point where the undergraduates in CS today make up something like 25 percent of all Stanford undergrads. So, it's bigger today than the entire Engineering School was in 2007 in terms of number of students. It's been the biggest contributor to the doubling or more of under-graduates in Engineering at Stanford, going from a historical 20 percent up to nearly 45 percent today. I think there are a bunch of reasons why that happened, but one of them certainly was the external world around us and the emergence of a lot of the social networking companies like Facebook and so on. There were really interesting job opportunities for students who could write code. Another part of it was the 2008 financial crisis, where students were certainly thinking about careers where there were exciting and well-paid job opportunities.

But a key factor was the fact that we had two indi-viduals—first Eric Roberts and then Mehran Sahami—who basically took charge of the undergraduate Computer Science program and transformed it into something that was really, really well done.[46] Students need to know how to use code, but they changed it so that they basically were writing code for interesting applications as opposed to silly homework assignments. The lectures in these introductory classes were incredibly well done. They're on YouTube, and students all over the world watch them. They turned the introduction to computer science experience into something that was a lot of fun. Students just flocked to it. I've heard literally hundreds of stories about students who said they came to Stanford and had no idea they would major in Computer Science. They took CS106, which is the Introduction to Programming course, and that did it—they were Computer Science majors from that point on.

I've actually sat in the classrooms and watched. Superficially, what they did is they made the curriculum have a lot more choice in terms of the application areas students could work on in Computer Science. They created a lot of tracks—everything from data mining to AI to machine learning and so on. After the students took the introductory classes, they could follow a pathway that was interesting to them. They cut back on the number of required courses in the major. That meant students had more choice and more flexibility. They put the students first. They basically said, "What do the students need to learn to be really good, in terms of contributing to a company like Facebook or any one of your favorite social networking companies?" They provided an educational experience that not only prepared students incredibly well, but also did it in a way which was really a lot of fun.

Today it's Mehran and the fleet of lecturers and other faculty who he's trained, teaching a class with 500, 600, 700 students in it. Having these students give that class one of the highest teaching ratings in the School of Engineering year after year after year is just remarkable. I think that had a big impact as well.

What was interesting was that all of that growth in Computer Science did not come at the expense of other engineering majors. It was not the case that the enrollments in EE and other departments fell dramatically because everyone was flocking to CS. Basically all the growth in CS happened because of students who would probably not otherwise have been engineering majors, which is pretty remarkable when you think about it. If anything, there was absolute growth in the other departments in the school as well, but not to the same extent that CS saw.

There wasn't any obvious way in which you could reallocate resources to address this growth. You cannot pull faculty billets from other departments, because they were arguably doing as much as they'd ever done in terms of undergraduate and graduate teaching and research. So, a lot of the resources that needed to be put in place—everything from teaching assistants to lecturers to new faculty billets and so on—had to come as incremental resources to the school. That was sometimes a hard sell. I can remember going to Budget Group meetings year after year and pointing to the enrollment numbers and everything else and arguing that we needed more general funds allocated for teaching assistants, and we needed more faculty billets so we could put them into Computer Science. Most of the people in the room were not from Engineering. They were often faculty from H&S [Humanities and Sciences] because up until very recently that was always by far the largest undergraduate program. They had handled 80 percent of Stanford students historically at the undergraduate level. They would say, "Well, this can't be right, because our classes are not getting smaller and we've got just as many majors as we always had." They were kind of in denial about what was going on. And, of course, they were wrong because it is a zero-sum game. Stanford wasn't suddenly admitting hundreds more students.

Figuring out how to get the resources to Computer Science was a real challenge. There was a struggle within the school, because the arguments not to take them from other departments were strong. And then outside the school, the arguments were strong because it is in many ways a zero-sum game. The provost was sympathetic, but there were lots of people around campus who weren't, who didn't want to see Engineering growing to the degree that it was. That challenge certainly continues today.

In the end, it didn't hurt that the president of the university was from Computer Science. It also didn't hurt that John Hennessy and I play golf on a regular basis, and we could talk about these things. He fully understood what was going on, but he was also a good enough politician in his role as president that he could smooth over some of these things and find ways to work with the provost to get resources channeled into Engineering without upsetting everybody else in the university.

CREATION OF THE STANFORD DESIGN SCHOOL

David Kelley showed up at my office one day around 2002/2003 and said we really needed to reinvent how we teach design.[47]

It should have a much broader impact than just mechanical engineering, he argued. We have a product design program, which has been going for a long time, but he saw it as a way of educating a much broader cadre of students to develop life skills that were going to be really useful to them throughout their careers. This was all about design thinking.

That was a huge opportunity that has grown into something that I think is very important today for Stanford. In some ways, the growth of the d.school and the classes they were teaching (which were mostly populated by non-engineering students) also contributed to this realization by the student body that maybe engineering was something more than just a bunch of geeks sitting there writing code in their little cubicles and never talking to anybody else in the world.[48] It helped to socialize engineering.

The thing that made it work was that Kelley didn't say, "I need $100 million and a building and ten faculty billets and we'll create something remarkable." What he said was, "Look, I think we need to do this, but we need to start out small. We need to do a bunch of experiments and find out what works and what doesn't work because we're not really sure how we're going to do all of this." That was a model I liked a lot because there were a lot of people in the school who were skeptical, to put it mildly, about design thinking and whether this was something Engineering ought to be involved in at all—much less make it a significant initiative. It's sort of the fuzzy side of engineering. People would say, "Where's the calculus in it? Where are the partial differential equations?"

The way we were able to make this work was, when people raised those kinds of questions, I would just respond by saying, "We're just doing some experiments, and they're probably going to fail, so don't worry about it. It's probably going to amount to nothing. But we ought to be in the business of doing experiments and trying things out." So, the d.school started in a double-wide trailer. They painted it all red inside and started teaching some very small classes. The student interest started growing, and they had a cadre of people in the Valley who were really excited, starting from Steve Jobs on down. They were really excited about what they were doing and became volunteers and mentors and coaches.

It took ten years and five physical moves on campus from the double-wide trailer to successive places where we could find space to house them, each being designed a little bit differently in terms of the physical infrastructure they were using. Finally, they ended up in the Peterson Building where they are today. It was very much an experiment that took place over a decade. I think, in retrospect, the reason that worked so well was because couching it as an experiment meant nobody worried too much about it and kind of dismissed it. Then as it grew and became popular, and other faculty saw it, they would go and hang out and say, "Gee, maybe I should look at this and see if I can learn something from it." It was something that grew at the natural pace that allowed it to be successful within all of the bureaucracy of the university. It was helped, of course, by a major gift from Hasso Plattner who funded the whole thing at the end of the day.[49] But he did that because he was just really excited about the concept and believed in it.

David M. Kelley, the Donald W. Whittier Professor in Mechanical Engineering, speaking at the opening gala for the Hasso Plattner Institute of Design (d.school)'s newly reconstructed building in May 2007.

PERSPECTIVES ON INTERDISCIPLINARY INITIATIVES

The Precourt Institute, the Woods Institute, and Bio-X are examples of interdisciplinary institutes or centers that have the common goal of trying to figure out how to get faculty together from different disciplines to work on really complex research topics. I think that we've learned a huge amount by going through that process. I wouldn't argue that we have it right yet, because I think the institutes are still evolving. While they've accomplished a tremendous amount, I think they still have a set of difficult issues. Their structure makes them, in some ways, less effective than they might otherwise be, but we don't have a better idea right now for what the structure ought to be.

The difficulty is that the institutes basically report into the dean of research. That's probably the right place, because they're research institutes and they have faculty from multiple schools involved. The common point then would logically be the dean of research. The problem with that is the dean of research doesn't make faculty appointments. They're all made in departments and schools. So, Bio-X and the other institutes have the mission of trying to build large interdisciplinary programs. And the premise is that to do that, they've got to involve faculty from Engineering and from some of the sciences, maybe some of the social sciences, maybe from the Medical School. Yet they don't have any ability to appoint those faculty to Stanford.

The quandary is that the institutes largely control space. Bio-X has the Clark Center, and the institutes have other physical space within buildings where they can house these interdisciplinary programs. But they don't have the ability to go out and search for a faculty member and hire that faculty member and put that faculty member in their space. There's some good elements to this because they've got to partner somehow with the schools, which do have the ability to appoint the faculty. So, you've got two entities: one that can appoint the faculty, and one that controls the space in which those faculty would be housed and in which they would do their research.

This only works if there's effective partnership between the schools and the institutes. In my experience, whether or not that happens really comes down to the individuals involved— that is, the people who are leading the institutes, the person who is the dean of research at the time, and the people who are the school deans at the time. It's not always the case that those partnerships are perfect. In fact, they may not even be really good, because every one of those individuals has other agendas as well. The institutes have a great mission, and they have lots of carrots they can put out there in terms of seed research funding, brand-new buildings to house faculty, and so on. However, they do not have complete control over their futures because they typically can't appoint faculty.

The schools also have other priorities. They want to be involved in the institutes, but they've also got to worry about departments and educating undergraduate and graduate students in disciplines in their departments and so on. So, there's this pull in many directions for all of the players in this structure. When it works well, it can be really successful. But there have also been examples where it did not work well because of the people involved.

Educating the Engineers
of the Future

Curriculum really is the responsibility of the departments as a starting point, especially at the undergraduate level. They're the people who deliver it, and the departments need to define what skill sets our graduates need to have in order to be productive citizens. The curriculum really starts with the faculty within the department. That said, there's a real tendency, especially in a research-intensive university, for faculty to essentially ignore the undergraduate curriculum because all of the reward systems in the university are set up to reward individual stars and the great research that they're doing.

The question then is: How do the faculty and departments come together to put together a coherent, interesting, and exciting curriculum? How do you encourage faculty to do that when the reward system doesn't really reward them for doing that? Aside from persuasion, which can be effective at times, I think part of the solution is that if we see really exciting curriculum opportunities that are not going to result from faculty in a department getting together and saying, "We need to do this!" then sometimes you need to do an end run and think about doing something at the school level that would involve creating curriculum. A good example is the entrepreneurship program. That's a school-level program, which started with Jim Gibbons. People thought it was critical for our students to know entrepreneurship, so Tom Byers came in.[50] He set up a whole bunch of courses, and their real goal is to provide entrepreneurship opportunities for a wide range of engineering and non-engineering students. Another good example is the d.school. They offer a whole set of classes, many of which actually aren't even for credit, where students can develop a set of life skills that would never arise within any individual department as a core requirement. The students value it greatly, and they take these classes.

A final example might be the Institute for Computational Mathematics and Engineering, ICME, that we established in partnership with the Math Department. All engineering programs have requirements for basic math skills. Traditionally, those courses would have been taught in the Math Department.

Every engineering school I know of complains about the quality of the math courses that are taught in math departments. The math faculty who are teaching these courses love pure mathematics. They basically want to teach math skills, and they really don't care much about how you apply partial differential equations to solving particular practical problems. We set up a series of courses that cover calculus and PDEs [partial differential equations] and so on, but they teach them very differently. They focus on applications. Yes, the students learn how to solve PDEs, but they learn how to solve them by working on interesting engineering problems in a variety of domains, from circuits to fluid dynamics. We saw it as a school-wide need, and we set something up that was beyond the bounds of a single department.

CHANGING FACULTY RECRUITMENT IN THE SCHOOL OF ENGINEERING

We actually made, I think, a pretty dramatic change in the way faculty are hired in the Engineering School. It had its origins in Computer Science which, for whatever reasons early on in my time as dean, started doing these "open searches." Typically, a faculty search is targeted in a particular technical area, and they started doing what we call broad area searches. If there's a faculty opening in Computer Science and you think you're a computer scientist then you'd be welcome to apply, and the department would hire somebody they thought was the brightest, smartest, most interesting and innovative person in the field, almost independent of what their research area was. Computer Science experimented with this, and sitting up in the dean's office, I was just blown away by the quality of the people they were finding from these kinds of searches. The research areas would obviously vary from one year to another, but most often they were in the emerging areas, because it would be young, exciting people who had just graduated and were looking to change the computer science field.

We gradually moved essentially all of the searches within our departments in the School of Engineering to that model—that is, open, broad area searches. Sometimes the job postings would say, "We have a preference for faculty in Mechanical Engineering in three or four areas, but anyone who is interested in Mechanical Engineering can apply." That made a huge difference across the whole school in the quality of the faculty we were able to hire. It continues today to result in constant improvement in the quality of the faculty. When you get to a position where the departments are highly ranked and arguably, you're competitive for any faculty member, then sometimes you can take a different strategy for faculty hiring than someone who's in a mid-level public university or something. They've got 500 students in Mechanical Engineering, and they've got to teach all these students fluid dynamics, so they've really got to hire somebody in fluid mechanics. In those searches, you end up with a much smaller, narrower pool, and you arguably miss the real all-stars. We were fortunate to have all of our departments be highly ranked, and all of them be competitive for anyone they wanted to hire.

A side benefit of doing these broader searches, which I hadn't really appreciated until we saw it evolving over time, was that it actually makes it far easier to improve the diversity of your faculty. If you've got say a great woman in some particular discipline of mechanical engineering graduating one year, and you do a targeted search that isn't in her area, she won't even apply. But if you do a broad area search, you get to look at her. Then she'll be in the pool. You can think differently about some of those diversity issues. So, it helped us to increase the percentage of women on our faculty and to attract more under-represented minorities.

I think the more focused on diversity we become in colleges and universities, the more we have to insist on diversity in the search process and committees. Candidates coming in who see nothing but old white males are going to think differently about the place than if they see an interesting collection of different kinds of people on the search committee. I certainly tried to make sure the search committees were diverse. We always try to have at least one member who is outside the school or department because that brings an outside-in perspective on things, which we've found to be very useful over the years.

Final Reflections on Time as Dean

The day-to-day business of being a dean is basically worrying about faculty appointments and worrying about budgets and worrying about fundraising. The timing of the development aspect of the job for me was basically perfect. We had a president who was an engineer and agreement with the central administration in terms of the things we were trying to accomplish. The Engineering Quad, for example, would not have happened if John Hennessy hadn't been in the President's Office and we had consensus between the players in the Engineering School and Building 10.[51]

If you look at the money that was raised, I was involved with raising it, but John was deeply involved with it, obviously. Without that partnership, the golden age we went through for fifteen years or so probably wouldn't have been as golden. So, I was really lucky in the sense that I was the Engineering dean at almost a perfect time in Stanford's history when the president was an engineer and when there were lots of really exciting growth opportunities happening. We were sitting in a location where there were lots of alumni who'd done incredibly well and who were excited about the initiatives and wanted to give back to the Engineering School and to the university. So, it was really a lot of fun.

I think it is really important to emphasize the partnership with John, because that was a unique time in Stanford's history to do some of these things in Engineering. It only really happened because he was in the president's office. And John Etchemendy too. He's a logician. I found him incredibly easy to talk to, and it was almost like having two engineers up there in Building 10: the president and the provost. That was part of the golden era.

But even more importantly, take the way the major campaign that John ran evolved. All of these university campaigns start from the bottom up. It's always "tell us your best ideas" and "throw all these ideas in the hopper" and so on. And what results from that is $50 billion of ideas, from all of the departments, the faculty, the staff, and everything else. Then the critical thing is how do you get from something like that—that wish list—down to something that is actionable and right sized that can actually turn into a successful campaign? That's actually the hardest thing to do. John, through his leadership, did a tremendously good job of that.

A lot of it was done through the Executive Cabinet, with the deans. I'd sit there around the table with all of them. One of the things that John brought to the table was that he had enough experience in industry that he understood top-down management. He'd been on boards. Of course, I had as well. And Bob Joss, who was the Business School dean, had been on boards. There was a subset of us there who understood top-down management from an industrial perspective, but we also understood the bottom-up chaos from a university perspective, and John was able to orchestrate the right balance. You don't get from a $50 billion wish list down to an actionable strategic plan without some serious top-down management. That has to happen behind the scenes. You can't do it overtly, and you have to let everybody think their ideas are as good as anybody else's. At the end of the day, you've got to sell the reduced actionable plan, which will disappoint a lot of people because their ideas didn't make the final cut.

He was really good at that, and I think he orchestrated the Executive Cabinet and the deans to think that way. Our job was basically to whittle it down into something we can actually go out there and get people to write checks for to build new buildings, build new programs, create Bioengineering, create the new Business School campus, and so on. I give John a tremendous amount of credit for how he led that exercise. At the end of the day, it was a group of ten or twelve people sitting around the table, but you know, the person who's in charge really needs to orchestrate the process of how you do that really well. And I think that's what he did.

CHAPTER 8

BOB JOSS

Dean of Stanford Graduate School of Business
(1999–2009)

Robert L. Joss is an American businessman and banker who was dean of the Stanford Graduate School of Business from 1999 to 2009. A former White House Fellow, he received his MBA and PhD degrees from Stanford. Prior to becoming dean, he served in senior leadership positions at Wells Fargo Bank and was the CEO and managing director of Westpac Banking Corporation, one of Australia's largest banks, for six years.

Moving from Business to Academia

It was an interesting experience for me coming from industry to the deanship. It is not completely unusual at Stanford Graduate School of Business (GSB), but it's pretty unusual in academia for people to come out of business and go into an academic role like a dean. We've had three or four deans from business at Stanford GSB over the years, and it's generally worked out pretty well.

First, it was a really different experience for me to go from a position of industry leadership to academic leadership.[52] They are very different kind of institutions—different values, different ways that people think and make decisions. That was very challenging in many ways, although I wasn't completely shocked. I knew the university pretty well. I'd been a student here and I got my PhD here, but I had never had a full-time academic career until I came back to be the dean.

Second, it was an interesting time, because 1999 was the peak of the internet bubble. Everything here was a little surreal/unreal. Our students all thought they could start some sort of internet company, whether it was dog food or anything else, and get rich. We had CNBC interviewing students on the lawn, and we had real cultural challenges in getting people interested in academics.

When you work in industry, especially when you're a CEO, you have several things that you almost take for granted: the way people think, the way decisions are made, the things you can delegate to people. You have a lot of senior executives who are eager to take on things, and they aspire to more senior roles in the company. But being a dean is not at all like being a CEO. It's more like being a managing partner of a firm like Boston Consulting Group or something, where you've got a lot of professional, highly educated people. You're the managing partner, but there's an awful lot you would not think of doing without consulting the partners.

In a school, of course, the partners are the tenured full professors. We have lots and lots of partners' meetings around who to hire, what to teach. Increasingly in business, it's not like CEOs run around giving a lot of orders. There's a lot of communication—getting people together and getting a common vision of where you want to go and getting people on board. In that sense, it wasn't completely different, but it's a really different culture in the university. People value things differently, spend their time differently, decisions are made very collegially and not very many are made by a single person.

Moreover, I do feel that having worked in Australia was really helpful to me. If I'd come right after my previous job at Wells Fargo to be the dean, I think it would have been much harder. I think having worked in another country and having wrestled with all the challenges of the different culture and realizing the importance of getting to know that culture and listening more—being better at asking questions, being a little more patient about things—was really helpful to me. I felt the university was almost like another country, and it was. The culture is so different from a business culture. You've got to really work hard to try to understand that culture and how things work, and the way decisions are made, and the way people get ahead.

There's a sort of coherence in business, where if you take care of the customers and you do a good job with employees, then the shareholders will do well. You have a vocabulary and a way of lining things up. What does it mean to be a great company? What's success in a great company? It's happy customers, happy employees, happy shareholders.

You talk about success in a university or school, and it gets very complicated. You've got many more constituencies. Here at the school, you've got faculty, you've got staff, you've got students who kind of feel like they're the customer, but they're not really the customer. You've got recruiters, you've got the rest of the university, you've got alumni who are kind of like investors but not completely, and yet you rely on them for a huge amount of your financial support. It's a very complex kind of constituency management role, particularly as you get into a senior school role.

I think there's a huge amount of trying to teach and talk to each of the constituents about the role they play and how they can help make it a better school. They need to understand other people's roles. Students are very short-sighted and focused on themselves and on having a good time and getting a good job. They ask, "Why do we have faculty that do research? Why don't they just teach?" Well, you can't be a very good long-run sustainable teacher if you're not pushing the boundaries of knowledge within your field.

You've got an awful lot of communication that goes on. That's true in any business or any industry, but I think it's particularly challenging in academia because of these multiple constituents who have different pressures and demands, and they don't really understand each other very well. So, it takes a lot of time, and there are very few people to delegate to. In business, you've got people who aspire to executive roles, but most faculty would just as soon not have anything to do with administration. They don't really want your job. They know we need a dean, or we need a provost or something, but they don't really want to do that themselves. They don't really understand too much of what goes on there, so it's difficult. And a lot of the outside world, they want to talk to the dean or the vice chancellor, or whoever it is. They don't want to deal with anybody else, which creates a huge amount of time pressure for the dean. I would say the demands of my time as dean were probably greater than they were as CEO of Westpac, just in terms of all the places you needed to be and the people who wanted to see you. The biggest challenge was managing my time.

IMPLEMENTING CHANGE INITIATIVES ACROSS THE UNIVERSITY

One of the challenges in any leadership role with regard to changing the place and making it better is that you have to get this healthy sense of dissatisfaction with the status quo. You've got to get people thinking, "We really could be better. We *want* to be better." When I joined Westpac, they were in a real crisis. They were in the news, and they'd gotten into all these problems, like suffering the largest loss in Australian corporate history. They knew they had to get better, and they were looking to me to be the sole director of that. So, you're going into a situation where people know you've got to change. In fact, it was almost too much that way. People would say, "Just tell us what to do, Bob." And I'd say, "I have a pretty good idea what to do, but you've got to help me understand some of the nitty-gritty details in terms of execution and what's wrong."

However, at the GSB, people were pretty self-satisfied. They thought, "We're great. We're one of the top schools in the world." So here you are in the role thinking, "Yeah, but we could be better!" I think the challenge there was that it's not a burning platform. You've got to take time to build up some thoughts and ideas and a constituency around what we want to do. The narrative becomes, "We are good, but we could get better. We need to get better."

Robert Joss, right, at a press conference in 1999 announcing his appointment as the dean of the Stanford Graduate School of Business, with outgoing dean Michael Spence, left.

I came not knowing for sure what we needed to do. I loved the school. I was a student here. I was on the advisory council. I'm an alumnus here, so I knew quite a bit about it. A number of my really good friends are on the faculty, so it wasn't completely alien to me, and I had recruited here. But I hadn't been a faculty member here.

I also had my own biases about what needed to change. The school was really good, but we weren't very involved in terms of *global* management. We weren't a very global place in terms of our thinking, our research, our teaching. Second, we weren't really doing much of anything around leadership, which was of strong interest to me. I thought we were exceptionally good on technical management skills—our accounting, finance, marketing, strategy, operations—the functional skills of business and industry. That's where our strength was—in the disciplines, in the faculty, in the research—kind of bringing it in an overarching way together in terms of what's *management* all about? But we weren't doing enough to explore what's *leadership* all about? And, is there something about being a *global* enterprise that's different than just local?

Those were the things on my mind. And over time, we were able to really do a lot of things by recruiting faculty and starting new courses, changing the curriculum, and pushing in those directions. But it's not like you can come in and announce, "I've got this strategy." People would just say, "Who the hell do you think you are?" It's not really the dean's role to do it alone. It's the faculty that ultimately determines the strategy. So, it's a lot of work in terms of just talking and teaching and pushing and cajoling.

From the beginning, we have always been a graduate school, kind of like the Law School and the Medical School. Stanford never had an undergraduate business program, and we evolved the curriculum and developed an approach and a philosophy around students who usually had an undergraduate major in something other than business. The MBA, which was our flagship degree, was focused on grad students.

Increasingly, we could see that a lot of students from other parts of the university really wanted to study aspects of business, but we didn't have the faculty or the size to do it. The Engineering School kept growing. The Economics Department and some of the other social science departments were growing, and they were interested in issues around leadership and group behavior. We started to have a lot of collaboration, and our faculty were often in joint appointments with a lot of these other places in the university. We never thought that we really could have the scale or the people to run an undergraduate bachelor's degree or something like it in GSB, but we thought, "We *can* have an impact throughout the university. We can do a better job of collaborating with Engineering, with Law, with Education, with Medicine." Between our faculty and their faculty, we could impact more students without increasing the size of our student body that much. We could actually touch more students.

We now have a lot of programs with joint degrees and joint classes and summer programs and programs in entrepreneurship. The Stanford d.school, for example, was a collaboration between our faculty and the School of Engineering. So, we tried to do a lot of collaborating around the university, which was not the case when I came here. The GSB was very autonomous—siloed. We would talk about the university as "across the street." And, in fact, the search committee when they were interviewing me and offered me the job, they said, "Bob, just keep the university off our back. That's your most important job as a dean. Protect our resources." We had our own endowment. We still do. So, we've always been a pretty independent place—but sometimes too much, I felt.

I suppose in one way I had the advantage of having been the group head in earlier roles, like at Wells Fargo. When you're a group head, you care about your *group.* You run it and you think, "What's wrong with the CEO? He doesn't understand *my group.*" And then when you're a CEO, you think, "What's wrong with those group heads? Why don't they think more about the whole enterprise?" So now as dean, it was like being a group head again.

When I was a dean, we had seven schools across the university. But I knew what it was like to be in the president's office and having to think about a greater university. It was one of the things I didn't expect would occupy my time, but I became more and more convinced it was really important to increase our collaboration between the Business School and the rest of the university. Part of it was just personal. I found I got to know the other school deans pretty well, and a lot of them asked me for my ideas or advice on things because they didn't have any background in management. They were all academics, and I'd spent my whole life managing in large complicated enterprises. So, I could see we could be more helpful.

One example is that we started this program, the Stanford Leadership Academy, for teaching current and future faculty and staff leaders. These are people from all over the university. When we began, the Business School had a reputation of being aloof and arrogant and off on our own, and that wasn't helping us at all. I would say to people, "You can't be a great school if the university is not also great. So, you've got to play a role in helping the university get better as well as the school."

There are some schools where I think the school is better known than the university. Take Wharton, for example. Most people can't even remember which university it is connected to: Is it Penn State, or is it the University of Pennsylvania?[53] And Kellogg School of Management at Northwestern University is a little bit that way, too. These business schools are actually better known than their universities. Then you have some other great universities that don't even have business schools, which I think is a mistake. I think business schools are the only place in academia where you really try to understand the questions: What does it take to make an organization work well? How do you go from ideas to actual execution and delivery? Other parts of the university often are immersed in the world of ideas and invention and discovery, but the Business School is the one place that knows a lot about organizations as the vehicles for getting things done and how to manage organizations for implementation. I think in many ways that we're about organizational performance. That is what business schools are all about: How do you get an organization to perform really well? There's a lot of openness and potential for collaboration between the other schools and the business school around that idea: How can we work with you and your faculty to help your students?

One of the things we do at Stanford is we periodically review undergraduate education. Every ten years we ask, "What does it mean to be an educated student in the world today, and what should we be doing in our undergraduate curriculum?" But we never reviewed graduate education. So, while I was dean, we actually had a group of representatives from all seven schools look at a review of graduate education: What is it about Stanford? If you come to Stanford as a graduate student, how should that be a different experience than if you go to Harvard or Princeton or Yale or wherever?

Historically, the answer to that question was that it was all departmentally focused. If you were in the Chemistry Department getting a PhD or master's, nobody else had anything to do with you but the Chemistry faculty. We surveyed a lot of graduate students, and I think it shocked a lot of the faculty in other schools to learn that most of their PhD graduates were not going into academic careers. They were going into industry, or research labs, or government, and they ended up working in large organizations where they felt really ill-prepared for organizational life. There are real questions there, like: How do you get things done in an organization? How do you lead? How do you work with teams? That's where the Business School can really make a major impact in educating grad students in all disciplines.

So, we ran a program in the summer—the Stanford Management Academy, a Management 101 almost—for Stanford graduate students that were nominated by other schools. We ran it in the summer because graduate students are here doing research during that time. They said, "We want some leadership training." The president actually financed that program to get it going because our key thing was that we had to pay the faculty to teach it. They were not going to do it for free. It was like an executive education program. We needed enough to pay the faculty, and the students were not going to pay tuition.

Of course, Stanford alumni loved this program. The alumni were all saying, "Yeah, this is the way the world works. It's interdisciplinary. It's collaborative. You've got to get people understanding each other. You can't just show up knowing about management. There's science and technology and there's innovation." We got a lot of alumni support because they saw that this was a great program, and they were happy to raise some money for it. Then our faculty realized that they loved it, too. They loved teaching engineering students. They were more quantitative, and they were more deferential than the MBAs who come out of consulting and investment banking firms. It was also a good way for our younger faculty to get trained who weren't quite at a point where they felt they could teach senior executives. They were having a hard enough time teaching MBAs and working on their research, but this kind of student body was great for them. It helped them develop their teaching, and not at a big cost to their research, which they were obviously working really hard on during those first seven years before tenure. Overall, it was a good complement for everything we wanted to do. It helped our faculty development and exposure to other students. It helped the reputation of the Business School vis-à-vis the rest of the university, and it was one of those things that was a win for everybody.

I think now, if you asked me what I was most proud of, a lot of people would assume I would say, "Building this new GSB campus." That is great, but really, for me, this collaboration of the Business School within Stanford and the reputation our school now has on the campus as a result of that and where we can continue contributing is the thing I'm most proud of. It is why Stanford has a business school.

Fostering the Interdisciplinary Agenda in the Business School

We got started early in the Business School in supporting the interdisciplinary agenda in teaching as opposed to research. For example, in the early days, one of our faculty members was very interested in biodesign innovation. He found a faculty member in Engineering and a faculty member in the Medical School that were working on this. They got this idea of having a course that would have a third of the students from Business, a third from Engineering, a third from Medicine. It was called Biodesign Innovation.[54]

The idea was that the medical students would come with a problem because by watching the operating theater they could see an unmet medical need. And they would say, "If only we could do X, this would be so much better. We could have better patient outcomes, better medical outcomes, and so on." On the other hand, the engineering students had a lot of tools, whether it's bioinformatics or nanotechnology or whatever it might be. And the business students would come saying, "How big is the market? Who would pay for this and what price would you charge, and could you make any money?" None of them really understood each other's discipline or field, and they didn't have time to learn each other's thing with a degree of depth. But they knew as a team—a business student, an engineering student, and a medical student—they could come up with something and see if they could prototype it.

This course got to be very popular. We put the spotlight on it. That's one of the ways you can make change at a university is to trumpet some things and write articles and say, "Look at these guys!" And then other faculty say, "What are they doing?"

Stanford had Stanford Bio-X, but it didn't have the Business School in it. Initiatives like this brought the Business School in. The experience those faculty members had teaching grad students from the three different schools ultimately led them to do some research together as well. I think developing a course in many ways was easier than starting off on a research track, which could take several years.

From our side, the way we would support this is that we would say to our faculty member who wanted to do this, "Great!" And we gave them a little time off or something to develop the course because it takes a lot of work. Teaching load is one resource we had a little bit of control over. "Instead of teaching your normal course load, maybe you could teach one less course so you can spend time figuring out how you would do this class, and how it would work." It's a pretty collaborative atmosphere at Stanford.

FACULTY HIRING AND DEVELOPMENT STRATEGY

One of the things I discovered when I came was that it was so critical to explain the various roles in a university, whomever I was talking to. If I was talking to MBAs, which was frequently, they would typically say to me that our teaching was not good enough. They loved the lecturers, and they would ask, "Why don't we have more of that and less of these academics?"[55] And

I would say to them, "Hang on a minute." They would all admit that some of their really best teachers were serious academics— they were challenging, they made them work hard, they felt like they had really learned a lot. As dean, talking about balance and about the kind of people that have really made us distinctive was important. "Our faculty are at the top of their field. They are highly respected. Our economists are as good as the economists in the Economics Department. Our psychologists are as good as the psychologists in the Psychology Department."

That was part of our faculty recruiting strategy. We don't just go recruit in business schools. We recruit from Harvard Econ, from MIT Econ, from Princeton Sociology. It's always been our desire to get the best of the social scientists and to convince them that they actually would have a more fulfilling career in a business school than in a narrow department. Because here they can work on the challenges of organization, and how do you get organizations to perform. It's exciting and interesting, and not just in an ivory tower.

A lot of the MBAs would say, "Why do we have PhD students?" I would say if we didn't have a PhD program, we wouldn't get the kind of faculty we wanted. The only way to have academic faculty who are at the top of their field and continually advancing the state of what we know is to have a PhD program. PhD students are also going to go out there and be future academics. You can't just rely on people coming in and telling war stories from having worked in the world of business. That is not going to be lasting. They will tell you what worked for them and what works today, but ten years from now, we're going to need to draw on something new.

There's nothing more practical than a good theory that stands the test of time.

So much of leadership is about teaching. Similarly, if I was talking to young faculty members who found the MBAs not very tolerant or patient, I would talk to them about what the MBAs liked and where they were going and what was going on in their worlds. It was the same with the alumni and with the rest of the university. It was just a lot of talking and teaching. I often found myself talking a lot about why it was so important for Stanford to have a business school and why it was so important for the Business School to be a bigger part of the university. It would add meaning to our purpose as a school. Why are we here? We're not just here for our own self-indulgence and to send people off on their way. We can help the university be better by helping our schools teach their grad students how to make things happen and get stuff done, so they aren't just individual performers all their lives. If they go into academia, they might be department chairs. They might be deans. Indeed, we expect that they probably will, and we want to have had an influence on that.

Something that also really set Stanford on the path to excellence was a change the school made to hiring in the 1950s or 1960s. We were pretty ordinary, and Harvard was way up there. At the time, there weren't that many business schools, but we were no match for Harvard and others, like Dartmouth and Wharton. But the president of Stanford at that time, Wally Sterling, was looking for a dean.[56] He was frustrated, and it took a long time to find someone through the search, as good candidates weren't coming up and the faculty were mostly retired businesspeople and/or academic accountants at the time.

At the same time, there was a big report that was funded by the Ford Foundation called the Gordon-Howell Report.[57] It was quite famous in business education at the time. Howell was a faculty member at the GSB, and Gordon was a faculty member at the University of California, Berkeley. The report said, "Look, business schools are just inadequate. They're not grounded in the social sciences with economics. They're not teaching in a rigorous enough way. The students who graduate are just practitioners, they are not thinkers. They don't think deeply enough." That really pushed universities to upgrade their business schools a lot. If you wanted an economics department, you had better go out and recruit the best economics person. If you wanted a department in organizational behavior, you had better go out and get the best social psychologist. If you wanted statistics, you had to go out and get the best people from the mathematics departments. In other words, you couldn't have second-rate people if you wanted to be a first-rate school in a first-rate university.

The dean that was eventually hired was actually from business: Ernie Arbuckle.[58] He was the dean when I was a student here, and I knew him really well. He was an unusual choice in some ways. He was a real people person, and he loved the school. He had gotten an MBA here, but he was not a very academic guy and not a deep intellectual thinker. But he was a real people person, and he understood the importance of getting the best people to Stanford. In those days, we had a goldmine because we could go to the University of Chicago and Carnegie Mellon and Princeton University, and we could recruit in the winter. We could bring them down here in the California sun, and they could buy a house for $45,000. It was unbelievable!

Anyway, Ernie just started hiring really top people. We got Ezra Solomon and Lee Bach, and some giants in various fields—Jim March, he was here for a long time, and Hal Leavitt, Alex Bavelas.[59] We got top psychologists, organizational behaviorists, economists, finance experts. We were just pulling them in. We increased the caliber of the faculty in terms of academic respectability and quality, and it made the university stronger, too. We built a school with a nice reputation. It was based on the fact that we were going to hire top academics and figure out how to teach what they knew in a business school. That's what really launched Stanford's Business School back in the 1960s and 1970s.

By the time I got here, I would say we were doing an exceptionally good job of teaching students how to think rigorously and critically, but we weren't doing a very good job of teaching them how to go from thinking to doing. How do you actually get things done? It's great to think it through, and that's important if you're a strategy person. But what if you have a group of people and you are in charge of getting things organized and moving? That's where I thought the leadership and global perspective in our teaching curriculum was a key missing link. I would say to the faculty when I was first here, "What about teaching leadership?" They really didn't like the idea. They would say, "No, you can't teach leadership." They used to call it the L-word, and we didn't want to use the L-word. So, I said to them, "Well, can you do research about it?" That was the first issue, because if you can't do research about it, then it wasn't going to appeal to our faculty. Anyway, some of the organizational behavior faculty said, "I do a lot of research around power," or "I do research around trust." I said that those were really relevant areas in terms of what it takes to do leadership. People have got to trust you. They've got to believe in you. You're in a position of authority and responsibility. The faculty said, "Yes, I hadn't thought about it that way. I guess if that's what leadership is, then we can teach it."

So, we had to do a fair job of lifting the sights of some of our faculty to areas that were important to leadership in business. Culture was another one. It always bugged me that we couldn't do more with the humanities faculty, particularly in anthropology. How do anthropologists study culture? One of the most important things in a business or organization is the culture. Couldn't we get some people in anthropology into the Business School? I finally gave up, because when I went and spoke to the anthropologists, they were more interested in studying the people of Papua New Guinea than business. But if you were a young PhD in anthropology and you got interested in studying the culture of JP Morgan or Goldman Sachs, you could really make a mark for yourself. And you could have consulting opportunities running out of your ears. You could work in a business school and make twice as much as in the anthropology department. But that's still a missing link at Stanford. We've done a great job in psychology, sociology, economics, some engineering disciplines, statistics, and political science. But we haven't had the chance to work with anthropology.

One of the biggest challenges we have had is that we are a relatively small school. Harvard is twice as big. With a small school, you have a smaller faculty, and a smaller faculty means you can't hire new people as easily. You don't want to just hire one anthropologist. You've got to have three or four or they're not going to have colleagues.

When I was dean, one of the things we tried to do to manage this was to support co-teaching between the departments. We had a faculty member who had an idea that how you act and how you present yourself had a lot to do with leadership. When you're in a position of power, getting people to trust you, believe in you, and so on depended a lot on your body carriage and movement and the use of your voice. It was called "acting with power," and she started to work with someone from the Drama Department.[60] I've always thought we had a lot more room for collaboration with the humanities like that, whether it's the visual arts or the performing arts.

One of my great teachers and friends over the years, John Gardner, used to say, "Leadership is a performing art. You're the instrument, and you've got to learn how to play that instrument and play it well. You can't play it well if you don't know it well."[61] That's why a lot of self-knowledge is so important in leadership. We need to take advantage of the humanities to address these issues. They've been studying this for 2,000 years—how people get creative and how people inspire other people. In business, we have only begun to worry about this in the last twenty years. Yet in so much of business now, especially when you're dealing with bright people, it is about: How do you inspire somebody? How do you get people to be more creative? How do you get them to take the initiative? In some ways, the humanities know more about that than we do, but they don't know how to translate it to us. How do you turn that into some artful recruiting? It's too hard to build up humanists as full-time faculty. You're probably better off if you could just find one or two people to help co-teach with the business school faculty.

Fundraising at the Graduate School of Business

Fundraising is a constant. Tuition seems steep to students, but it doesn't begin to cover the cost of delivery. That's a challenge for all universities. The economics of education is difficult. It is very labor intensive, and student/faculty interaction is what it's all about. If you have to teach 1,000 students, you don't have that interaction. Stanford has 420 students in its MBA class. We just believe in the kind of education we offer. We believe in a lot of engagement and a lot of challenge and critical thinking. If you have a classroom of 100 as opposed to sixty or fewer like at Stanford, there's less magic in it. Graduate education is not about standing up and doing lectures; that is more undergraduate. Graduate education is more about teaching people how to think and challenging them. If you're going to help people be group leaders and practice that, you need to give them constant feedback. These are pretty time-intensive and people-intensive exercises.

It takes a lot of fundraising to support that kind of effort. We are fortunate that virtually all of our fundraising is from alumni. It covers a whole range of things. Some of it covers scholarships or fellowships for students, some of it is to endow professorships, some of it is general support, and some is for buildings. It is critical to the budget. The tuition covers no more than a third of the budget. The earnings from the endowment we have built up at the Business School over the years cover about another quarter of the budget. Another quarter is annual giving. We have lots of alumni functions and five-year reunions. Getting people back to campus and getting them engaged and interested is really important.

Finally, executive education is an important source of general funds. It's really valuable for four reasons. First, it does make a margin of contribution, and it's just unrestricted funding because it is general revenue. It's not restricted to a fellowship or faculty. Second, it enables our faculty to teach a different group of students. They can teach senior managers and executives, and they learn a lot by doing it, beyond just teaching MBA and PhD students. They are teaching executives who have different issues and challenges and questions. Third, it's a really good source of revenue for our faculty. We pay them well to teach, and they don't have to go out and sell themselves. Executive education is a great source of additional income for them. Fourth, it often leads to contacts where people ask them to come and consult or do research. So, executive education is a really important part of what we do.

The big problem with this model is that the way academia is run, it is what I would call procyclical. When things are good, everything is up: the students have done pretty well, they arrive with some assets, so they don't need as much financial aid. The alumni are feeling good so they're making more contributions. The endowment is performing better, and companies are spending on training and executive development and sending people to executive programs.

If it turns, everything goes the other way: the students need more financial aid, the alumni are feeling stressed, companies cut back on executive development, our endowment doesn't perform as well if the market crashes, and so we have to throttle back how much we draw from the annual payout of our endowment. It's very procyclical, and you've got to watch that. When times are really good, you've got to build up for when you do have a downturn.

CHAPTER 9

PHIL PIZZO

Dean of the Stanford University School of Medicine
(2001–2012)

Philip Pizzo, MD, is the David and Susan Heckerman Professor and Founding Director of the Stanford Distinguished Careers Institute. Previously, he served as dean of the Stanford School of Medicine and the Carl and Elizabeth Naumann Professor of Pediatrics and of Microbiology and Immunology.

Joining Stanford

I am a physician scientist. I spent most of my life at the National Institutes of Health as a researcher, mostly in the lab as well as doing clinical work in childhood cancer and AIDS research. I came back to Boston in 1996, where I had trained in the early 1970s, intending to spend the rest of my career there. I was, at that point, the physician-in-chief at the Children's Hospital and chair of Pediatrics at Harvard.

In the spring of 2000, I got a call to gauge my interest in becoming dean of the Medical School here at Stanford. My first response was, "No, I'm not interested." I had no clue as to why I was even on that list. I had no interest in being dean. I knew a person on the search committee, so somehow my name surfaced. Then I got another call asking whether I would at least come out for a short visit. I did, and it was transformative. On the way back, I thought, "There's something interesting about this institution, this culture, which is very different from what I'm experiencing."

I had left NIH with hopes of creating interdisciplinary, innovative teams to look at different ways of solving problems that affect children. But what I found at Harvard was a very traditional mindset that said, "We do things in a certain way." After meeting John Hennessy, I realized that this was a very different environment. I knew many people at Stanford, but I didn't know the culture very well. It was much more of, "We like to try new things. We are not focused on the past, but are really thinking more about the future." I found that to be very intriguing.

That said, the reason that they were reaching out was because the Medical School and medical center were in significant trouble, and they had decided that they were going to go outside Stanford to bring in a new leader. In the years just prior to that, Stanford and UCSF had attempted to merge their hospitals and clinical faculty, practices, and programs, but not the two medical schools. UCSF and Stanford were two very different cultures, one public and the other private, and the merger was largely being guided by the two institutional leaders: Dr. Joe Martin, who was the vice chancellor at UCSF, and Gerhard Casper, who was the president at Stanford. Basically, they were at a conference together, they took a walk in the woods, and came up with this plan to form this merger, which made a lot of sense to them, but not to the people below them. The Medical School clinical department chairs and faculty at each institution eventually rebelled against it, and a couple of years of work and a lot of financial investments by both institutions were squandered.

Historically, Stanford Medicine had been great in terms of research. In 1959, the university had moved the Medical School from San Francisco to the Stanford campus. Most of the clinical faculty decided to stay in San Francisco where their practices were. Stanford then recruited a handful of faculty who were transformative, including the entire Department of Microbiology at Washington University. Six people came here to found the Department of Biochemistry—two won Nobel Prizes, and the other four all had very distinguished academic careers. They, in turn, began recruiting people with a very strong scientific bent. It really gave the Medical School a very strong scientific underpinning. Stanford Hospital and Stanford Medical

School were in the same brand-new building at that time, but most of the patients were being cared for by community physicians. Quite honestly, the faculty were quite happy with that, because they were mostly interested in doing research as their primary focus with a lesser amount of patient care; they weren't interested in traditional healthcare delivery. That was the end of the 1950s into the 1960s, and as the years went by, the nature of academic medical centers began to change.

In the 1990s, it became pretty apparent that Stanford Hospital was becoming a liability; the financial underpinnings were not that strong, and it wasn't that competitive. It didn't have, except in a handful of areas, outstanding expertise. There weren't the go-to physician leaders; UCSF was much stronger in that way. At one level, the university was grappling with questions like, "Do we need a medical school? Do we need to have an academic medical center?" An academic medical center needs hospitals aligned with a medical school and sometimes other professional schools. So, those were the kinds of questions that spawned this merger to take place, and when it failed, it became even more of an issue. It was in that setting that I was invited to come here.

John Hennessy was on the search committee. He was provost at the time, and he was the person who offered me the position. John was brand-new to his role. Given what happened to his predecessor, Gerhard Casper, whose own path forward was altered when the merger went down, I think John felt that the medical center and Medical School were important, but he wanted to have a little bit more distant relationship with it. Moreover, John Etchemendy, who was an outstanding provost—they were both extraordinary leaders—by his own accounting, knew nothing about the Medical School when he took office. The university did not have very positive views about the Medical School and medical center.

After the de-merger, Stanford Hospital was losing $20 million per year. I was told before I came that it was all going to be balanced and everything would be okay, but when I arrived in April 2001, cash-on-hand for the hospital was four days, and the deficit was $20 million. The Packard Children's Hospital had a deficit of about $5 million. So, the university faculty looked at the medical center as a real liability. Stanford is the sole member of the corporation, and even if it's not for profit, they had a reputational risk on top of financial challenges.

FACING UP TO THE CHALLENGES

Thinking about the future—and crafting a vision—has been one of the things that I've done throughout my career. It was really trying to say, "How do we rethink the way academic medicine is constructed?" I served as dean for twelve years—two-thirds of the time that John and John were in place—and things changed. The Medical School went from being in a deficit to having surpluses in the hundreds of millions of dollars.

From December 6, 2000, when I signed the offer letter until my arrival date, April 2, 2001, I spent every other week at Stanford, meeting with people, listening to areas of interest, and formulating what became the outlines of the strategic plan, which I announced in my first newsletter published on April 2. It went to everybody. To this day, when I see people, they still remember that and talk about the importance of receiving my biweekly *Dean's Newsletter*. Often, there's little dialogue and communication, particularly to staff and students. My newsletter was a very important way of respecting and listening to people.

I looked at ten different areas that required emphasis and work in terms of strategic planning. I did not engage with an outside consulting group and decided to do it within Stanford over the course of the first year. We put together ten working groups of faculty, students, and staff that dealt with everything from undergraduate medical education, graduate education, postdoctoral training, and continuing medical education, to research based in clinical patient care, communications, finance, administration, and public policy. All of these efforts culminated in the first of what were twelve strategic planning meetings that I led every winter thereafter. John Hennessy came to the first of those in January 2002, and that was the beginning of the transformation of Stanford Medicine.

One of the things that I did early on was assemble a Dean's Office leadership team. When I got here, there was only one senior dean left, and I didn't carry that person over. I recruited senior associate deans for faculty affairs, education, basic and clinical research, finance and administration, communication. The roles actually matched those ten areas that I described. Members of that leadership team were almost all internal hires. That was important, because bringing in more outside people probably would not have been a good plan at that time. They were all highly respected individuals, and we worked wonderfully together. We met every week as a group. I also met with them individually. They had delegated responsibilities to oversee these different aspects of the team. This was a multibillion-dollar operation between the Medical School and the two major teaching hospitals: the Stanford Hospital & Clinics and the Lucile Packard Children's Hospital. You can't do it all yourself. We had joint leadership teams between the Medical School and the two hospitals that met every week for hours, planning the clinical strategy. We met with the clinical chairs every other week, and with the Joint Executive Committee of both clinical and basic science leaders every other week. This was a way of keeping everybody reasonably aligned.

We had to address some big strategic issues regarding medical education. On the day after I signed the letter agreeing to come to Stanford, I received a call from one of the faculty who had been on the search committee who asked if I knew that Stanford Medical School was at risk of losing its accreditation from the LCME, the Liaison Committee on Medical Education. Apparently, Stanford had been put on notice that by only one vote it had avoided losing accreditation. It had everything to do with its facilities, which had not been renovated since the school moved here. The LCME said, "If you don't do something about this or give us evidence of what you're doing in the next year, we're going to take your accreditation away."

In response, those who preceded me had developed a program to renovate some of the old buildings for medical education. It had been approved by the Board of Trustees. My job was going to be to go out and raise close to $200 million to basically renovate a 1959 building that had little conceptual planning to meet the changes in medical education. No one knew what the curriculum was going to be. No one knew what the real needs were. It was just kind of throwing spaghetti up against the wall and saying, "This is how we're going to satisfy the LCME."

I came back in February 2001 to John Hennessy and said, "I advise you to go back to the board and say, 'We're not going to do this. We need to start over.'" Then the burden fell on me, of course, because I had to go to Washington—I hadn't even started my job here—and meet with the LCME and in a supplicant mode say, "Look, give us a reprieve of at least a year to develop a new plan." That led to defining a new curriculum and coming up with the conceptual design for what an ideal facility would look like, which became the Li Ka Shing Learning and Knowledge Center.[62]

This strategy emanated from another pretty comprehensive planning group, very interdisciplinary, that looked at, "What do we need to create the future?" A big part of what we needed at that time was a lot of flexibility. Part of it was to create classrooms that were not fixed entities, that could be expanded or contracted accordingly. We wanted a building that would house a state-of-the-art simulation center. The ground floor of the Learning and Knowledge Center probably today is still among the finest simulation centers in the world because we were able to build it from scratch.

Another major challenge was that the Medical School was ranked number eleven whereas all the other schools at Stanford were ranked number one or two. During my tenure, the ranking in *U.S. News & World Report* went from number eleven to number two. That, by the way, was not with any change in people or organizations. It was about figuring out how they did the ranking and then persuading the statisticians at *U.S. News & World Report* to use a different methodology that measured faculty quality rather than just faculty size. That became important, because it allowed the Medical School to be seen as an asset, as compared to a liability.

The methodology the statisticians used for medical schools was different than in other settings. They used total amount of NIH funding as a third of the score, so a medical school like Stanford, which had a very small faculty, could never compete. The faculty at Harvard was more than ten times the size of the faculty at Stanford. In engineering, *U.S. News & World Report* used a blended funding methodology—per faculty member and total funding. I presented the data to *U.S. News & World Report* and that changed everything, because it equilibrated size versus quality. Stanford had always had the highest NIH funding per faculty member. I knew that the more emphasis on that, the better we would do. When it became equilibrated between the two, that significantly affected the ranking. Afterwards, John Hennessy began looking at the Medical School differently than when it was seen as either a financial or a reputational vulnerability. We were on par with the other schools. I knew that we could never get above two in the NIH ranking unless they changed some of the other components of the system, but two was okay. The best students want to be at a top-ten school.

One other thing that's important to know is that the Medical School and the Business School, in Stanford parlance, are so-called "formula schools," so they stand on their own financial bottoms.[63] That meant that I was responsible for everything—for putting together all the plans for financial improvement, for working with the leadership to find funding for the buildings. Important parts of the Medical School campus are new. None of this existed when I first came here in 2000. These were all parking lots. This was part of the university's big transformation. In terms of the Stanford Challenge campaign that John was responsible for, we had to align with that, but also conduct our own fundraising in parallel. We were obviously operating under the umbrella of a university-wide campaign, but when it came to meeting with people, creating the funding paths, all of that had to be done together.

What I think John brought to that part of the work was bringing the different schools together in unified and coordinated planning. That's when the concept of creating interdisciplinary institutes was formulated, so that different schools, rather than operating on their own bottoms, began to think more collaboratively. That exercise of thinking of the university as a different kind of playing field was, to me, a really important opportunity.

FOSTERING INTERDISCIPLINARITY

We went through a process of redoing the Medical School curriculum, and we reorganized a lot of the graduate education programs. We created a group of interdisciplinary institutes within the Medical School—a stem cell and cancer institute, and then ultimately a comprehensive cancer center, a cardiovascular institute, a program on transplantation and immunology, and the first neurosciences institute that started here and then extended to the university. It was a matter of creating institutes within the Medical School that in turn reached out to other members of the university.

At one point, I had envisioned that we would migrate all the departments into these institutes and abandon departments. I actually proposed it at a retreat. Everybody listened attentively and then made it very clear: "That would be over my dead body!" Departments are still an anchor. I basically decided that that was an idea too far ahead of its time. You have to make compromises along the way.

Stanford School of Medicine Dean Philip Pizzo, left, School of Humanities and Sciences Dean Sharon Long, and School of Engineering Dean James Plummer, right, discuss interdisciplinary programs at the Academic Council meeting in Kresge Auditorium in 2002.

The dean of the School of Engineering, Jim Plummer, and I played an important role in starting the very first joint department between two schools. There may have been one many decades ago, but that had disappeared. Bioengineering became an exemplar of a department for which there had been lots of antecedent thinking. We wanted Bioengineering at Stanford, but it had always been, "We want it in the Medical

School," or "We want it in the School of Engineering." Basically, we put together some planning groups that said, "What is the fundamental essence of the Department of Bioengineering that would make Stanford unique?" We didn't want to do something traditional like a biomedical engineering focus on devices. We wanted to do something that was more in the realm of quantitative biology and systems biology and really think about how to apply engineering concepts and sciences to solve medical problems. That department, which recruited its first faculty members in 2003, to this day is probably among the best departments at the university.

John Hennessy and John Etchemendy, their role was to enable us to let that happen because we had to break down many rules. We had a formula school—our own financial bottom—and a non-formula school in Engineering, and we had to figure out how to make the infrastructure work in ways that would make it seamless for the people who were going to be leading it. We didn't want the faculty to feel like they were split between the places but actually working in an environment that was a shared entity between two schools. Someone could have said, "You can't do it this way," but that wasn't the mindset. Once we had the data from the task force that said we should create the department, we said, "We're not going to let anything get in the way of achieving it; we simply are not going to let all the nickel and dime things that come along the way stop us." We created new kinds of models that allowed the two schools to operate collaboratively.

The very first thing was to appoint two chairs of the Bioengineering Department who would serve as co-chairs. That was a tactical decision for the first handful of years, so there would be equal vetting between someone appointed from the Medical

PHIL PIZZO

School and someone appointed from the School of Engineering. Now that it's more established, there's a single chair
and a co-chair, but that was the model initially.

Then we decided to have a national search for the first
faculty. We had such an outstanding number of people applying
that although we were looking for one person, we took three.
The first was Steve Quake, who was a tenured, named professor
at Caltech who had gotten his doctorate here at Stanford. If
you look up Steve Quake and look at the trajectory of his work,
he transformed this whole place. He basically created the plat-
forms for doing DNA sequencing that changed the whole cost
structure and began finding ways of finding DNA sequences in
blood for early diagnostics. The second was Karl Deisseroth,
who was here already. He did not have an engineering background, but he was an MD/PhD, which was another really
important thing that we were looking for. He was a neuroscientist. Within a few years, he created the field of optogenetics, which is one of the most fundamentally important
areas of neuroscience that applies engineering principles to
solve neuroscience and many other problems. The third was
Jennifer Cochran, who was in the Department of Biochemistry
at Caltech working in protein engineering. She's currently the
chair of Bioengineering today.[64]

They've recruited an array of people that are just extraordinary. One of the really important parts of Stanford is, rarely
do we choose people on a programmatic basis. It's almost
always, "Who's got the most innovative ways of thinking about
this?" The faculty in our Department of Biochemistry here,
which is one of the best in the world, would always say, "We
want to bring somebody here who is better than the rest of us."

Transforming the Clinical Side of the Medical School

Transforming clinical sciences is much harder, because there you don't have that flexibility. An additional part of my job was to begin the transformation of the clinical faculty. Quite honestly, when I first got here and people would call me for referrals, I'd say, "How about Boston or California or San Francisco?" We had to change both the quality of the faculty appointment system (which we did) and the recruitment process to bring really outstanding clinical leaders here and to have them valued by people in the institution. That work began in the early 2000s; it's still continuing to this day. This is a very different place. In the 1970s, people used to joke and say, "At Stanford, MD stands for 'mouse doctor.'" But they don't say that anymore.

My basic philosophy on recruitment is very simple; if you recruit A+ people, they're going to continue to recruit A+ people. If you begin compromising and you recruit A people, they're going to recruit B+ or B people. For the leadership group, just get the very best people you can, and then they take on the role of recruiting people on their teams.

I spent a lot of time recruiting institute directors, clinical chairs, science chairs from around the country. I think they were attracted by a couple of things. Stanford as a university was already on the rise. I think the last twenty years have moved it even further. The entrepreneurial spirit in Silicon Valley was a real attraction to people. People want to be in an environment that looks like it's going to be transformative, where they're

202

going to make a difference. I think my job was to present that mindset to people—the excitement of coming and being on the ground floor of making a difference.

It was the clinical side that needed that reputational difference, because it required some stretch of the imagination to think that you were going to be valued here and that you were going to be able to build programs of excellence. Thankfully, we had good partners in the hospital administration that began collaborating and saying, "Yeah, let's begin to do this in a different way." A big part of that was laid out in strategic planning processes focused on finding key leaders and creating connectivity between the clinical programmatic areas and the scientific programmatic areas. I focused primarily on building the cancer, neuroscience, immunology and transplantation, and cardiovascular areas. Clinically, these were pretty much the differentiating areas—it's where we had the scientific complementarity, and to be blunt, it's also where the money was. As time went by, it became about building up more of a health system, the primary care areas, which was not the emphasis at the beginning.

Expanding the Medical School Campus and Programs

There were limits to expansion. At the beginning of the 2000s, every building had to go through an approval process for the amount of square footage, which was fixed against something called the "general use permit." We had a very fixed amount of space that we could build to. It was enough to meet almost all of the needs that we had, but we did not have the funding. John told me many times that he didn't think we would succeed in getting that funding, but we were able to get it. A big part of it came from Li Ka Shing.[65] I spent a lot of time meeting with him over the years to create that funding platform.

The Li Ka Shing Center [LKSC] didn't open until 2010. That building housed the simulation center on the ground floor. We put classrooms on every floor because we wanted students to be embedded everywhere. The first floor is largely classroom settings. The second floor is a large conference center. The third floor is where the administration is, and there are more classrooms. And then the fourth floor is where the students have their health and exercise facilities, meeting rooms. It's the best space on the entire campus. I wanted that to be for the students.

Even the placement of the building was purposeful. We wanted it to be physically proximate to our research labs. We wanted it to look out across the campus to engineering and basic sciences. If you look at LKSC, you'll see that it has an overhang. My vision was that it would look at what would ultimately become a new quad. The neuroscience building used to be a big energy facility, and I knew that it was going to go away at some point. I wanted there to be a physical connection between the Medical School and the Science and Engineering Quad—the new quad that had been built on the west end of campus. The Clark Center came up after I arrived as well. It's an interdisciplinary area which now looks out onto the Biology Research Building. We focused on physical proximities to create this nexus.

There's a brand-new hospital, which was the biggest building project of all. The approvals took five years. There were some big needs: creating a facility that would be a model of excellence, that would have high-tech single patient rooms, that would ensure lots of dignity for patients and families. It's probably among the most beautiful places in the world right now for a hospital facility, but it was a huge effort to get there.

The research funding and the nature of our recruitment program were interconnected. Rarely (if ever) did funds for recruitment or anything else come from the central university to the Medical School. We had to fundraise. Even though the hospitals were in big trouble when I came, the Medical School, thanks to the people before me, already had a significant endowment, so it had resources. It was possible to get things started. When I came, we faced a $20 million deficit in the Medical School, so without that endowment it would have been impossible.

Research and education in academic medical centers are major cost centers. A research program, even with faculty who have the highest amount of per capita funding in the country, still requires an additional 30 to 50 cents on the dollar. In general, where does that cross-subsidization come from? It comes from endowment, gifts, royalty income, and clinical sources. At that time, when the clinical programs were not doing as well, there wasn't a lot of cross-subsidization, other than money that the hospital would put into the recruitment of clinical faculty because they were going to be generating clinical income by building these programs.

For example, there was no National Cancer Center–designated cancer institute when I came here; there is now. That happened during the first five years. I brought in an external group of people that I know. I'm an oncologist by background. They said, "No way, it's never going to happen here." But it did. It happened because a handful of people shared the vision and began recruiting people, both scientists as well as clinicians. Cancer turns out to be 30 to 50 percent of the revenue stream of most academic hospitals. People in hospital administration are willing to invest in that area because they see the return on investment on that. They tend not to be so invested in primary care practice—things that are revenue losers.

The Biodesign program was something that we helped to support and that is more design thinking on devices. We also supported a program called SPARK, which was a similar approach but for the development of drugs.[66]

Finally, the institutes helped to formulate where we were going. For example, the Lorey Lokey Stem Cell Research Building is a testament to two institutes: the Cancer Institute and the Stem Cell Institute. We took advantage of the fact that in 2003, President George W. Bush basically trashed stem cell research, and that spawned a huge effort in California to form the California Institute for Regenerative Medicine. That was a $3 billion investment by the state in funding research and stem cell biology research, and we probably had more funding here than any place else. I appointed Irv Weissman, who was already a highly recognized stem cell researcher, to be the director of the Stanford Institute for Stem Cell Biology and Regenerative Medicine. Irv began recruiting people—with impeccable taste. This became, and is still, the world's leadership group in stem cell biology. It's a consequence of having a big idea with a big vision to create ways of unshackling it from traditional departmental barriers.[67]

INTEGRATING RESEARCH
WITH CLINICAL PRACTICE

I helped integrate research with clinical practice by building cultural connectivity. I spent a lot of time during the first years meeting separately with the basic science faculty and departments, and separately with the clinical departments, and then bringing them together. Every other week, the basic and clinical science chairs met in a shared meeting. Our very first retreat had ninety people—all the basic science chairs, all the clinical science chairs, people who were likely going to be appointed to various leadership roles, junior faculty, senior faculty, students, members of the Board of Trustees, hospital administrators, and administration from the university, the provost, or the president. Midway during that retreat, two things happened that I think were transformative. One is that people began saying things like, "You know, I finally understand what this is about. I can see the connection of my basic science thinking to this clinical program." Second, I remember the very first dinner at that very first retreat, people sat in their comfort zones, in their clusters, but by the second night people were beginning to sit together. At all twelve retreats that I led thereafter, participants viewed themselves as colleagues, a community.

The culture of basic science is very different from clinical medicine. People began to exhibit a willingness to understand each other, and that had a huge impact on how things progressed. It enabled us to do more joint planning, to make the case to make shared investments in capital and people. The interconnectivity was critical, because Stanford is a very small place. Once the willingness was there, the culture changed.

One of the things I insisted on was, when clinical departments were going to recruit a basic science person, there had to be joint appointments. The basic science department had to have faculty on search committees, to make sure that the quality of the people coming in was equivalent. That enabled basic and clinical science departments to have more shared values with each other.

We also had to change the criteria for clinical investigation. When I got here in 2001, there were two faculty lines. One was called the university tenure line, UTL—the traditional model. It was very small; approximately 300 people. Then there was a second line that had been created in the mid-1990s called the medical center line or MCL. The problem was that the people in that line were not recognized by the University Academic Council, and they couldn't be principal investigators, so they couldn't apply for grants. We made the case to the Faculty Senate to change the rule to allow MCL faculty to become principal investigators around 2004. That was transformative, because the university had a cap on the number of UTL faculty. Once people could become principal investigators on the clinical side, I could recruit people in an ever-increasing number. Grants covered part of their costs—that, coupled with their clinical activity.

Then we created an additional line called clinician educators. These were people who were largely doing clinical care and some education. They were not even considered university faculty; they were basically called staff physicians. We elevated that group to have an academic title with an appellation; they became "clinical faculty." That became the largest-growing group. The mindset was, "Let's really expand this group. Let's develop criteria for their promotion and value them." And then we decided to recruit people at the interface between the lab and the clinic, including clinical trials. That became the clinician scholar line.

Those were essential changes in allowing integration to happen. We also had to make essential changes in the funding arrangements between the Medical School and hospitals that allowed people to be compensated on a basis that was both competitive and commensurate with their roles. These huge, under-the-hood kinds of things were essential. They all came about because of that strategic planning process.

FINAL REFLECTIONS ON TIME AS DEAN

Overall, I tried very hard to reach out to people across campus, to break down barriers. One of my predecessors said, "Don't waste your time going across the university." I did not listen to that. At my very first meeting at the Faculty Senate, an economics professor said, "The Medical School is basically growing like weeds." I had to spend time trying to demonstrate that we brought value to the university. That meant creating lots of bridges. That's why building bridges with Engineering was important; that's why building bridges with my co-deans was really important. And I think we worked, quite honestly, wonderfully together. John Hennessy played a major role in helping to facilitate this. The group of deans that I was part of got to know each other personally. We had social events at each other's homes on a regular basis. We worked collaboratively on the Stanford Challenge campaign together. It was really bridge-building and not silo-building. That was the biggest difference I felt between Stanford and Harvard, where there was not a lot of interest in sharing. Here there was much more of an interest in sharing and connecting, and I've personally valued that.

CHAPTER 10

PAM MATSON

Dean of the School of Earth, Energy
and Environmental Sciences (2002–2017)

In her current role as Goldman Professor of Environmental Studies and senior fellow in the Woods Institute for the Environment, Pam Matson leads the graduate program on Sustainability Science and Practice. As dean of the School of Earth, Energy and Environmental Sciences, she built interdisciplinary departments and educational programs focused on resources, environment, and sustainability, and co-led university-wide interdisciplinary initiatives.

Laying the Foundation for Interdisciplinarity

My involvement with John Hennessy's decade and a half-plus of leadership started before I became dean. Shortly after John became president, he started a needs assessment and a planning process that would ultimately lead to what became known as the Stanford Challenge. I had very great admiration for his approach.

Along with John Etchemendy and the Board of Trustees, he set up a process whereby Stanford's schools could bring their communities together and think through what they really needed in order to achieve their goals in the next five to ten years. Very brilliantly, John set up several cross-cutting committees as well as the needs assessment efforts within the schools. I was a member of the Interdisciplinary Themes Committee, and our job was to engage across all of the schools to identify research themes that could be addressed best by all of us working together. That committee ended up identifying something like twenty themes; we articulated them to John and John and the board, and after iteration they selected just three that became part of the Stanford Challenge. The planning process was very much owned by John and John. Any strategic planner will tell you: the leader has to own the planning process. They owned it, and they reached out in nontraditional ways and looked for ideas and needs beyond the schools.

Outcomes of this process that were included in the Stanford Challenge were an initiative on environment and sustainability, an initiative on human health, and an initiative around the arts, and a couple of others that emerged over time. I believe the environmental initiative turned out to be the clearest example of an initiative in which all seven schools could be engaged. But the brilliance was in reaching out beyond the school-by-school planning approach and changing the more typical way of thinking about where the university needed to go and what resources we needed in order to accomplish it. Once those themes were identified, a huge amount of work and iteration went into identifying exactly what the needs were and, for the cross-cutting initiatives, how we could best work together.

As this process was moving along, I was asked to become the dean of the School of Earth Sciences—now Earth, Energy and Environmental Sciences, which we call the "School of Earth" for short. As I took on that role, I was already very engaged in and excited about John's vision for Stanford and the strategy that he had developed for meeting that vision. At about that same time, John engaged a committee of faculty members from across the schools, including me, to build the initiative on environment and sustainability. It became our job to articulate, through an iterative process of engaging faculty around the university, what the initiative would address.

We had all-hands meetings where we invited any faculty member who was interested in an environmental initiative from any part of the university to join in roundtable discussions about what was needed in terms of new faculty, organizational structures, resources, space, and so forth. We thought deeply about the institutional changes that would need to take place for this initiative to succeed.

Alumni were very involved in both giving feedback on our plans and encouraging them. Many of our alums understood and recognized how important it was for Stanford to engage in research and teaching on environment and sustainability issues, and they were thrilled that Stanford was working and moving in that direction. They wanted us to get real about doing it. They got involved in a variety of ways, to the benefit of the university, themselves, and the world. Our Stanford alums love the university! As a dean, that was something that astounded me and that I valued; alums from around Stanford got involved because they cared about our research and teaching efforts on environment and sustainability. I suspect that was true for the arts and for the human health initiative as well. It was amazing.

The Interdisciplinary Initiatives and the Stanford Challenge

Many people think the Stanford Challenge was just a fundraising campaign, but initiatives underlying that fundraising campaign were real. They were about harnessing the strengths of our university and using that new knowledge to help solve problems. That became something that was recognized and rewarded and acknowledged, so that faculty could pursue solutions-oriented research and be rewarded for doing it.

Our School of Earth Sciences had always done use-inspired fundamental research. Our research was designed to discover how things work in the world but also to help find solutions for societal challenges. With the environmental initiative, more of the university moved in that direction, and it became much stronger in our school, too. Stanford became very widely acknowledged for valuing interdisciplinary approaches, with the recognition that no one discipline could address these really complex problems alone. We became known for making interdisciplinary research and education work well. And I think we became known for actually caring about linking the knowledge we were creating in the university to action outside of it. As we did that, I think we were setting up for the university's next steps that are underway today.

The fact that John supported and encouraged all of us to build these interdisciplinary initiatives, and then went out and got the resources to support them, has made us a world leader in real-world problem solving. The Stanford Challenge was one of the mechanisms by which that happened. But it wasn't top-down; nobody said, "You've got to do this." This was bottom-up, too, going all the way back to that Interdisciplinary Themes Committee. It was a fabulous connection of bottom-up ideas that faculty really wanted to go after and top-down acknowledgement and valuing and working hard to fund them. What we did in the last fifteen years could not have been done if we hadn't had a president who was committed and leading the way. But they also couldn't have been done if there weren't faculty who wanted to get them done. It was an essential combination. Those things together led over time to a shift in the kind of faculty we have and the ways we think about our role in the world. It was an absolutely fabulous partnership and collaboration between the university leaders and the university's faculty and students.

And, of course, it was a collaboration with our alumni and donors. Another brilliant aspect of the Stanford Challenge was the way it engaged our alums, including early in the planning process. Events all over the country and all over the world brought Stanford to our alums—lectures, dinners, receptions, and other ways for people to engage with and learn from faculty and students and connect with John. John went to dozens of these events, and he was superb. And, of course, a wonderful group of people in the Office of Development and alumni volunteers made it all work. I think that for universities to be successful in engaging their alums and other donors, they need to bring them into the fold, remind them of what their university can do, share knowledge and excitement about what we are doing and learning, and let them meet and know the president, the provost, and others—that worked for us, and it was fun!

ESTABLISHING INTERDISCIPLINARY STRUCTURES

One of the outcomes of the initiative on environment and sustainability was the creation of the Woods Institute for the Environment. That was something that John put his stamp of approval on very early, talking about it as an "institute of the seven schools at Stanford" focused on environment and sustainability challenges. It became the Woods Institute when Ward Woods stepped up to lead the funding of it, but it was launched by John before that. Later, the Precourt Institute, supported by Jay Precourt and others, joined in with a focus on the energy transition. These interdisciplinary institutes were made up of a large number of faculty members from all the schools at Stanford; the institutes in effect helped mobilize the university's strengths around environment and sustainability challenges. We acknowledged that interdisciplinary/multidisciplinary approaches were necessary and that we needed to work together to address them effectively. The founding directors of the Woods Institute were Jeff Koseff and Buzz Thompson. Lynn Orr was the founding director of the Precourt Institute.[68]

At the fifth anniversary of the Woods Institute for the Environment in 2009, Dean of the School of Earth, Energy and Environmental Sciences Pamela Matson speaks with Jay Precourt, founding donor of the Precourt Institute for Energy and Woods Advisory Council member.

The institutes have done a great job of engaging the breadth of Stanford's faculty expertise in research, reaching out to faculty all over the university and providing seed funding and other opportunities for engagement in multidisciplinary research. At the same time, the fact that the institutes were able to hire highly successful researchers—senior fellows—and usually did that in partnership with the schools, made it possible for us to hire new faculty who could fill critical expertise gaps and bring fresh perspectives as well as diversity to the university. Many faculty in the School of Earth came to the university in joint positions where half of their position was in the school and half was in the institute. It was a very, very successful innovation that John and John made possible.

With the institutes, the focus on interdisciplinary approaches and growing numbers of faculty, staff, and students working in environment and sustainability areas led to the need for a new, special building for the initiative. Soon after I became dean, John Hennessy gave me the job as lead dean and member of the faculty planning committee for building what would become the Yang and Yamazaki Environment and Energy Building—Y2E2. This building was to be the first of the four buildings making up the Science and Engineering Quad and would house faculty from many of the schools at Stanford. We had incredibly fast-paced design and building processes, and we were committed to building a high-performance "green" building that would be highly efficient in energy use and water use, with sustainable materials, good light for everyone, shared spaces for interdisciplinary interactions, and so on. And we needed to do it with a budget that was about the same as for any other Stanford building. We were really excited and dedicated to proving that Stanford could afford to build all its buildings as green buildings. The planning team had to grapple with lots of trade-offs in order to get the most important sustainability features, but I think we succeeded pretty well—and Stanford learned from the process. Most new buildings now are as good or better.

As we were building the interdisciplinary Y2E2, we were also building new departments or rethinking old ones to become multidisciplinary and focused on environmental and resource research and teaching. In the School of Earth, we built a new department called Earth System Science to include faculty already in the school but in other departments, along with new faculty hired during the Stanford Challenge. That department included lots of different disciplines all focused on understanding and addressing global environmental change, even some social science disciplines. A bit later, another of our departments transitioned from doing mostly oil and gas research and education to being a broadly based energy resources department with new kinds of expertise. And Civil and Environmental Engineering, in the School of Engineering, also broadened its directions and disciplines.

We also made remarkable progress in interdisciplinary education but still retained disciplinary educational programs. In 2000, the School of Earth created the Interdisciplinary Program in Environment and Resources—later called the Emmett Interdisciplinary Program in Environment and Resources (E-IPER) thanks to the Emmett family's incredible gifts to support it.[69] E-IPER is a far-field interdisciplinary PhD program, unlike anything else in our university or any others. PhD students in it gain deep knowledge in two or more areas, usually one in a policy-related field and the other in science and technology, and then they combine that knowledge to carry out their research. Those students have been remarkably successful. And then E-IPER added a joint master's program in Environment and Resources, and students in Stanford's MBA and JD programs can add that master's degree to their professional degree. Hugely successful!

Later, in the last years of my deanship, we launched an additional interdisciplinary program called Sustainability Science and Practice. It's a master's program that draws graduates from undergraduate degree programs from all over the university. Sustainability Science and Practice is a highly structured program that prepares students to be sustainability leaders. It's designed around three elements: understanding environmental and sustainability challenges from a systems perspective; understanding decision making and leadership for change; and designing and innovating for sustainability transformation. Students develop expertise in each of the three areas and carry out a practicum as well. Since it was launched, it has doubled in size each year. The student demand is incredible!

TRANSFORMING THE SCHOOL OF EARTH SCIENCES INTO THE SCHOOL OF EARTH, ENERGY AND ENVIRONMENTAL SCIENCES

At the time when I became the dean of the School of Earth Sciences, environmental and sustainability issues were part of my conception of what the school should embrace. The fact that John Etchemendy and John Hennessy selected me as dean sent a message that the school should expand to become as much a school of the environment as a school of earth science. It was a very purposeful move. They recognized that Stanford needed a home to build faculty expertise and that very few other units on campus were hiring faculty members with interests in environmental concerns.

The School of Earth Sciences at the time had a long tradition and was very well known in the areas of energy resources, earth hazards, geophysics, geology, and hydrology. We recognized that at Stanford, the School of Earth Sciences was the right place to build new strengths in areas like climate change, water resources, agriculture and land use, ocean and forest systems, and so forth. I think that there was a lot of pride in the school about who we had been and a little bit of worry about where we were going. On the other hand, I argued then and I still would argue today that if you look at the school's history, it was a school that had always been focused on problem solving and not just on scientific discovery, and it had always evolved and changed as societal challenges changed.

I think change is hard in a university, and the School of Earth, Energy and Environmental Sciences actually had more change than any other school, in large part thanks to the initiative on environment and sustainability. We hired many new faculty members, added and changed departments, and became the hosts of the interdisciplinary educational programs that are valued by faculty all over the university. We also went through a very long process to change the school's name! I have to say thanks to John and John for being there every second, just encouraging us to keep going forward.

One of the factors that helped us shift the school was society's increasing concern around whether we had enough water or food, or about droughts and climate change, or other environmental challenges. For a long time, Stanford had a few really impressive people spread around the different schools working on environment-related research—well-known people like Paul Ehrlich, Perry McCarty, Ken Arrow, Hal Mooney, and a number of others. But we lacked expertise in a number of important areas. One was climate science. We had Steve Schneider, a fantastic climate scientist, but basically nobody else working on climate change issues. We—the broader community of people around campus working in the environmental initiative—realized we needed to expand our expertise to be as great as we wanted to be and could be. As the dean of the School of Earth, I needed to say, "Let's get the resources to add new faculty expertise in these areas."[70]

That happened over and over again as we identified really critical areas of expertise that any twenty-first century university would need to have. Many of them ended up being hired in our school. Adding a greater focus on resource and environmental questions was a kind of no-brainer. Universities are in many ways ruled by the faculty, and a dean really can't do anything that the faculty simply do not want to do, so it can be hard to launch in new directions. I would not be able to say, "We need a climate scientist. We're going to hire one." I would instead encourage faculty to consider and argue for the need, provide opportunities for the departments to actually engage in that search, and make it very clear that they weren't losing anything by hiring climate scientists. So, we didn't have to say to a department, for example, "When your next faculty member retires, you can't choose who you want to hire next. We have to use that billet, that money, that position for climate science."

This is one of the key issues actually: the best way to change a school is to allow it to grow. We had the resources to add new positions, rather than to replace older but still important areas of research, thanks to the Stanford Challenge and because the economic conditions up until 2008 were fantastic. Our school had endowments that grew, and it gave us some funds to add more faculty. The Stanford Challenge funds were very important, too, and the Woods Institute was very important because of the joint hiring we did with them—we sometimes could afford to hire two new faculty rather than one. But funding and the ability to grow aren't everything. We struggled, for example, to build expertise in the environmental social sciences. We hired some great people, but knew we needed more, and for that, a different departmental structure would probably be needed.

RECRUITING FOR DIVERSITY

Our recruitment strategy focused not just on areas of expertise but on diversity. We dramatically increased the number of women in the school—and made some more limited progress in other areas of diversity, too. We made great progress in gender diversity not just because we were able to hire new people in new areas—some of which had more women PhDs in them than some older and more traditional earth science areas—but also because John Etchemendy had a fund to help incentivize diversity in hiring. In other words, the university decided to invest in this, and it really paid off. And we started looking very hard and very carefully for excellent women and found them all over the place. Fifty percent of our hires have been women over the last eighteen years or so. That's a big difference from the situation in the past—a really huge difference—and because of it we now have enough women on the faculty and involved in faculty searches that equity happens automatically. We are far from that point in terms of diversity of underrepresented minorities, but we have to keep focused and we'll get there.

It's an interesting and slow process to change universities, and it takes patience and stick-to-itiveness and resources. I just can't say enough about the fact that John Hennessy and John Etchemendy kept their eyes on that goal and made it possible for the schools to change who they were so that we can deal with the challenges of the twenty-first century. It's a long-term process to change a university and to change a school, because it often has to happen one faculty member at a time.

RESPONDING TO CHALLENGES

Prior to the 2008 financial crisis, we had been roaring along and succeeding remarkably in bringing new resources into the university. When you have financial resources, change is a lot easier than it is otherwise. After the financial collapse, we all had to pull back. I think we were led very well through that process. The approach that John Etchemendy used—basically, to take the hard hits right away and make some dramatic cuts—meant that we didn't have to be cutting for the next five or ten years, which was a brilliant thing. But there were some hard decisions right up front. I think a lot of us were able to look for the silver lining—to use the opportunity to end things that needed to be ended anyway, and that kind of thing—but still it was very hard. Of course, that changed faculty members' mindsets or outlooks on life, going from a place where resources are there to help them achieve their goals to a place where we have to cut back. From my perspective, we had made great progress, and we were able to continue making progress. We still were able to hire some positions, not nearly at the rate we were before, but our students were still coming and still doing great. I didn't have a feeling of a total slowdown; certainly, I had no feeling of failure during that time. It was a different environment, but still great.

I think what probably got difficult for me in the last five years of my deanship was that we had grown and diversified a great deal, but we knew more was needed. We saw more exciting opportunities and important directions, but the university had slowed its major fundraising initiative and there was little appetite for forward motion. There were still new donors and new commitments to new buildings, but there were very, very few. There wasn't a university campaign to drive that, and the Stanford Challenge was over.

We couldn't do a lot of new things. For example, in our school we had been saying for years that we really needed a new building. Our main School of Earth building, the Mitchell Earth Sciences Building, was and still is decrepit, and we had outgrown the facilities it offered and the space needed for our expanded community. We needed to replace it, but we were never able to actually get the resources to do that. There was a lot of hard work to try to get there but without in the end succeeding. Replacing and expanding our space will hopefully happen in the initiatives led by our current president and provost.

Another thing that we all recognized and did not succeed completely at was finding avenues for faculty members and the research community broadly—faculty research associates, graduate students—to connect with decision-making worlds outside of the university. Many of us understood that we could be more useful if we were in a conversation with decision makers so that we actually understood what they needed, what their challenges were, whether state or federal government agencies, or corporations, or nongovernmental organizations. We began to seriously think about how to make those connections between the expertise of the university and the needs of the outside world around environment and sustainability challenges much more apparent. I think there was quite a shift in our own perspectives about what our job was. It's not just to create new knowledge, but hopefully to make sure that some of that new knowledge is useful and usable and used by decision-making communities who are trying to do a better job. We're still not there, but definitely many more of our faculty have an interest in doing that—rethinking the university's role. That, too, will hopefully become possible in the future.

TELLING EACH OTHER'S STORIES

One of the things that I valued most as a dean during those years with John Hennessy and John Etchemendy as our leaders was the fact that we deans were partners; we worked together. We were a collegial, collaborative cabinet. The Executive Cabinet of school deans and vice provosts was a very close community and very dedicated to working together.

It's an amazing thing when I think back on it. We almost never argued just for our own school. We didn't feel like we were competing for funds. We were helping each other out. We were telling each other's stories, and we were working together for the university. That approach was led by John, and it was a very, very important part of the leadership team that he built and kept going. The same is true for John Etchemendy. They were great together, and they built their leadership team together. It was pretty fun. And it was unusual, I think, in universities. I think it made everyone feel like they were part of something really special and really important.

CHAPTER 11

DEBORAH STIPEK

Dean of the School of Education
(2001–2011, 2014–2015)

Deborah Stipek is an emeritus professor of education. Prior to coming to Stanford as the dean of the School of Education, she was a professor at UCLA for twenty-three years. Following her tenure as dean, she was the Peter E. Haas Faculty Director for the Haas Center for Public Service. Throughout her career, she has been involved in education policy initiatives at the state and national level.

Becoming Dean of the School
of Education

I had spent twenty-three years at the University of California, Los Angeles, perfectly happy. I had no expectation or desire to leave, and I had no aspirations to become a dean. When Stanford called, I said, "No, I'm not really interested." The person who was the co-chair of the search committee said, "Well, I'll call you back after you've had time to think about it." I said, "I'll just think about the reasons why I don't want to be a dean!" In the spring of 2000, they encouraged me to come and spend a day here, just to get to know folks. I spent a day talking to people, and I fell in love with Stanford. That day totally changed my view of what I wanted to do in my future work.

I was hired based on my personal values and history, what I'd done, how I had organized my own career and profession, and what I believed was important. We had a lot of challenges in education to address, and we needed people who had important tools from their disciplines to really dig in and try to address them. I feel that if you live in an ivory tower, the work you do is not going to be as relevant as it would be if you're interacting with the people who are actually out there implementing what's being learned by researchers.

I think this perspective partly reflects the values that I grew up with. It's why I'm at the Haas Center for Public Service right now. My advisor when I was a doctoral student was very much involved in policy and had been a central person in creating Head Start, so I was trained to engage with policymakers. I spent a year working in the U.S. Senate for the experience of being in a real policy setting. For ten years, I directed the laboratory elementary school on the UCLA campus, so I had really jumped into practice. I was running a research center at UCLA, but it was a research center that was embedded in classrooms, where researchers collaborated with teachers.[71]

At Stanford, the issue that attracted me was the desire on the part of the administration and of some faculty for the school to move further in its efforts to be more relevant to the practice of education. In the 1970s and 1980s, one of the ways that some schools of education had gained some respect on campuses—not a lot of respect, but more than they had—was to become less practitioner-focused and do more of the type of work done in traditional academic departments. For example, when I was hired at UCLA in 1977, they were hiring psychologists, economists, sociologists, and anthropologists—they were not hiring people who had PhDs in education. Stanford, like UCLA, focused on the kind of scholarship that would be published in regular disciplinary journals. When I arrived, junior faculty shared with me that they were told, "Don't publish in education journals. You'll never get tenure if you do that. Publish in discipline-based journals." There wasn't a lot of direct interaction with the world of practice, aside from our teacher education program. Now, a faculty member in the School of Education at Stanford being reviewed for promotion who has only published in disciplinary journals and doesn't have anything that is related to educational issues could be disadvantaged. That is a big change. Other major schools of education have moved more toward being engaged with practice as well.

One of the challenges is: How do you do really rigorous research that is respected by people in the disciplines but also has practical value? That's the tightrope that we are walking. Sometimes when you're working in the real world, things get really messy, and it's hard to maintain the kind of rigor you can have in an experimental study. But I think Stanford walks it well—probably better than any other school of education in the country.

At the time I was being recruited as dean, Stanford was developing a new center, the John W. Gardner Center for Youth and Their Communities. Milbrey McLaughlin was the founder of that center; she was also the co-chair of the dean's search committee, so I got to know her fairly well, although I had known her by reputation before. John Hennessy was clearly supportive of that initiative. The Gardner Center, which still exists, essentially embeds or connects researchers to community leaders—mostly local, although I think they've done some national work as well now. So, it's not researchers saying, "I think I'll ask this question and find the answer and then share the answer with whomever might be interested." This is Stanford researchers sitting down with community leaders in Redwood City or San Francisco or East Palo Alto or Mountain View and saying, "What are your challenges?" and then developing plans for embedding research in the community that would help them address the problem. It's a very different model for research than is typically done in universities. I love that model, and I was inspired by Stanford's level of commitment and enthusiasm.[72]

Deborah Stipek

The Executive Cabinet

It's hard to become a dean from the outside because there's so much to learn. Getting to know Stanford was a challenge. There was a sort of drinking out of a fire hose aspect to it—trying to figure out who's who and what's what. One thing that I was impressed with right from the very beginning at Stanford was the Executive Cabinet, which at the time included the president, the provost, the deans, and the vice provosts. It was a sounding board for university-wide decisions. The provost and the president divided their responsibilities: John Etchemendy really ran the academic side of things, the nuts and bolts of the university; John Hennessy was the fundraiser and visionary and very good at it. Of course, there are many decision-making bodies around, but the Executive Cabinet was sort of the president and provost's kitchen cabinet, a place where they could throw out ideas, get feedback.

A couple of things struck me about how it worked. One is the degree to which the deans focused on the bigger picture of Stanford. This was not a situation where each of the deans was jockeying for resources or leadership that would benefit their school. There were actually times when a dean might say, "I don't think this is going to be good for my school, but I think it's the right thing to do for the university." I had a friend who was dean of education at Harvard at the same time; she could not believe how cooperative and mutually supportive and helpful Stanford deans were. She described a much more competitive situation at Harvard.

233

Collaboration didn't occur just at those meetings. If I had a question, I could email or call any dean, anytime, and say, "Has this ever occurred for you? Do you have any suggestions?" I would have an email back in minutes: "Here's my cell phone, here's my home phone, feel free to call." I felt that kind of response basically reflected the culture across the university. Whenever I called anyone or asked for help, they couldn't always help me, but they always seemed eager to try. It is just a very supportive environment. I think part of it was organizational; the Executive Cabinet met on a regular basis, and we got to know each other fairly well. The issues were framed as collective issues. It wasn't, "What are we going to do for the School of Education today?" It was, "Here's the dilemma that the university faces." It demanded that we look at dilemmas from the university's perspective. Clearly, we brought our own lenses to it; we had responsibilities to our schools. But because of the way it was presented and the context in which it was presented, you had this feeling that you needed to look at it through two lenses: your school and the university in general.

CREATING A FUNDRAISING INFRASTRUCTURE

The School of Education had a very weak fundraising infrastructure and history when I arrived. They had not developed a strong group of loyal major donors. We started almost from scratch. I was really fortunate to have the help of some people who were really good citizens of the university. John Levin, who at the time was a trustee and had been chair of many boards, helped me start a School of Education Board of Advisors—a group of people who understand the school, what it's trying to accomplish, its challenges—to guide us and begin to develop a fundraising arm. He took on that job just to launch it. Then I had the good fortune of having support from Maddy Stein, whose husband, Isaac, was the chair of the Board of Trustees. There were many really incredibly good things going on at the school, but not fundraising. At Stanford, that's a major part of what deans do, and that's the only way we can really grow and develop new fields.

Maddy Stein and John Levin were my mentors. They were very respectful and collaborative. The first step was to establish a board and get people involved. They helped identify people who might be good board members and talked to them. Obviously, if Maddy Stein and John Levin were involved, that attracted people. If it was just the School of Education who called potential donors, their responses were tepid, even though they may have graduated from here. I needed Maddy's and John's clout, and they were willing to use it.[73]

The Advisory Council created a group of people who saw themselves as stewards of the school, both in guiding the way we thought about new initiatives and in helping us raise the resources that we needed to be able to actually implement new initiatives. It probably took two to three years to really get that nailed down. I had the benefit of some very strong, very wise people who were willing to come over to the School of Education and help it gain the visibility, respect, and support it deserved.

Ironically, a call from the comedian Bill Cosby was another milestone in our development. I got a call from John Hennessy who said, "You're never going to guess who just called me." And I said, "Who called you, John?" He said, "Bill Cosby." I said, "Yeah, right!" And he said, "Yeah, that's what I said, but it really was him. I recognized his voice!" Bill Cosby made a cold call to John Hennessy and asked, "Would you like me to do an event to help raise scholarships for teachers?" We said yes, but I didn't have staff who had experience doing a major event at Stanford. This was in 2004, many years before the revelations regarding Cosby's sexual misconduct surfaced.

Loyal Stanford citizens came to the rescue. Maddy Stein and Linda Meier got together to work on this. Linda Meier is incredible; this woman could run a Fortune 500 company. At the time, there wasn't an event at Stanford that she wasn't basically running. She's absolutely extraordinary. I said, "Do you want me to bring some people to work with you?" And, they said, "No, we'll bring our own people." Linda had this group of people who were always there. They were eager to work with her because they knew it would be a class act and extremely well-run event.

We ended up putting on a really good event that raised a lot of money. It all went for people who were training to be teachers in our one-year post-BA teacher credentialing program called STEP, the Stanford Teacher Education Program. Teachers don't make very much money, so the idea was to do what we could to minimize the amount of debt that they have when they finish that fifth year. The event definitely put the school on the map, and people started paying attention to us. It was an opportunity for us to showcase what we do.

CONNECTING TO PRACTICE AND GROUNDING RESEARCH IN REAL-WORLD PROBLEMS

One initiative to connect the school more directly with practice involved expanding STEP. It prepared only secondary high school teachers at the time, so we expanded it to prepare elementary teachers. That meant we needed to hire some new faculty who were able to prepare teachers, so they needed to know a lot about practice.

A second initiative involved one of the major donors to Stanford, the Halperin family. Phil Halperin worked a lot with the San Francisco Unified School District [SFUSD].[74] He said, "Are there any faculty who are doing research in the San Francisco Unified School District?" I said, "Probably. Let me find out." So, I sent out an email. About eight or ten faculty members were working in SFUSD. We didn't realize the extent of the involvement, and the San Francisco School District didn't know they had that many people from Stanford who were working there. Some of it was more basic research, but some of it was working collaboratively with administration or teachers.

With Phil's help and funding from his family foundation, we created a partnership between SFUSD and Stanford where we raised funds for research, but the research questions were provided by the district. They would say, "Here are our priorities. Here are the challenges that we're facing. Here's where we think some information or research could actually help guide us in addressing this problem." That list would be circulated to the faculty. We created a whole proposal process where faculty would send in a proposal, explaining the study they would do related to an issue shared by SFUSD and how much it would cost. A review panel that included both people from SFUSD and the GSE would review the proposals. The idea was to do research that was practically useful but had broader implications. So, it wasn't an in-house research group doing research just for SFUSD, but scholars who were interested in answering questions that would be useful to Los Angeles or Chicago or Nashville or other districts as well.

We didn't bring in new faculty positions; fundraising just paid for the research itself. It was maybe $800,000 a year for a certain number of years divided across a number of projects. It often paid for graduate student research assistants. Every year we have a conference where all the findings from the research are presented and discussed with both SFUSD staff and GSE faculty and students. It's still going on; it's a long-term commitment. Many, many really good studies and a deep relationship with the district have come out of it. SFUSD has been through at least three superintendents since we started the collaboration. Typically, these kinds of university-district partnerships fall apart when the superintendent leaves. We were working at many levels in the district; you could have turnover with the superintendents, but the partnership stayed in place because it was valued by people at many levels in the district.

The new dean, Dan Schwartz, has taken on some other districts in an expanded version of the San Francisco partnership.[75] I thought that these partnerships were very valuable because the faculty were forced to grapple with real-world problems that districts were facing. Long-term collaboration yields benefits because Stanford researchers and district staff get to know and trust each other. Initially, faculty would get, say, $100,000 to do a particular project. Five years later they're on their third project, often externally funded, because they've developed these relationships.

EDUCATIONAL LEADERSHIP INITIATIVES AND THE EAST PALO ALTO ACADEMY

We developed a program for practicing principals where a group of principals came to campus once a month to engage in conversations with Stanford faculty. Each cohort lasts for three years. A lot of them valued it as much for the collegiality with other principals as they did for the Stanford people that we brought in. We also created an executive education program for superintendents with the Business School. These kinds of programs engaged Stanford faculty and students directly with education practitioners in leadership positions. What we learned from them about the real challenges they faced informed our research and our ability to share findings in a way that was useful. It has allowed Stanford to use its expertise and resources to support the larger community.

We were also involved in starting a charter school, East Palo Alto Academy [EPAA]. This was in 2001 when charter schools were relatively new in California. Linda Darling-Hammond was the lead person at Stanford. She started EPAA in collaboration with a charter school organization called Aspire. East Palo Alto had no high school. Years before, for purposes of desegregation, they had closed the high school because it was all kids of color, mostly black. When they closed the local high school, they bused the kids to all the nearby high schools in the community. The East Palo Alto community wanted their own high school, and Aspire was interested in starting a high school there. The idea was to create something where Stanford would play a role in developing innovative practices and studying them; Aspire would run the nuts and bolts. After a number of years, Aspire and Stanford got a friendly divorce. It was mostly because Aspire was getting bigger, and they wanted to create strategies and approaches that would be the same across all of their schools. The idea of having Stanford experimenting with things ran into conflict with their desire for consistency.[76]

Linda Darling-Hammond, professor of education, speaking at the Brown v. Board of Education Fiftieth Anniversary Symposium in 2004, as panel moderator Sally Dickson, associate vice provost for faculty development, looks on.

When Aspire moved on to develop other charter schools, we created a 501(c)(3) called Stanford New Schools that was independent of but associated with Stanford.[77] The nonprofit entity was needed to oversee the charter school. The dean of the School of Education was automatically chair of the board for Stanford New Schools. We also started an elementary school at that time. As long as I was dean, we maintained the Stanford New Schools oversight. The university was incredibly generous and provided some funding. In addition, we raised money because we couldn't meet the students' needs on what the state provided, although the state has raised their contribution a fair amount since then.

The high school is still there and thriving. It eventually moved from the Ravenswood School District to become a dependent charter in the Sequoia-Union High School District. This was more efficient as it meant that Sequoia-Union picked up a lot of back office costs, allowing more money to go directly to student education. When the school became a dependent charter with less autonomy and more district oversight, Stanford New Schools was no longer needed. It was dissolved in 2017. Some of us who had been working with the school are still deeply engaged, however. The elementary school no longer exists. The Ravenswood School District didn't like charter elementary schools because they pulled kids and their accompanying funding out of the district schools. When the elementary school came up for reapproval, they turned us down.

When Dan Schwartz came in as dean, I don't think he was that enthusiastic about playing an active role in running a school. I think the benefits for the GSE diminished over time. There weren't that many faculty who were involved, and it was a fundraising burden. Up until then, my view was that the charter school actually benefited the GSE's fundraising because it sent a message to donors who cared a lot about public education that the faculty at Stanford were willing to get out and get their hands dirty. It was not an ivory tower bunch of researchers. I think he believed that the charter school had run that course, and the GSE had developed other initiatives that connected faculty and students to practice.

IMPLEMENTING CHANGE IN THE SCHOOL OF EDUCATION

If you want to change a department or school, you do that through faculty; you don't change the faculty you have. You don't say, "Okay, you are going to do a different kind of research." But, as one of my colleagues said to me, "You can't herd cats, but you can move the cat food." The SFUSD partnership essentially put some cat food in front of faculty. They might not have naturally sought out research that was in partnership with the district, but when somebody said, "Do you want $80,000 to fund your graduate students to do work that you might want to do anyway? All you have to do is tweak it a little bit and work with this district," they went in that direction. You can move what's being done in the school a little bit with resources; that's one reason why fundraising is important.

The other way to make change is through new faculty positions. To a substantial degree, when a faculty member retired or left, the faculty felt compelled to replace them. If we had someone who did X, they wanted to hire a new person who does X. So, it was hard sometimes to move in new directions.

But we did raise money for faculty chairs. I made that a high priority. It didn't feel to faculty like a replacement; you could talk about new directions. Policy was one area that I wanted to grow, and we did that partly by raising funds for policy research and an endowed chair. Over that period, we really became known as one of the major places in the country in education policy.

The learning sciences and technology design areas also were growing and developing a lot over that period. We brought in some folks, like Jonathan Osborne who is an expert in science education, and created some organizational structures to highlight technology and education, including a master's program and a doctoral program.[78] Dan Schwartz has really pushed in that direction. He's in a much better position than I was to do it, because he really knows the field, whereas I know policy. I think deans tend to move in the direction that they feel they know and are comfortable in.

During my tenure, we had a major campaign, the Stanford Challenge; breaking down disciplinary barriers was a central theme. The deans and trustees came up with three areas to focus on: the environment, human health, and peace and security. But potential donors kept saying, "If you're going to solve big problems, why aren't you taking on education?" So, they added a fourth dimension to the focus areas. We were deeply involved in that and created some cross-campus collaborations and teams of people to begin to flesh it out. Out of that campaign came two major initiatives in the School of Education. One was the policy initiative, which engaged scholars both in and outside of the GSE. That resulted in the Stanford Center for Education Policy Analysis. The other educational area included in the larger university initiative was teacher professional development. We had a very strong teacher education program, but we weren't doing much in teacher professional development, so we created the Center to Support Excellence in Teaching, CSET, which also still exists. Those two big initiatives came out of that major university campaign.[79]

When I stepped down, Claude Steele took over, but he was only there for about two years and then he got an offer to be provost at Berkeley, so I got called back to resume as dean until they had time to find a new dean.[80] I had my ten-year stint, and then I had an almost two-year subsequent stint before Dan Schwartz was hired. When I became dean, it was the School of Education. Claude Steele renamed the school during his tenure. Stanford has the Graduate School of Business, and he saw that as the model. He wanted this to be known as the Graduate School of Education, and it is now. I think he felt that changing the name of the school would give it more status.

I actually wouldn't have done it, because when I was dean, I was trying to deepen our engagement in undergraduate education. We created an undergraduate minor in education and hired someone to oversee that. Undergraduates would occasionally end up in graduate education classes, but there was no one guiding them and there was no formal process for recognizing their coursework. So, we created this minor and developed a set of courses that were particularly appropriate for undergraduates. I was moving away from thinking of the School of Education as a graduate school and thinking of a School of Education at Stanford that provided educational opportunities for a broader array of students.

CENTRAL ADMINISTRATION DREAM TEAM

I felt like I had the dream team as far as central administration. John Etchemendy was such a wonderful provost, in
part because I always felt like he was both a mentor and my
boss, and those two didn't seem to conflict with each other at
all. I really felt like I didn't have to make things look rosier
than they were. I could go to him with any problem, and he
would guide me. He's a very ethical man. He's very kind. He's
very supportive.

The other thing I love about this university is that there is a
can-do entrepreneurial culture. I'll give you an example. I went
to John Etchemendy, telling him that I'd like to start a minor
for undergraduates in education because there were so many
students who were interested in taking education courses. He
said, "Well, there's a rule that you can't have a minor if you
don't have a major." Before I could even start to argue with
him, he said, "We'll have to change that rule." There wasn't this
attitude of, "No, we don't do it that way." He was so thoughtful
and such a good listener. I'm sure he made a few mistakes, as I
did, but he was very well respected.

There were times when I couldn't move John Hennessy, like
on the need for a new building for the School of Education.
That annoyed me. Also, he is not always the best listener. He
had strong opinions. He would sometimes express his opinion,
and then he'd say, "What do you all think?" He'd go around
the table, and we'd tell him why it was a bad idea, and then
he would say, "Well, here's why it is a good idea!" [laughs] I'd
think, "You didn't really want our opinion, did you?"

But he was very supportive of the GSE, and he did bring resources to the school. There was one woman who was interested in a loan forgiveness program for undergraduates. John Hennessy was the one who steered her towards the School of Education. He said, "What about a loan forgiveness program for teachers? They're not going to make very much money."

And he was very supportive of the charter school. I happened to have a meeting with him once right after I'd been called by the principal of the charter school who told me, "Three of our kids got picked up yesterday for armed robbery." I said to John, "I think I should probably let you know about this because there may be some questions coming in." He said something like, "Did anybody get killed or did they shoot anyone?" I said, "No, no guns were fired." He said, "Oh, okay." I think a lot of presidents would have said, "Oh my god, this is going to be a PR nightmare." I was grateful for his constant support.

CHAPTER 12

LARRY KRAMER

Dean of Stanford Law School (2004–2012)

Larry Kramer is an American legal scholar who served as the dean of Stanford Law School between 2004 and 2012. Prior to joining Stanford, he was Russell D. Niles Professor of Law at New York University. He now serves as president of the William and Flora Hewlett Foundation.

Joining Stanford

I was on the faculty and an associate dean at NYU Law School. But I had friends at Stanford and had been out there a couple of times to present papers. I was also fairly close with Jack Rakove from the History Department, who was helping me understand history as I made a switch in my scholarship to focus more on that, and I was toying with the possibility of coming to Stanford as a faculty member. They had not made me an offer yet, and it was not clear that they would have, but we were in conversation and I was planning to visit.

Anyway, the dean of the Law School stepped down, and I got a call to come interview. What I think happened was that Jack Rakove was on the dean search committee. He had already invited me out here to teach one of his classes, and he said to the committee, which hadn't moved along very far, "As long as the guy's coming and he's on the list, why don't we interview him while he's here?"[81]

So, I did an interview with the committee. It went really well. You don't always know whether that's the case, but I just felt like everything clicked. I was pretty excited about it. I think it went well on their side, too, and it helped kick the process into gear. They pretty quickly focused on a couple of other candidates. I knew who they were because we all talked, and then they made me the offer. It all happened pretty fast—that was probably April/May 2004—and I accepted the job right away.

Top of mind when I arrived was that even though Stanford was already one of the top three law schools in the country, I still thought we were underperforming. It was an incredibly strong school, given the faculty already there, but not fully achieving all it could. Plus, it seemed a little out of the flow of things. The faculty were here at Stanford, but they weren't out on the circuit. You weren't getting exposed to their scholarship unless you had some reason to look for it, there weren't that many events happening here, and so on. So just fixing that would do a lot.

EARLY DECISIONS

I tried to do some simple things right away to generate goodwill. For example, one bathroom had been designated for the dean's use. I turned it over to the faculty which, believe it or not, meant a lot to people. It said something. I don't think anyone had intended it to mean quite what it had come to mean. But it represented a notion of the dean as special and privileged. That was literally my first move—to rekey the bathroom so that everybody's key would work as of 12:01 a.m. on my first day.

I also started to do some things to engage the faculty with each other more. There had always been a Wednesday lunch with a workshop, but I created another lunch that was just for eating together, with no program. Everyone would come and just hang out together. I did a few small but hopefully mean-ingful things like that.

The third thing I did was to create a kind of cabinet. My predecessor, Kathleen, had only had a vice dean who was responsible for the curriculum. I asked Mark Kelman to take that position.[82] He was one of the most well-respected members of faculty generally, as well as someone I already knew a little and trusted. But I also created several other associate dean positions. There was a curriculum dean, a dean for the clinics, a dean for the international students, and a dean for academic life. I didn't do this because we needed all those new positions. It's a small school, and there wasn't that much administration. But I needed advice and honest input and feedback, and I picked people who were liked and trusted in each of those communities. This gave me a really solid base to talk things through and make sure I wasn't missing anybody's views or any important points of conflict, and also a way to communicate back to everybody. Those were early moves.

I learned right away that Stanford was about to launch the Stanford Challenge campaign and that the Law School needed to plan for it. That had been put on hold at the Law School during the year before I arrived because everybody agreed that it didn't make sense for an outgoing dean to plan the campaign. So, we had some catching up to do.

I'd learned over the summer both what the major themes of the university campaign were going to be and what the major issues were in the Law School. It became pretty clear where the overlaps were, and I put together subgroups around each of the Law School themes in the campaign that mapped onto the university's themes. The university campaign was focused on making the university more interdisciplinary and more international, as well as more public service and practically oriented. So, we created a subgroup on interdisciplinary work, a subgroup on international work, a subgroup on public service, a subgroup on clinical education, and a steering group.

We started to meet. I wanted this to be informal, so we met for brunches and dinners at my home. Each subgroup met once

a week. We'd talk through where the Law School was, what we
needed to do to become better, and so on.

INTEGRATING THE LAW SCHOOL WITH
THE UNIVERSITY: SWITCHING TO
THE QUARTER SYSTEM AND
IMPLEMENTING JOINT DEGREES

Another piece which I began working on pretty early
concerned the academic calendar. I had spent almost a decade
at the University of Chicago—as a student and in my first job
teaching—and, like Stanford, it teaches on the quarter system.
I had then moved to Michigan and NYU, which were both
on semesters. So, for me, the difference between quarters and
semesters was not a big deal. They both work just fine; they're
different, but they both work. When I came to Stanford, I was
surprised to discover that, while the university was on quarters,
the Law School was on semesters. Since all the plans we were
talking about for the campaign involved integration with the
larger university in one form or another, that difference didn't
make any sense to me.

Let me back up for a moment, because there is another
point that puts my desire to shift to quarters into context. When
I interviewed for the job, they asked me what I saw as the Law
School's major challenge. I said that the major challenge was
size and specialization. When I had gone to law school in the
1980s, law schools were all doing pretty much the same thing,
a kind of soft trade education focused on a set of analytic skills

we describe as "thinking like a lawyer." And, in that context, the small law schools dominated the large ones, with the exception of Harvard because it's Harvard. The small law schools were to the large law schools what espresso is to coffee—a more concentrated, more potent version of the same thing. But in the years since I graduated, specialization had increased, together with demand from students for more variety. The world was evolving in ways that would have the big law schools dominate the small ones because they could offer more choices and opportunities—more teachers, classes, centers, clinics, student organizations, and so on.

This was not limited to Harvard. I'd been at NYU, and while I was there, the dean had basically conceptualized NYU as striving to be to other law schools what New York is to other cities: not the best in everything, but the best in some things, up there in most things, and with more of everything than anybody else.[83] And that was what we had built. That model allowed NYU to shoot up in the rankings and attract faculty. So I said, "The problem is, how are the small law schools going to compete as offering variety and opportunities becomes what students and faculty want?" They came back and said, "So what's the answer?" And I said, "I have no idea what the answer is. I'm just saying, that's the challenge, and we'll need to figure out an answer."

When I got here and learned more about Stanford, the answer became clear. It was the rest of the university. Students didn't need more law classes. Yes, there was some sense in which they could benefit from offering more specialized law classes, but we could supply that with adjunct professors. What students really wanted and needed were opportunities to learn about things taught in other disciplines. If you were going to be a business lawyer, you needed to know accounting and organizational behavior and finance. If you were going to be a technology lawyer, you needed to understand something about technology policy. And so on. Whatever you were going to do, you needed to know and learn things outside the traditional law school curriculum, but things that were actually taught in other parts of the university—in schools and departments that were, in their fields, as highly thought of as the Law School. Plus, students wanted clinics; they wanted public service opportunities; they wanted a chance to try different things. Stanford Law School's opportunity came from sitting inside a university that had top-five schools and departments in every single discipline that mattered—schools and departments that were top three in most, and number one in quite a few. To not take advantage of that was a huge mistake.

Larry Kramer, dean of the Stanford Law School, teaches a session of "Thinking Like a Lawyer" in 2007. The course was designed to expose graduate students in other parts of the university to core legal concepts.

All that made clear to me that we should switch to the quarter system, because we couldn't do any of that effectively while on a completely different academic calendar. The first challenge was just getting the faculty to agree to switch. But I was naïve. I thought that would be easy. It turned out not to be the case at all, and it took me five years to get it done.

To appreciate the reason, you need to understand that faculty are, generally speaking, really conservative when it comes to institutional change. They may be quite radical in their scholarship and their intellectual work, but when it comes to their institutions, they generally don't like change. They have their lives constructed and don't want to disrupt them. At the same time, they generally won't oppose changes that don't affect them directly. For most proposed changes, then, you'll get opposition from that small portion of the faculty that are directly affected, but everybody else is fine. But changing to the quarter system required 100 percent of the faculty to redo their classes completely, so everybody's initial reaction was "Whoa, no! I don't want to do that." It's not an entirely unreasonable reaction, and it took a long time to bring people around.

Part of doing so simply entailed emphasizing that it was just a one-time switch, after which things would again be stable. A much bigger factor in changing people's minds came from realizing some unobvious benefits. On the semester system, everyone was teaching for the entire school year—the typical load being a class in one semester and a class and a seminar in the other. Most people assumed that on the quarter system, they would need to teach one class every quarter with a seminar during one of the three quarters. But we didn't actually need more classes. If anything, we already had too many classes, and there were complaints that classes were too small. So, on the quarter system, faculty would teach one class during one quarter, a class and a seminar during a second quarter, and have one quarter off from teaching. That was a huge benefit for faculty in terms of their time for research. But it was also a benefit for students, who could take more of the classes that were offered. Those insights turned around most of the faculty, although it was still a really long process.

There's no reason to go through all the machinations, but we had some really challenging faculty meetings. In the end, I proposed a compromise, which was to delay the implementation for three years, because full implementation required changing a huge number of moving parts. Not only did faculty have to change their classes, but the school had to change the day schedule and the week schedule. We had to change the credit requirements and rework the first-year calendar. Plus, if the goal was to make the whole university accessible, we needed to line our days and weeks up as much as possible with the rest of the university. A lot of interrelated things needed to be changed in order to make it work. Mark Kelman, who was my vice dean and was the single most vociferous opponent of making this shift, was the person most responsible for figuring this all out and making it work, and, to his credit, once the vote was taken, he did so wonderfully. He's really good at that kind of administrative thinking, and he figured it out along with other people's help.

The shift opened up a great many benefits for students, more than we initially saw and more than just integration with the university. In the semester system, students needed the whole first year for basic law, after which they had only four semesters. So there was only so much they could do and little time for anything outside the Law School. With the quarter system, we could reconfigure the first year to allow more electives early, so students could begin to explore and experiment, and they had six additional quarters, which is to say 50 percent more classes, to go wide or deep or both. And by making use of the whole of Stanford, students could take those classes with the very best faculty in other disciplines, with the very best students in those disciplines, students who would be their future clients and colleagues. Rather than a course in "business" taught by a law professor or an adjunct, which is what most schools were doing, Stanford students could take accounting and finance and organizational behavior at the GSB. It meant more, higher-quality offerings than any other law school could meet, except for possibly the University of Chicago, which uses the same calendar.

The flexibility also allowed us to develop a wide range of three-year joint degree programs, allowing students to get a JD master's in many different disciplines. We created something like thirty-five options, I think, everything from a JD-MBA to JD master's in computer science, health policy, education, and multiple disciplines in the humanities and social sciences. Along the way, we developed a joint degree template that other schools at Stanford could use. Now if you look around Stanford, there's tons of other joint degree options between other schools using our template.

The key to making these work was recognizing that each discipline, on its own, already allowed students to earn credit toward a degree for a certain number of hours in another discipline. By allowing students to earn credit toward both degrees for these classes, that is, by "dual crediting," we created a kind of Venn diagram that enabled students to earn both degrees in less time while still fulfilling 100 percent of the requirements toward each of them.

We also created a number of new JD-PhDs, though these had potential revenue implications. We used the same dual crediting for the course requirement portion of the joint degree, but the typical PhD program also provided five years of fellowship support. So, the basic structure was to have students do their first year at the Law School and pay full tuition, then begin their fellowship support for the next five years. During those five years, they would finish the course requirements for both degrees and work on their dissertation. Students could thus earn a JD-PhD in six years, but the Law School would lose two years of revenue, because the student would not pay for their second and third year of legal education. It's a huge allure for students: "Come do a JD-PhD at Stanford, and you only have to pay for one year of law school."

But to get approval from the university, we had to address the revenue issues. Because there would never be a huge number of JD-PhDs, the Law School promised to take an additional transfer student for the second and third year, which, given the low marginal cost of additional law students, replaced almost all the revenue. We wanted to add some transfers anyway, essentially bringing in great students we had missed in the initial round of applications, so this too was good for the Law School.

All this was made easy by a unique aspect of Stanford's operations. Most universities budget by having every school operate on its own: it brings in its own money through tuition and fundraising and has only what it brings in. Stanford uses a "one university" model. The tuition all goes to the central university, which then provides general funds to each school based on needs. That model makes it infinitely easier to have students and faculty moving among schools, because you don't have to compensate another school if you want one of their faculty to teach a class at your school or want them to let some of your students take classes there. This wasn't true for the Business School and the Medical School, which do operate on their own bottoms, so we had to work out special deals with them. Fortunately, the Medical School class is so small compared to the overall operation that they just said, "Let's not worry about it." So, it was really only the Business School that needed a special deal, and we were able to negotiate things that worked pretty easily.

There were lots of other changes we needed to work on to take full advantage of the calendar shift. For example, we needed to get course information to everyone at a time when they could still use it. How can we expect students to cross-register if they don't have information about offerings at other schools or, as turned out to be the case, if the registration periods of the schools are on different systems and at different times? So, the deans agreed as a group to ask the registrar to create a single system for information and registration, where all the information would be released and everybody could register in the same system, at the same time, on the same days. There were a ton of similar issues that had to be resolved as we went along. So that was the multidisciplinary piece.

LARRY KRAMER

CLINICAL EDUCATION AND THE
PROFESSOR (TEACHING) LINE

Traditional legal education took place entirely in a classroom. There was no real hands-on teaching about how to do "lawyering." Think of a doctor doing rounds: there was nothing like that in law school. Clinical education was the answer to that, a way of providing practical training in law school.

Stanford Law School had been an early pioneer in clinical education. The original legal clinics were less about teaching and training than about providing legal services to people who couldn't afford to hire private attorneys. So, the original clinical movement was pretty much limited to poverty law, and Stanford had been a pioneer in that in the 1960s. Then, precisely because it wasn't really considered intellectual enough by most law faculty—it was considered social activism—Stanford had essentially let its clinical program lapse. The students started a community law clinic in the 1980s, but it mostly limped along on its own, with little faculty support.

Then David Mills was drawn into Stanford by Paul Brest.[84] David strongly supported clinical education, and he had a lot of support based on strong personal relationships with people on the academic side of the faculty. With their backing and the support of Kathleen Sullivan as dean, they began to build a clinical program. It was still relatively small when I arrived, and we decided to enlarge it. NYU was a leader in clinical education, so I had experience at a school where I had seen what it could be. Even though I had been associated mainly with the academic group at NYU, as opposed to the clinical or social justice groups,

I had a pretty deep appreciation for clinics. So here was another opportunity to capitalize on growing momentum and build something new and different and better.

At first, the clinical faculty and their supporters opposed the shift to quarters. "You can't run a clinical program on a quarter system," they said. "It's too short on time." But Larry Marshall was now at Stanford.[85] He had been a visiting faculty member the year before I came, and we hired him my first year as a tenured professor to run the clinic. He came up with a really smart solution. In a semester system, students would take a clinic alongside other classes. Suppose, Larry said, we have students take a clinic for a quarter but make it the only thing they do that quarter? Since they would not have end of quarter exams, we could run the clinic through the end of exams, which would make it effectively a semester in length. The student experience would then be immersive and better for that, while with five remaining quarters, they could still take more than enough regular academic classes. It meant we could have a stronger and better clinical program.

A key issue that emerged as we grew the clinics had to do with clinical faculty appointments. At many or most law schools, clinical instructors were contract employees. At places where they were given academic appointments, the academic faculty tended to look down on them because they weren't "real" academics in the sense that they didn't do much research and writing or did mostly practitioner-oriented articles. That was not surprising, because clinical teaching is much more time consuming and intensive. Giving clinical faculty regular academic appointments was putting a square peg in a round hole. Hence, the dilemma.

Stanford University offered a solution in its "(Teaching)" line. A "Professor (Teaching)" is a formal position at Stanford, a line defined around and for positions whose primary focus is teaching. It was already used in some other schools and departments but hadn't been used at the Law School. So, we brought it in. It didn't completely eliminate the tensions, but you could appoint people into a recognized faculty line without feeling like you were being asked to ignore the actual requirements of that line and treat someone whose main work was not research as if it was. Better still, it solved the tenure standards problem by giving us a set of criteria to evaluate people by that fit the job we were actually asking them to do.

Building this kind of clinic was expensive, and so this became a key part of our part of the Stanford Challenge. We needed to raise money for faculty positions, for supporting fellows, and for fees and other costs associated with litigation. And, of course, we needed space. Part of the Neukom Building plan included a whole floor dedicated to clinics.

Each clinic ran twice a year for a quarter, so clinicians got the same quarter off as other faculty. We wanted our clinicians to do academic writing in their fields, and the expectation was that they would do so during that quarter. There was still a salary gap; these are different markets, after all. But we progressively closed it as best we could, so the compensation was reasonably close.

THOUGHTS ON ADJUNCT FACULTY

Most law schools supplement the courses taught by regular faculty with adjunct teachers, usually practicing lawyers.

Different deans and different schools have different feelings about how to use adjuncts. When I was at Chicago, for instance, there were very few because people thought teaching needed to be done by full-time academics. NYU had a lot of adjuncts, but it was a matter of real controversy and there was constant pushback from the academic faculty.

My own experience had led me to conclude that adjunct faculty could add a lot of value. You could have bad adjunct teachers, of course—the kind who would teach by telling war stories from their practice. But a thoughtful, accomplished practitioner could offer students something the regular academic faculty could not. Full-time faculty are great at teaching students a field's deep structure and underlying theory, and they are also good at showing students sophisticated ways to think about theory and analysis. But I used to say to people, "You take Civil Procedure from me and then take Advanced Civil Procedure from me, but it's essentially the same course twice—because what I'm teaching you, what I have uniquely to offer you, is a way to think about procedure." The doctrine in the second course is different, but that's not as important as learning new ways to think about that doctrine. A really good practitioner will take students deep into the practice in a way that is not just nuts and bolts or war stories, but that is also different from what I can do. Good adjunct professors help students take the kinds of things they learn from me and other academics and deploy them in context. So, I became a fan of using experienced practitioners as adjuncts for advanced classes. It was another way to increase students' choices and opportunities in the context of a small law school.

Internationalizing the Law Program

Everyone talks about the need to be a "global" school, and Stanford needed to do more in this regard. One change seemed easy and obvious: to increase the exposure of our students to lawyers from other countries by admitting more LLM students. The LLM is a master's degree in law, and it's common to admit lawyers from other countries who want to earn such a degree from a U.S. law school. Stanford typically admitted only a few such students, and we increased enrollment to a number equal to 15 percent of the second- and third-year classes. These international LLM students were older, and they had typically been practicing in their home nations for a few years already. So, this was a really good way to expose American JD students to lawyers from other countries, from whom they could learn.

Doing the converse also made sense, so we created exchange opportunities for our JD students with good law schools around the world—in Singapore, Chile, France, Japan, China, Germany—basically, in major legal markets with good law schools. Unfortunately, only a few U.S. law students took advantage of those opportunities. Mostly, they didn't believe that the quality of legal education was as good as what they would get at Stanford.

Lastly, we added new faculty teaching international law classes and increased the size of the international curriculum with new classes in things like trade law, international human rights, private international law, and so on.

This is all well and good, but it doesn't get to the really hard question: What does it even mean to be a "global lawyer?" In the long run, the laws of different nations will likely converge to a point where knowing the law in one country will allow you to have a good feel for the law in another country. Something like this happened in the U.S. in the nineteenth century. In the early years of this country, the tort law of New York and the tort law of Illinois were dramatically different. By the late nineteenth century, the economic integration in the country was such that there actually were a set of tort law principles that you could learn that would give you 90 percent of what the tort law was going to be in any state. So, you could study this general "tort law" at law school and then go learn the particulars in an individual state pretty easily. In some areas, international law is already like that—antitrust law, for instance, or securities law. But in most areas, the laws in different countries are still like the laws in different U.S. states in the nineteenth century. So that's a challenge: it's still too early in the convergence process to teach "global" law.

We tried to think of other ways to expose students productively to law and lawyers in other countries. One was to take advantage of how difficult it can be for first-year law students to get jobs at American firms. They don't have enough skills yet. So, we thought, why not work out deals with law firms around the world to get our first-year students jobs abroad? They could spend the summer after their first year in another country practicing law, which would be great experience.

We started to build that network, and I was really excited about it. Then the economy collapsed in 2009, and the legal market with it. We had to shelve those plans and work doubly hard to make sure the second- and third-year students were getting jobs. We didn't have the bandwidth for this new big effort.

On the whole, I thought we did a couple of things that were good. We made the student body more international, created these opportunities for study abroad, and enlarged the international curriculum. But it was well short of what needed to be done. When Liz Magill came in as dean, I said to her, "The biggest place to improve the Law School is its global program and presence, because Stanford is still very U.S. focused."[86]

PUBLIC INTEREST LAW

Public interest law, like clinical education, had become associated with liberal social activism. It was not considered intellectual, and, as a result, it was not highly respected at Stanford. The school had the kinds of things almost every law school had. It had a public interest law foundation and an annual conference, but it was all student-run, though there were a couple of faculty who were into it. But if you listed schools that had a significant public interest focus or that helped students develop public interest career opportunities, few would have thought of Stanford.

I was coming from NYU, which has a very strong public interest law program, so I had a sense that this, too, could be good and important, not to mention helping to attract students. To do so, however, we needed to get out of the mentality that public interest law is just for a small subset of students who want (as they liked to put it) "to do good rather than do well." The message I wanted to send is that there are opportunities to contribute as a lawyer to the public interest no matter what kind of career you want and that doing so will increase your

career satisfaction as well as enabling you to do good in the world.

So, we built a public interest center—the Levin Center for Public Service and Public Interest Law—meant to speak to the entire student body and to integrate public interest thinking into everybody's legal education. The clinics were part of it, so we wanted everybody to take a clinic. And there were specialized courses, though these were much broader than you might think. We also brought in speakers and held conferences and tried to get every law student in the school to engage with the Levin Center. There was a very talented woman, Diane Chin, who had been working in the career development office helping students who wanted to find public interest positions.[87] I made her the head of the center. She is super-entrepreneurial, and she built it into a real powerhouse and before long other schools were copying us.

APPROACH AS DEAN

By the time we finished the planning process for the Stanford Challenge, I had a clear idea in my head of what we wanted to do and how it all held together. Implementing it, however, was another matter altogether. I knew from my experience at several law schools that if something affects the faculty members' lives, they'll likely oppose it, because they're generally conservative when it comes to institutional change. If it doesn't affect them, they'll usually let you go unless you offer a theory about why the change is desirable, because they're trained in critical thinking and so rise to the argument. It's the natural thing to do, and once they start arguing, they often talk themselves into a position. So, rather than present some overarching theory of legal education and invite fruitless opposition, I focused on the individual pieces and kept them separate. The people who didn't like a particular change would oppose it, but the rest of the faculty would be fine, and nobody was opposed to every single piece.

Over time, I was able to move almost everything along that way. Plus, lots of it didn't affect anybody directly. Building clinics didn't affect the current faculty, who could see and agree that it offered more opportunities for our students. The same was true of joint degrees and bringing students in from other parts of the university. As to that one, faculty quickly discovered that having students from other parts of the university was great, because they are still really smart but also a bit different from law students in how they think. So, I was able to move on each of the pieces by never presenting it as, "Here's an overarching plan, and when we're done, here's what we'll look like."

It was equally important to show patience. I never forced anything, and if there was too much opposition to something, I would either let it go or try a different version. In the debate over moving to quarters, faculty who were opposed came back with something they called modified semesters. Since that was better than what we were doing and I will always take a half loaf over none, I proposed that we give it a try. By then, however, most of the faculty wanted to make the move. Still, rather than force the opponents to change, I proposed a compromise. We would vote on moving to quarters, but since so much needed to change to implement that move, we could use the modified semester plan for the three years it would take to get everything ready. If, at the end of that, people thought we didn't need to change more, we could always vote not to finish the shift to quarters. That got support from all but one member of the faculty and made the subsequent shift three years later go down a lot easier, even for those who still didn't like it. Patience went a long way towards making that move a success.

Relationship between the Law School and the University

I had been on the faculty at Chicago, Michigan, and NYU and had also visited at Columbia and Harvard. Stanford was my favorite university. I was really blown away with the breadth and depth of excellence. I'd never seen anything quite like it.

That was reflected in things like rankings. When I was thinking about the quarter system shift, I looked at the rankings of all the Stanford schools and departments that were directly relevant to the Law School—I think I counted fifteen of them. All fifteen were top five; thirteen were top three, eight were number one. There was no other university close to that.

I also liked Stanford's sort of spirit. Stanford embodied what everybody said about the West—it was nimble, and it was flexible. You could do new things, and you'd get support. One of John Hennessy's favorite lines, which I loved to quote, was "Stanford has the benefit of not being burdened by a glorious past." I thought that was exactly right. It totally captured the spirit of the place. And then there was that "one university" financial model, which created opportunities that were more difficult to implement elsewhere.

The weather made a difference, too. When I first arrived, I said to faculty, "Don't recruit by talking about the weather," which is something people had done with me. "We don't want people to think that *we* think the reason they should want to come here is the weather. That sends the wrong message." After a couple of years, though, I found myself recruiting with the weather. It's just so nice and it makes the quality of life so nice.

More seriously, the Bay Area weather turned out to be important in making a multidisciplinary program work. I had been at the University of Chicago, for example, and I can tell you that from October to April, you didn't want to leave your building if you didn't have to. Here, I could just walk out of my office, no coat or bundling needed, almost any day of the year. That helps generate a culture in which people easily move to other schools or departments, and lots of intellectual and personal benefits flow from that. It was interesting to experience that.

It also helped that Stanford is a relatively small, compact campus. We had someone start from the front door of the Law School and walk to each of the other schools and departments that mattered to law. All of them took eight minutes or less except for the Medical School, which was a twenty-minute walk.

Put all these things together, and they conspired to create the perfect conditions for the kind of multidisciplinary program we wanted to build at the Law School. It helped, too, that I was part of a group of remarkable fellow deans, all of whom were on board with what we were all trying to build jointly.

Everybody was willing to bend and make space, and sometimes push back at their faculties to help. There was a lot of that.

The two Johns—Hennessy and Etchemendy—were critical in all this, of course. I do have one criticism of John Hennessy, though, which is that he didn't really like the Law School. Or maybe it's just lawyers he didn't like. He didn't mistreat the school in any way. He didn't give us fewer resources or provide less help when I asked for it or anything like that. But he didn't have much love for our profession. The deans would give presentations at retreats, and John would always sort of heckle me throughout mine. I don't think he even realized he was doing it, but he's an engineer and a business guy, and he had that old-fashioned businessman's contempt for lawyers and what they contribute.

At the end of the Stanford Challenge, when we were doing the university-wide events all around the country and all around the world, John would talk about all the amazing things being done at the university, pulling something from every school and institute. At the first event, he literally left the Law School out. I was so furious. I went to Martin Shell, almost yelling, because I had faculty and students that were doing amazing work and donors who had stretched to support our campaign. The Law School had undergone a remarkable transformation, and I felt like we were just unappreciated. They added some references into the speech after that, but it always felt wrong that I had had to ask.

One last thing to note about this period. Those years, 2004–2012, turned out to be the end of the golden age of Silicon Valley. Obviously, Silicon Valley had been growing and booming all through the 1990s, but those years were really something, with Google and Facebook and a slew of other major innovative companies bursting out. This was before the bad stuff started happening—with disinformation and privacy and the like—or at least it was before we were aware of it. There was just a lot of excitement about integrating everything we did into and with the Valley.

At one point, I was recruiting someone from Harvard. I said, "When the Constitution was adopted, everyone in politics had a choice: Do you stay in your state, or do you go to this new national government?" Conventional wisdom said to stay in the states. They had been the center of power and where everything important had happened. So, Sam Adams, one of the leading revolutionaries, decided to stay in Boston. He became the governor of Massachusetts. His cousin, John Adams, made the opposite decision and went to the new government. John Adams became a world historic figure, while Sam Adams has a beer named after him. "Harvard is the states," I said, "and Stanford is the new national government. You should be coming here." He didn't come, unfortunately, but I think that was and still is true. We're in the midst of a world historic moment that's happening right here. Stanford is at its epicenter, and it was really exciting to be part of it.

CHAPTER 13

RICHARD SALLER

Dean of Humanities and Sciences (2007–2018)

Richard Saller is the Kleinheinz Family Professor of European Studies at Stanford University and the former dean of the School of Humanities and Sciences. Previously, he was provost at the University of Chicago.

Moving to Stanford and Early Perceptions of the University

I knew John Etchemendy because he and I attended what was known then as the "nine provosts" meeting. These were the nine private research universities—the Ivies, plus Chicago, Stanford, and MIT.[88] I was provost at Chicago, and I'd known him for about four or five years. There was a change in leadership at the University of Chicago in 2006, and in the fall of 2006, John phoned me and asked me whether I would interview for the job here as dean of the School of Humanities and Sciences. My immediate response was, "Why on earth would I want to do that?" It's not a natural step for a provost to move to a dean's job.

He said two things. He said that the university was about to announce a $4.5 billion fundraising campaign, so there would be new money to do things with. In my eight years as dean at Chicago and five years as provost, I had never had anything but deficits to wrestle with. So, the idea of actually having resources to do something that wasn't already being done was very attractive. The second thing he said was, "You can talk to the other deans, and they'll tell you that they're happy and collegial." Again, that was a change from Chicago, where there were some sharp elbows. Then I said, "I'm married and I'm not moving without my wife." He said, "I've already checked on that. I don't think that will be a problem." He had done his homework, and he really was a master recruiter.[89]

By the time I'd been here for a few years there were actually three ex-provosts from top-20 universities serving as deans here.

John was able to assemble people with experience. Claude Steele came from Columbia, and Lloyd Minor came from Johns Hopkins.[90] He was right, that group was collegial. It was a different experience for me. In Chicago, I had been on the faculty for ten years before I started as dean, so I knew a lot of the people there. When I came out here, I may not have known more than five people. It's a very different experience administering a group that you've only just met.

There was a search. In the end, John offered me the job. I'd made up my mind that I wasn't going to be part of the new regime at Chicago. I'd also watched Hanna Gray and Geof Stone, former president and former provost, stick around at the University of Chicago after they had finished their terms, and it was hard on them to watch other people making different decisions.[91] So, I thought maybe putting 2,000 miles between Chicago and my new job would be wise. In retrospect, I think it was exactly the right decision.

RELATIONSHIPS WITH THE SENIOR MANAGEMENT TEAM

John Etchemendy was terrific in my view. One of the things that has made Stanford such a good place for me is that John had a terrific sense of when he could intervene to smooth over collaborative friction between deans. There were times when I felt that because I had such a big and diverse school, I had the other school deans coming to me saying, for example, "Will you hire a spouse in Theater?" There was no hope that the other school would ever reciprocate; it just didn't work that way. John Etchemendy, as provost, would intervene in those cases and figure out a way to make it costless or near costless to me.

We had monthly Executive Cabinet meetings, and that included the seven school deans plus the director of the Hoover Institution, the two academic vice provosts (for undergraduate education and graduate education), and the dean of research. John and John listened to us. John Etchemendy, who I think was the prime mover in hiring new deans, was very careful to try to appoint deans whose personalities would encourage collaboration.

In general, relationships within the senior leadership team were much better than at Chicago. There was one evening there that I will never forget in the late 1990s when there was rebellion amongst the faculty against the president of the university who hired me. The same evening, I got a phone call from the president and from the leader of the faculty rebels saying, "Whose side are you on?" At Stanford, John and John managed to set a tone so that I never had anything like that kind of experience or strain here. It makes the work so much better.

By and large, John Etchemendy's promise of collegiality was kept. Any time it looked like it might not be kept, I could go to John, and he would smooth things over without having to take my side in a visible way. I think in terms of the different institutes, I had a really good working relationship with Ann Arvin and I would hope she'd say the same. I felt like we were almost always on the same page. Because she was the dean of research, she had responsibility for the independent labs, the institutes, and so that worked well.

When I arrived, I started having individual meetings with all the deans. That didn't continue. It got to the point where the pressures on their time and my time meant that it was easier just to communicate by email and we could solve problems that way. Occasionally we decided it was better to have a face-to-face discussion or a telephone call. I've lived through twenty-four years of full-time administration, and email really does change the interpersonal dynamics.

TACKLING CHALLENGES

Apart from the fact that John wanted to make the change sooner rather than later—I actually started midyear rather than at the start of the academic year—I didn't know that there were issues. The senior political scientist in the Political Science Department, Barry Weingast, came in to see me and said, "The School of Humanities and Sciences is ungovernable."[92] That was a bit of a shock. I came to understand over months and months that there was a profound distrust of the dean's office among the faculty and the departments of the school. And there was a mistrust from the top administration about H&S's ability to run its own affairs.

My first job was to try to put the administrative house in order to try to gain some trust. We did that. The administrative executive dean took another job, and I happened to hire somebody, Adam Daniel, who was absolutely terrific at the job.[93] Over the first few years, I think we managed to gain trust. In fact, in year two or three I suggested to Adam that we do a consumer satisfaction survey among the departments. Apart from a few wrinkles, it came back almost completely positive, so I think we really had established some trust there.

I told Adam that we needed to respond to every email, inquiry, and request from a department chair or faculty member within twenty-four hours. The answer might be that it would take some time to find the answer, but we were going to be responsive, and we were going to get an answer to them, whether it was yes or no, as soon as we could. I later discovered that the previous administration, rather than giving no for an answer, just didn't give an answer. The departments and the faculty felt like they were dealing with a black hole.

The other thing that I found out, and this took a couple of years, is that the dean's office was believed to have reneged on written agreements with faculty. What could be more fatal to developing a relationship and trust than to be going back on written commitments? Faculty members were told that if they were recruited, they would get X, Y, and Z, and then they didn't get X, Y, and Z. I arrived in April 2007. Within a year and a half, the recession hit, and we were in retrenchment mode. But even when the endowment fell by about a third, we didn't renege on any written commitment we had made. Another challenge was a lack of regularity in process. Departments needed to know what to expect, how decisions were made.

My starting principle is that the foundation for a great university is the quality of the faculty more than anything else. There are other things; quality of students, quality of facilities are important. But the quality of faculty is the sine qua non. When I got here in 2007, it was the "Wild West," where faculty in some departments—not all, but many departments—thought that the only way to improve their situation was to get offers from Harvard or Princeton or Yale. In the year that I arrived, there were fourteen departures of tenured faculty to the same position in another university. We tried to establish a really cooperative relationship with the department chairs who were negotiating to keep these faculty members. In a few cases, we decided to let them go elsewhere, but for the most part we wanted to keep them. Within two years, we'd sent the departure rate down to two to four per year, and that's where it stayed through my time as dean. Hanna Gray, the formidable president of the University of Chicago from 1978 to 1993, told me that she thought that the net flow of senior faculty was maybe the best single indicator of how well you were doing. It was good to see that the departures had declined.

If you've got constrained resources, it's logical to think that you will do better by focusing those resources on fewer, more expensive hires and enabling scholars like Gary Becker and Bob Lucas and Jim Heckman to do their research rather than expanding. The economics department in Chicago was about two-thirds the size of MIT when I was there. Actually, it was about half the size; it expanded to be two-thirds the size. But it was able to compete on reputation because of the extraordinary quality. A long time ago, Jonathan Cole published findings that the top 5 percent of scientists in the United States generate 50 percent of the science. I guess the basic principle is that bigger is not better, which runs against faculty instincts. They always think if they can hire this one additional person, it'll make their department stronger. That may be true in the individual case in a serial way. It's not true in the long term, in the aggregate.[94]

Whether that means saying no to student growth or teaching loads after a certain point due to faculty growth constraints depends a lot on how the teaching works. At Chicago, what we had to do in economics, and we've had to do that in some of the sciences here, is go to a category of nonresearch teaching. The university is in the process right now of changing some of the titles. Senior lecturers are reasonably well paid, and they're not hired by the usual tenure standards of research. To keep the really good ones, you need to offer long-term contracts and job security. But you ought to be able to get six courses rather than four from them, and they're likely to be more attentive to the students if you've hired well.

The departments were generally strong when I got here. Rankings are a sort of game, but the two rankings that I take seriously are, first of all, the Shanghai rankings, because they are based on countable things, and they're not designed to sell magazines. They're designed to baseline the Chinese effort to build quality. The second are the graduate program rankings from *U.S. News & World Report*, which are based on reputation. When I arrived, *U.S. News* was ranking eleven of our graduate programs within H&S, and all eleven were ranked in the top five.

In general, I think a dean at a first-rate university needs first to be responsive to his faculty and departments. I learned this at the University of Chicago, where I started as dean in 1994 at the age of forty-one with the Economics Department in my portfolio. At the time, that department had four Nobel Prizes among the senior faculty. That taught me the lesson right away that it would be crazy to think that I as dean was going to tell this department where it was going to go. When I moved out here, of the eleven departments, I think six of them at one point were ranked number one in the country. It was an amazingly uniform set of strengths. For that group, I was just trying to listen to them and make judgments about how far we could support what they thought their agendas should be.

The weaknesses were in the arts, because we don't have a dedicated arts school; religious studies, because we don't have a divinity school and our department was tiny by comparison with the Ivy League; and international studies, because we had no department of Middle Eastern Studies or South Asian Studies. The year before I arrived, the Center for South Asian Studies had a budget of $10,000, and it didn't spend it all. I think we had one faculty member in Middle Eastern Studies, and that struck me at the time as a gaping hole. And East Asian Studies was in decline. Stanford had played a pretty noticeable role in the U.S.'s engagement with China in the 1970s, but the department, probably because of personal quarrels, had declined. So, it was time to rebuild. Of course, that was in 2007, when it looked like China was on a never-ending rise, and there was a greater interest in Chinese Studies and Chinese language among students. I decided that we couldn't be a first-rate university and not have some additional presence in those fields. I talked to John Hennessy about that, and he agreed.

I actually had an external review committee come in for Middle Eastern Studies. They talked about two models: one was to have it organized by religious parameters (in particular, Islamic Studies); the other was to do it as a regional thing. I didn't have the resources to create a new department. With Middle Eastern and South Asian Studies, there was no constituency. There was no existing department, so there was nobody taking up the agenda. I decided that in order to build those programs, it had to be through new resources, because I couldn't have my number-one departments saying, "The dean is taking away our strength in order to build his dream departments." So, we went out and we fundraised.

The second thing that we realized was that building a fully functioning department would probably require hundreds of millions of dollars in new endowment to generate enough of a revenue stream to hire the right size faculty for each of them—South Asian and Middle Eastern Studies. Instead, we decided to appoint faculty in various existing departments in those areas. They would be additional free appointments to the departments, but they had to be appointments that were related to South Asian or Middle Eastern Studies. The first thing that we did was hire Thomas Hansen, who was at the University of Amsterdam, a distinguished South Asian anthropologist.[95] He wasn't really the founding faculty member because the center already existed, but it was so vanishingly small that he really was the one who built it. We made it attractive, partly by hiring his wife, but I also told him that we would be fundraising in order to make more appointments. By the time I finished as dean, he had made several additional appointments, and he told me—and of course I have no way to judge this—that the South Asian Center had become a kind of vibrant envy of some of the older, stodgier departments around the country that didn't have the ability to do something cross-disciplinary and new.

There was another need in the humanities. For eight years in a row, the *Times Higher Education Supplement*—and I don't know whether it's still the case—ranked Stanford's humanities and arts departments number one in the world.[96] But we knew that we were losing students to engineering, probably more after 2010. So, another building push that I had was to strengthen our educational programs in the humanities and make them more visible. There had been a decades-long decline in humanities enrollments, so we made an effort. My senior associate dean in the humanities had most of the ideas. We did things like start a high school summer program to put Stanford humanities on the radar of students applying to college.

FACILITATING UNIVERSITY-WIDE COLLABORATION

John Etchemendy told me that he was making a major effort along with John Hennessy to make it easy for schools to collaborate. Stanford does not have a policy school, and disciplinary departments generally have a hard time making appointments of faculty whose primary publications are in policy and application, rather than in pure science or the equivalent. With that fundraising campaign that I mentioned, the Stanford Challenge, a lot of the funds were targeted to new institutes designed to provide a venue for faculty from different schools, and even senior fellows who didn't have a departmental appointment, to discuss and collaborate. There was the Woods Institute for Environmental Studies, for example. There had already been the Freeman Spogli Institute for International Studies, and that got a big boost. And the Stanford Institute for Economy Policy Research (SIEPR) already existed when I arrived.[97] Then

I cooperated with other deans to establish the new ChEM-H institute: chemistry, engineering, and medicine for human health.

Parenthetically, I'm very dubious about the notion that top administrators have visions about what needs to be done at a university. I think much more often, they are responsive to their outstanding faculty. ChEM-H is an illustration of that. In maybe 2011 or 2012, Yale tried to recruit Chaitan Khosla as part of their effort to build their sciences.[98] He's in chemistry and chemical engineering. He showed the relevant deans, including me, this masterful PowerPoint that he showed to Yale that caused them to commit tens of millions of dollars to build a new institute for him. Our response was, "Well, you have much more of that already here. Why don't you stay, and we'll commit additional resources, additional appointments." So, we made some very high visibility appointments, and the new building opened a few months ago. We established ChEM-H and the Neurosciences Institute, the two together, both of them cross over into H&S.

ChEM-H was probably the single biggest collaborative project. In the end, it turned out to be a nine-figure commitment. Chaitan's starting premise was, you have the chemists who are seeking to understand what's going on at the molecular level in the cell, and then you have doctors at the other end who are providing clinical care, and the trouble is that they're not talking across that divide enough. So, you have the chemist working at the molecular level, you have the biologist working at the system level and cellular level, you have the engineers who are increasingly getting involved in bioengineering, and then you have the medical school docs doing basic research and clinical care. Their idea was that you really needed to bring them together. What I had heard was that a lot of the work in pharmaceutical research was a matter of just trying everything and seeing what worked. Chaitan's notion was that if you understood the chemistry, you'd get to solutions a lot faster rather than just trying everything that you could think of. That made intuitive sense to me.

When Chaitan did this presentation, which he had crafted for Yale, we said, "Not only does this make sense, but Stanford's genuinely unique comparative advantage is that we have all the schools on the same footprint, and the faculty can literally walk across the street to do these collaborations." If you look, there is no other top-notch university that can do that. Harvard's medical school and hospitals are separate entities. Yale is not top-10 in some of the basic sciences. The University of Chicago not only is not top-10 in some of the basic sciences, but it doesn't have engineering. Princeton doesn't have a medical school. I could go down the list. Stanford is the only place where this could happen.

ATTEMPTS TO EXPAND STANFORD'S GLOBAL PRESENCE

There were things that were discussed, but not pursued. I was always happy to go along with the New York campus project, but I was never convinced that it was the right thing to do. I have yet to see that dispersion rather than concentration is a good strategy for a research university that's really aimed at generating new knowledge. John Hennessy wanted to do it and that was fine. While it was in process, I don't think I expressed any negative views to anybody or any doubts, but when the whole thing came to a close, I heaved a sigh of relief.

First of all, it's important to understand Stanford's place in the ecology of higher education. The main universities that we compete with for the best faculty all have stronger endowments per capita than we do. So even though Stanford is a very rich university, it is resource constrained. Spending money to establish outposts in a big way didn't seem to me to be optimal.

The other thing is, back in the early 1990s when Singapore was pursuing its strategy of bringing in some leading universities to set up local programs, the Chicago Business School was invited in, and I went as a representative of the University of Chicago. It was a very interesting visit for me, because it wasn't the Chicago experience. Business programs can be taught by parachuting in faculty for two weeks, but for a medical or an engineering program, you need faculty who will move there and set up offices and labs permanently. I think they were expelling Johns Hopkins, or they did soon after. I heard from the Georgia Tech representative that it was a big problem for them to get faculty to come over and establish the kind of presence that Singapore wanted.

Generally, with these opportunities, unless there is comparative advantage and guaranteed quality faculty, my inclination is to say no. If there's not enough faculty interest, it's almost hopeless. You need enough of a group. We had two faculty members who were instrumental in establishing a Stanford presence on the Peking University campus (PKU), but we also wanted them to teach on campus. They did long stints there as directors, then the student interest disappeared. One of the ideas was that our China abroad program for undergraduates would be stationed at the new center on the PKU campus. Within a few years, that fell apart, partly because of staff problems and partly because we couldn't get enough students to sign up. So, they moved it to the Chinese University of Hong Kong, and before they even got their first student in the door, they delayed it because of the trouble in Hong Kong.

That showed me that it was not easy. I thought, rightly or wrongly, that we would get more for our resources by devoting money that we wanted to spend on dissemination by bringing international students here to campus to get a genuine Stanford experience rather than going to the expense of setting up campuses elsewhere. A third of our graduate students in H&S are from abroad, and if we had more money, if we had more resources, we could expand that.

ONGOING CHALLENGES

A couple of things were troubling long-term trends. One was the cost of living in this area, which just made it increasingly hard. We kept increasing the mortgage subsidies to prospective faculty or for retention, but we could never get ahead of the game. Especially for young faculty with families, that just got to be a bigger and bigger problem. Although, I always watched the yield rate on job offers for faculty; even in the year I left, it was above 60 percent and probably closer to 70 percent in offers-to-conversions.

The other thing was the drift away from the humanities. A lot of our most devoted alumni who were generous supporters of the university had humanities degrees. When I arrived, the Engineering School was graduating 20 percent of the students or a touch less. H&S was graduating nearly 80 percent. Now, engineering has 40 percent and H&S has 60 percent. This is happening across the country—the notion that the only way to get a job upon graduation is a computer science (CS) degree. What's interesting is that when I arrived, economics was the biggest major in the university, and it declined by more than half by 2015. They were losing students to CS. Political science lost about half of its majors to CS. The reason I was more concerned about the humanities is that I think it's easier to make a utilitarian case for economics or for political science than it is for the humanities.

This has a couple of implications—some not so bad, some I think not so good. In the category of not so bad, one of the things that we saw in my last few years as dean was a steep increase in the number of humanities minors. Students majored in computer science for the purpose of vocation, but they were really interested in literature or history or foreign languages, so they minored in that. We saw the number go from eighty to well over 300. I don't see that as a bad thing.

The bad part of it is, I think CS on its own leaves our graduates badly undereducated. All you've got to do is listen to the national political rhetoric now. I'd like to think that the more exposure we give to students about other cultures, the better citizens, and maybe even the better employees, they'll be in the future. I know there's some disagreement about that, but it seems to me that having students know something about Chinese culture or South Asian culture would be important. You think about all of the issues that our tech companies in the

Valley are tied up with now in China or in South Asia. If they don't have employees who know something about the history and culture there, they're more likely to step on a landmine.

I was director of the Confucius Institute, which got me an interview with the Permanent Subcommittee on Investigations when Senator Robert Portman was chair. I had to explain to them why medieval Chinese poetry wasn't really a threat to national security. Cultural exchange can be cultivated at a much lower cost, not only in terms of cash but in terms of time and effort, by bringing over more foreign students. Right now, only about 10 percent of our undergraduates are from abroad. Having a more diverse international student body would help.

Now for a final reflection—and, here, I'm going to boast. I think between the University of Chicago and Stanford, I've been dean to more Nobel Prize winners than anybody else anywhere. It's pretty amazing. There was a moment at the University of Chicago when half of the economics faculty over the age of fifty had Nobel Prizes. When I was dean at Stanford, two Nobel physicists—Carl Wieman and our former Secretary of Energy Steve Chu—asked to come back to Stanford. If I, as dean, had needed to make the decision about whether to fund it—because both of them were expensive—it would have been a hard decision. But this is where the provost swept in. John Etchemendy just covered full costs. So, the two of them came back. Then we hired Al Roth in Economics from Harvard just as he was winning the Nobel Prize. He'd actually already physically moved here, but he hadn't changed his affiliation quite yet. That's the only time I've seen an appointment file that was quite that strong. Actually, I had already tried to hire him when I was at Chicago. I think, but I don't know for sure, that the strength of our Statistics and CS departments motivated him, given the modeling work he was doing. And he had actually done his PhD here.[99]

In general, I thought we should be encouraging the departments to hire young. I was looking at the age distribution of the school, which increased while I was dean. There was a presumption that we would hire young. But the two Nobel physicists asked to come. What's telling about that is that never happened to me in Chicago. The Stanford environment, the strength of the programs here, the power of the intellect of the colleagues is a magnet for people to come.

Provost John Etchemendy, Nobel Laureate Alvin Roth, Economics Department Chair Jonathan Levin, and School of Humanities and Sciences Dean Richard Saller meet with reporters at a 2012 press conference to discuss the work that led to Roth's award of the Nobel Prize Memorial Prize in Economic Sciences.

PART FOUR

CROSS-UNIVERSITY FUNCTIONS AND INTERDISCIPLINARY INITIATIVES

CHAPTER 14

JOHN BRAVMAN

Vice Provost for Undergraduate Education
(1999–2010)

John Bravman earned his bachelor's, master's, and PhD degrees from Stanford. He had a successful career as a professor in the Department of Materials Science and Engineering and served as Stanford's vice provost for undergraduate education for eleven years. He left Stanford to become president of Bucknell University.

EARLY DAYS AT STANFORD

I was at Stanford for thirty-five years. I'm a first-generation college student, second-generation American. I went to Stanford as a freshman in 1975, and I stayed continuously until 2010 when I left to become president of Bucknell University. Incredible good fortune. I had no idea what I was doing in picking a college; my parents didn't go to college.

There is a story that I told endlessly to students and others about having to deal with failure. I went to Stanford because I was rejected by MIT. It hurt very badly at the time, and it ended up being the single most important factor in my professional life. I grew up in New York City and on Long Island, and I badly wanted to go to MIT as an engineer, scientist, something. I had heard little about Stanford as a boy because in the 1970s, it didn't have the profile it does now. A good friend of mine in high school took a family vacation to California the summer before our senior year in high school, and he came back with tales of California and the California coast and the redwoods. But he also said, "We need to go to Stanford. It's the most amazing place." In the pre-internet days, all you could do was look at books and stuff like that. Long story short, I ended up applying. I got in, but I got rejected by MIT. He was rejected by Stanford, and he went to MIT. It's not MIT's fault, but he was so miserable that he dropped out after the middle of our sophomore year and disappeared. I literally don't know what happened to him.

But the fact that MIT rejected me, and I went to Stanford—and they made it possible by providing enough financial aid for my family—changed the course of my entire life. I went to Stanford as a freshman, I think it was September 21, 1975. I came home for a few summers during my undergraduate days, and then after my senior year, I stayed there because I started in the doctoral program. Just a remarkable turn of events. I physically lived on campus for nine years as a student—and a good part of my time as a professor, because before my PhD was finished, I won a professorial search and ended up on the faculty.

It was just mind-blowing, my history of good fortune and hard work. Amazingly, they had a search in my area; amazingly, I won that search and got tenure, then got promoted to full professor early. Most of the time that I was there, I lived on campus as a resident fellow—we lived in a dorm or I rented a house on campus. So I spent most of my adult life literally living on the Stanford campus. Thirty-five years went by remarkably fast, and it was the best thing that ever happened to me.

Transitioning to an
Administrative Role

Early on, I got involved with administration of one type or another. I was associate chair of my department. I was chair. I was senior associate dean in the School of Engineering, which is where I met John Hennessy, although I knew him before that. I was a member of the Engineering faculty, as was John Hennessy, albeit in different departments. We had talked at events, but at the time there were 230 faculty or so in Engineering. It was obvious to me that he was going to become the dean. It was no surprise. He had started MIPS; he was famous, and his reputation preceded him.[100] I remember a conversation with him in the elevator of the Terman Engineering Building. I was already senior associate dean, one of four in the School of Engineering. I said to him, "My job is to keep problems off your desk." And he said, "Well, that's a good thing." I think he was dean for only three years before becoming provost. That wasn't surprising either.

Jim Plummer took his place and may have ended up being the longest-serving dean of the Engineering School in Stanford history. Jim's the gold standard in so many ways. Very different from John, he would never want to be provost or president. He's a brilliant academic, just a fantastic engineer and scientist, and one of the best teachers I've ever had. Just a few months after John became provost, Gerhard Casper announced he was stepping down as president after only eight years, which really surprised people. I said to John, "There's absolutely no way you're not our next president." He said, "No way. I just became provost." And of course, he became president.

This was just based on my growing familiarity with him as a leader. I just—I mean, the word is "knew." I didn't intuit. I knew he was going to be picked to be president. A good mutual friend was actually on the search committee. I was not. He told me that John was really, really nervous in the search, which surprised me because I've never really seen John nervous. But I was not surprised at all when he became president. He was president for sixteen years. I became vice provost in 1999, and John became president in 2000.

I was vice provost for eleven years at a very important time in the development of undergraduate education at Stanford.

I served directly under John Hennessy and John Etchemendy, whom I also knew. He was a very different man than John Hennessy and brilliant in his own way. They're both borderline geniuses in my opinion, but in different ways. My boss was John Etchemendy, the provost, but I worked with both of them and a whole bunch of other people simultaneously. Gerhard had started a campaign for undergraduate education, which at the time was the only undergraduate education–focused campaign of a billion dollars or more. John Hennessy actually ran and delivered the campaign, and that's how I got involved with development activities. That probably led to my presidency at Bucknell because I happened to be in charge of undergraduate education at that time, so I had a big role in that campaign. I spent a lot of time on the road with development people and alumni, and that really brought me into association with the leadership of the university, including the board. It really made my life.

I owe a lot to John for keeping me on. I worked with John almost daily in one form or another. We also played golf once or twice a week almost every week, and a lot more in the summer, for ten years, so I literally spent thousands of hours with him. I knew him in all different ways. Just a remarkable leader, a remarkable person.

THE COMMISSION ON UNDERGRADUATE EDUCATION

When Gerhard Casper became president in 1992, research universities often were seen as having not paid sufficient attention to their undergraduate mission, as they had become so focused on doctoral education, research, and scholarship. In the 1993–1994 academic year, he established the Commission on Undergraduate Education (CUE), and I was on it. As I recall, eighteen people were on CUE, mostly faculty. Jim Sheehan was the chair.[101] He was a professor of history, a very highly regarded historian. We talked about foreign language and writing requirements, small seminars, undergraduate research, establishing a separate structural entity, and some other things, too. Of course, we never implemented all of it. It really became, not a detailed blueprint, but more of a guiding document about where we were going to go. We had to raise a lot of money to put resources behind it, and that was the campaign. The Commission on Undergraduate Education led to the creation of the vice provost for undergraduate education (VPUE) position.

There had been deans of undergraduate education and what have you, but this was different because it was at the vice provostial level. It was a separate unit independent of the schools that ended up having significant resources. Ramon Saldivar, professor of English, was the first vice provost and started implementing the recommendations of the CUE report.[102] I took over from Ramon and served in the position for eleven years, from 1999 to 2010, when I left for Bucknell. I had been senior associate dean for undergraduate education in the School of Engineering, so I had served in a role at the school level in undergraduate education already. I think it's fair to say I had developed a reputation as someone who cared a lot about undergraduate education and was a good teacher and advisor, so that was part of where my heart and soul was.

The biggest thing was to create an office that was not beholden to or underneath any of the deans of the schools. Stanford has seven colleges or schools, three of which offer undergraduate degrees: Engineering, Earth Sciences, and of course, Humanities and Sciences. Humanities and Sciences offered most of the degrees. From the beginning, there was a tension between the new vice provostial area and particularly Humanities and Sciences, because—quite understandably, and in many ways, rightfully—they saw themselves as the heart of undergraduate education. A quarter or so of the undergraduates graduated from Engineering and Earth Sciences, but the core curriculum of writing and English and foreign language and all that was mainly delivered through Humanities and Sciences. There was tension from the beginning as resources grew in VPUE. Yet, the area was not set up to have its own faculty, so everything we did had to engage faculty from the seven schools. We had many faculty from the four professional schools engaged; it wasn't just the three schools that have undergraduate majors. We had faculty from the School of Medicine and then smaller numbers from the Law School, the Business School, and the School of Education engaged in undergraduate education, too. The key feature was that the vice provost for undergraduate education was its own entity that, like the deans of the seven schools, reported to the provost, and so at least administratively was nominally equal. When you don't have faculty, of course, you never can be equal. It was a hybrid model.

The Campaign for
Undergraduate Education

Gerhard launched the Campaign for Undergraduate Education. I think he was called the convening co-chair. We did twelve roadshows in one year. It just about killed all of us. These were quite elaborate roadshows, not just a cocktail hour with a speech from the president. Scores of faculty and students and theatrical-grade sets were brought in to conduct seminars in front of our audiences. I think we had about 8,000 visitors in those twelve cities. Having learned from that, in the subsequent Think Again campaign, which I was also heavily involved with, roadshows were limited to four or five per year, although we had a larger total number of visitors.[103]

For the first time, I got involved deeply with development work. I also became the lead person with regard to the parents' board, because that board is undergraduate-centric; it has nothing to do with graduate education. I was constantly speaking in front of the parents' board and in front of development audiences. I did a lot of one-on-one development work. It was in that context where I traveled with John for the first time extensively and saw him work firsthand off campus. But in countless regular meetings on campus at the decanal level and above, I worked with John and saw him doing his job extremely well.

I think it's fair to say that the campaign was very well received by alumni. I think people generally agreed that we had strayed a little too far from the core undergraduate mission, and so people embraced it. We brought faculty on the road, and they gave seminars like we were giving on campus and the alumni just ate that up.

We had a thing where sometimes John, sometimes I, would interview three or four students in front of a plenary session, sometimes in a big venue that could accommodate 800 or 1,000 people. Then they broke up for small sessions, and then there were dinners with entertainment. It was a daylong extravaganza. About 80,000 contributed to the campaign, but 8,000 were at these events. I think it was a very, very important thing to do.

I think the first one was in Portland, and as I recall, fairly small, maybe 400 people. It was open to everyone. We would just mail all our alumni and current families in the greater Portland area and say, "We're having this event." It was completely self-selecting. Ninety-five percent of the money comes from 3 to 4 percent of people. They're typically not involved in these events. These campaign tour stops have a broader messaging purpose of getting the word out and exciting people. We would just invite people in the general area and announce events in *Stanford Magazine*, and what have you. They were broad invites; everyone could find out easily where the twelve stops were and what dates they were. In New York City, I think we had 1,200 to 1,400 people; Los Angeles may have been bigger—1,600 or something. We had some really big ones, and some with 400, 500, 600 attendees as well. Stanford has a pretty talented alumni body with pretty deep loyalty to the institution. The invitation was there, and people were loyal and curious, and they showed up in pretty good numbers. The same for the next campaign—it was the same basic structure.

There was a very light development touch at these events. It was mentioned probably by John or a speaker over dinner. But it was not like, "Okay folks, now take out your checkbooks."

It's a very light touch with development at big events like this. People know why they're being invited or why this is being done, but we don't hit that message hard. It's more just about exciting people with what we're doing.

Most of the money comes from a relative handful of people. Some of those people I was directly involved with, and they are good friends to this day. Once, with John sitting next to me— he asked me to do it—I gave the pitch for a $100 million gift. Stanford is a very well-oiled machine, amongst the most successful development organizations in the world. They often would take me on trips where we were hoping for $100,000, $500,000, $1 million, $2 million gifts. Generally, at any institution, the president is probably talking to the people at the very highest level, and at Stanford, that means $25 million, $50 million, and more.

Gerhard had secured, as I recall, five large gifts as a nucleus fund for the campaign from people like the legendary Peter Bing, Bob Bass, Chuck Schwab, Jerry Yang.[104] They made these big seed gifts, which every campaign has to have, and that was all done before my involvement. I spent a lot of time traveling in Europe and Asia raising money with a development officer. I think it's fair to say I was involved with some big final gifts. I closed out the campaign with a large gift out of Hong Kong.

DISTRIBUTING THE FUNDING

Funds from the CUE were allocated to programmatic support, new professorial billets, and financial aid endowment. We wanted to work on the access issue, which is so much more critical today, but even twenty-five years ago, it was a really big deal. A key component that came out of the commission was that these incremental lines *would not* be filled with people specifically aimed at improving undergraduate education. It simply was to increase the total available person hours to teach undergraduates. Departments would compete for them; they would make proposals, and if they were given a new line, they were obligated for some period of time to show how they were delivering more—and more innovative—undergraduate education than before they got this line. The idea was to increase the professorial capacity of those departments.

They were completely standard faculty, which at Stanford means very heavily research-oriented. You can't succeed at a place like Stanford unless you have a very powerful research presence. But the glory of Stanford is that it has faculty who do that and actually can also work great with undergraduates. But the people hired had no particular obligation to embrace the mission; it was that somewhere in the department, you were freeing up or creating time at the professorial level to do better at undergraduate education. Most were junior hires.

The Freshman Seminar Program was kind of the hallmark program. But there was also a greatly expanded undergraduate research program, improvements in writing and foreign language education, overseas studies, and a new core curriculum were all programs that were partially to substantially funded out of the Campaign for Undergraduate Education or VPUE. Funds covered faculty time, administrative staff, programmatic costs, direct grants to undergraduates to do research, travel, staff time, the whole thing. When I left, the core team at VPUE was probably sixty or seventy people. We built an office to run and develop some of these programs, but our core tenet was to deliver as much as possible through faculty. We also had to spend money on faculty buyouts: if you're going to teach here in a VPUE program, then your department has to be compensated so they can teach the courses that you're no longer teaching.

Freshman seminars were pretty popular. I think it's fair to say there was a broad embrace of what we were doing, but there was a lot of skepticism too, and even a lot of, "Why are we doing this?" We overcame the resistance and these kinds of views over time. The only way that works in academia is not by force majeure, but just by saying, "These are the opportunities, would you consider doing this? Talk to Dick. Talk to Jane. They've had a good time doing this." A good friend of mine is on the Law School faculty. He's a brilliant legal scholar, but he ended up being a great teacher for freshman seminars, and he also lived in a dorm for three or four years. Some people discovered that they really liked this. No one's a good teacher or anything else unless their heart is in it, so you don't want to twist people's arms. In any one year, we probably had 200 faculty engaged in one program or another, if not more. It was a good fraction of the Stanford faculty. My job evolved over time, but running those programs, development work, the piece on campus of asking people to be involved and explaining why it might be good, that's what I did for eleven years.

Expanding the Residential Education Program

I'd say the philosophy of residential education is the development of the whole person, not just the mind, not just the academic piece. I think residential education—in terms of having faculty live in dorms—dated from the 1960s at Stanford. Of course, Yale and Harvard and Oxford and Cambridge have been doing it much longer. For the most part, dorms that were not built like Harvard or Oxford colleges had cottages built and attached to them, in which staff or faculty would live. They were supposed to direct the intellectual programming of the dorm unit. When I went to Stanford as an undergraduate in 1975, the residential education program was already five or seven years old. Jim Fox was my resident fellow.[105] He was a linguist who spoke twenty-seven languages. So, as a student, I saw that model.

As a faculty member, I lived in dorms twice. For three years, I lived in an undergraduate house that had no freshmen. It was an upperclass house and small, only about forty students. Then I created a new residential education program and got permission to run it in the fall of 1999. Soon after, I was asked by Gerhard and John to become vice provost. Because a piece of the commission report had to do with improving residential education, I created this thing called the Freshman-Sophomore College.

What I had in mind was: What could I do that was as close as possible to a Cambridge or Oxford college? One of my advisors for my PhD was Bob Sinclair; he was also my undergraduate advisor.[106] He was British, and he had gone to Cambridge. I became aware of that world, and I started reading books like *To Serve Them All My Days* and watched a lot of British television like *Brideshead Revisited* about this world gone by. Those colleges, I just became enamored with them. I wanted to create something like that as best I could. Out on the west part of campus, there was a group of four upperclass undergraduate dorms, sophomores through seniors. I asked for and was given two of them, and I lived in a house that Stanford owned across the street. We did a lot of events at my house that were social, intellectual. We couldn't have the grand structures that Yale and Harvard have, but I wanted to create something similar at Stanford, and it became quite successful.

For the eleven years that I was vice provost, I also was dean of the Freshman-Sophomore College. The dean of the Freshman-Sophomore College reported to the vice provost, so I always joked that I had a staff meeting by talking to myself in the mirror. That program continued after I left, but the dean was no longer the vice provost. I was really proud of building that program. It had no elements that were different than residential education in general at Stanford, but we really took it to the next level.

John Bravman, Vice Provost for Undergraduate Education, poses with some of the Freshman Sophomore College (FroSoCo) student staff as they welcome incoming freshmen in 2007.

Increasing the Size of the Student Body

There was a time under John's presidency when we very explicitly talked about modestly increasing the student body size by approximately 400 in total, so 100 per year. The faculty and others largely rejected this. At the time, we had 18,000 applications for 1,650 slots, which seemed like all the numbers in the world. The thought of catching up to Harvard seemed impossible.

Eventually, the student body grew anyway, but slowly. One of the considerations was we wanted to maintain some quality of residential experience. Living off campus, which is common in most other schools, is so financially impossible in the Bay Area that we should expect to house every student for four years. So, the availability of housing was an issue.

I think the student body today is over 1,700 per class.[107] As the number of applications grew past 30,000, we felt we had an obligation to let somewhat larger numbers in, because these are all hypertalented students, for the most part. We're hurting ourselves; we're hurting them. Let's just do it. I suspect it was just done by fiat over time, without an internal lengthy discussion. The size and quality of the applicant pool grew so fast, I think it just became "How can we not do this?" It wasn't like we doubled the size or something like that.

Overcoming Challenges

We had to deal with various challenges. Local politics—that was ugly. We had to deal with the downturn in 2008. John and

John, I think it's fair to say, were very happy with how I handled that in my unit. It really became a model for how others should think about their units.

We were badly hurt at the VPUE because much of our money was new endowments. As new endowments, they did not have years or decades of growth and appreciation, so a lot of our endowments were under water within six months—they were worth less than when people had given us the money. By Stanford policy, the income you can draw from underwater endowments is highly limited, because in effect, you'd be eating into the principal, as it were. So, my budget was badly hurt.

I had to lay off nineteen people, and I did all the layoffs myself. I think I had PTSD for a week. I rearranged from eight or eleven units to five. That allowed us to be more efficient, and that's how I streamlined the staff. I think John and John would say that we moved quickly and soundly and did a lot to keep the great work going, albeit with a reduced budget. That was really painful. There were a lot of ups and downs. I can't say they were the best years of my life, but I so enjoyed working for and with John and John and the other people.

LEAVING STANFORD

My decision to leave Stanford was really painful because I'd been there for thirty-five years. In the coffeehouse, there's a bunch of caricature paintings of faces on the wall, and I'm still there. I expected to spend the rest of my career at Stanford. I think people were really in shock when I left. I expected to stay there for the rest of my life. For years, I had been called to interview for presidencies at smaller schools three or four times a year, and I always said no.

But I was fifty-two. I'd been in my job for eleven years. No one in his right mind expects to become provost or president of Stanford or Harvard or Yale. To count on that is stupid, and I was too young and too poor to retire. I wasn't keen on going back to the faculty and returning to full-time teaching and research. I really had come to deeply enjoy helping to run and support the university. When the next opportunity came along, I actually tried to talk my way out of it, but the headhunter was persistent. The then-chairman of Bucknell's board was going to be in San Francisco, and so I kind of reluctantly agreed to take a meeting with him. Rather than the promised thirty minutes, we talked for three hours, and I remember walking in and telling my wife, Wendy, "Maybe our life just changed." Sometimes things happen for a reason.

It worked out. It could have worked out very differently, of course. It was a very, very hard decision to leave Stanford. This university made me who I am, made my entire life; three of my four sons were born there; my oldest son went there. It was a very painful and hard decision, and some days I still regret it. Like now, when things are really bad again, in some senses, I still wish I was there, digging in: "Let's solve this. Let's fix these problems." I'm a loyal alum, and I love the place. To me, it's just the most amazing place in the world.

REFLECTIONS ON JOHN

John is one of the most remarkable men I've ever met. He can do the kind of superdetailed work you have to do as an engineer and a scientist, and then he can flip a switch and completely get his head out of the details and look at the big picture. That's how he started the company MIPS, and that's how he became president of Stanford. He can just go back and forth. Remarkable energy and drive. It is a real privilege to call him a friend. I learned a lot from him. There were four or five of us that spent thousands of hours golfing together. I really miss that camaraderie. He's just a remarkable human being. And his wife, Andrea, she's remarkable, too.[108]

CHAPTER 15

HARRY ELAM

Vice Provost for Undergraduate Education
(2010–2020)

An award-winning teacher, scholar of theater, and theater director, Harry Elam joined the Stanford faculty in the Department of Drama in 1991. He served in various administrative roles, including as the director of the Committee on Black Performing Arts, the Institute for Diversity in the Arts, and the Introduction to the Humanities Program before his appointment to the Office of the Vice Provost for Undergraduate Education, first as senior associate vice provost in 2007, and then as vice provost in 2010. In 2017, his portfolio expanded to encompass two additional leadership roles, the vice president for the arts and the senior vice provost for education. In 2020, he was named the president of Occidental College in Los Angeles.

Early Foundations

I was born and raised in Boston, Massachusetts. My mother was a librarian. During my childhood, she came to be in charge of all the public-school libraries in Boston. My father was a lawyer. He became a judge and the first black chief justice of the Boston Municipal Court. My mother made sure that students of color had books that looked like them, that were written by people like them and about them. My father started an organization, Project Commitment, aimed at keeping young black men out of the court system. So that sense of social justice, that idea of commitment, informed me growing up.

My parents also cared deeply about education. After second grade, they were able to send me to private schools. It was a great experience for me, in terms of the learning opportunity, in terms of preparation for college. From there, I went on to Harvard, thinking at that point I was going to be a lawyer.

Harvard was formative in a variety of ways. I think it's like Stanford in that the people are what made it incredible. The people I met have been friends for life. Harvard did not have a concentration at that point in theater, so all the theater I did was totally extracurricular. I was vice president of the black drama organization there and did plays in my dorm, Leverett House, and I also did performances for a black drama troupe. Theater was a big part of my Harvard life. I majored in Social Studies. It was an interdisciplinary major, and it gave me the freedom to take different things that related to my interests. I took a course in playwriting, and I wrote about theater subjects, including black theater performance history, in other courses.

I didn't really think about graduate school till I realized that the only thing I liked about law school was the drama of the courtroom, and that was senior year. So I decided to get a PhD in drama at UC Berkeley. I really got into it, and I loved all the things about academia. I loved the idea of doing research on theater and performance, I loved the connection with students when I got to teach, and I loved the idea that you could mix theory and practice so that I could actually direct plays as well as critically engage them. It was not just the theater program that drove me to graduate school at Berkeley, but it was Berkeley the place. Berkeley in my mind stood out as ground level in the struggles at that time for social justice, racial liberation, and free speech. It was a key place for all sorts of energy and excitement and fervor around social change. At Berkeley, I met a guy named Carlos Morton, and he wanted somebody who was a director to work with him for this Chicano Studies class. In the class, he was working on texts by Luis Valdez and El Teatro Campesino, the Farm Workers' Theater, around what they called *actos*—short skits depicting and agitating around political issues. The plays were very similar in form and content to those that I had seen and put on in the black theater of the 1960s. I saw this incredible parallel around raising awareness of issues through theater to help the struggle for social change. So that became the subject of my dissertation. Also, I looked at Workers' Theatre in the 1930s around unionization, around the Great Depression as another example of the genre I termed social protest theater.[109]

I fell in love with California, but a job opened up at the University of Maryland, College Park. It was a very different orientation in terms of theater than I had experienced at

Berkeley. The department's orientation was much more around the practical side, not the theoretical/critical side of theater and performance.

As a result, I learned quite a bit about directing there—things that affect me now in terms of being an administrator. One of them is transparency; you have to tell people how you feel. In terms of how I understand directing and administration: I don't see directors as autocratic or dictatorial, but as collaborative, at the center of this collective experience. What the director is trying to do is to incite the best work out of all the other members of the production team—the designers, the cast, everybody—all towards a common end. That, in essence, is what I tried to do as an administrator and as head of the VPUE [Office of the Vice Provost for Undergraduate Education] at Stanford. A different appreciation of directing, a different appreciation for engaged, collaborative leadership for me came through theater and performance.

Joining the Stanford Drama Faculty and Early Administrative Experiences

I came to Stanford in 1990 as an acting visiting professor for a year. I filled that role, and then they were doing a search, and I was an internal candidate. I did get offered the job, and I joined the faculty in 1991. Since the beginning of the 1980s, Stanford has been the best PhD program in theater and performance studies. This year, 2020, in terms of the applications for the program, we yielded all our top applicants. We got 100 percent, and that's not unusual in terms of our past record. I'm also very proud of the fact that we are probably the most diverse department at Stanford, percentagewise. Currently, 60 percent of our department is people of color, 30 percent African American, and that's because my colleagues saw this as being important to excellence. They didn't separate diversity but saw diversity and excellence going together. It wasn't me pushing them. It was this belief that this is part of what we do as a department.

As a Stanford professor, surrounded by committed scholars and researchers, I worked diligently at becoming a better scholar. I tell graduate students all the time that your career is about embracing the word "scholar." I felt the pressure—and it was a good pressure—to be seen for my academic achievements. That vision of being a scholar and my encountering all sorts of examples of productive scholarship in the department—everyone on the Drama faculty had written at least two books—was a very powerful influence on me.

Scholarship became the most important thing, but my faculty position included being the director of the Committee on Black Performing Arts, which had been around Stanford since the 1960s. It was both an administrative position and an artistic one. I directed a play each year, so that was part of it. But again, this idea of the scholar and the director coming together.[110] Things evolved over time, and, with Charles Lyons, former chair of the Drama Department and others, I created the Institute for Diversity in the Arts (IDA) and became the leader of that. IDA continues to exist as one of the key elements in the arts at Stanford.[111]

For whatever reason, Stanford has been very good at identifying people's potential for administrative leadership and enlisting them. I was put on the original committee to look at the change in the required program for all first-year students from the Cultures, Ideas, and Values curriculum to what became I-HUM, the required Introduction to Humanities sequence. That committee met every week for two years. There were fantastic people on it: John Bender from Comparative Literature; former university president Richard Lyman; Condoleezza Rice. It was a great committee to be on in terms of the working relationships that we formed, and also people there on that committee perhaps saw my potential as a leader. As another testament to Stanford's encouraging my leadership skills, I became a University Fellow during that period, too. People in my term as a fellow included John Bravman, who was my immediate predecessor in this role of vice provost and now is president at Bucknell; Patti Gumport, who went on to be the first vice provost for graduate education; and Tim Warner, now the vice provost for budget and auxiliaries management. So, it was a really interesting group, if you followed each person's trajectory at Stanford and beyond.[112]

Based on being both on the I-HUM committee as well perhaps as being in the University Fellows, I was selected to be the first leader of the new Introduction to Humanities program. This role enabled me to really reach out to people across the humanities at Stanford in ways I hadn't before. I'd met people, but you're pretty insular sometimes, limited to your department. But this broadened that range in terms of the humanities. Trying to design or think about what this program could be brought me in contact with faculty across the campus.

ROLE AS SENIOR ASSOCIATE VICE PROVOST OF UNDERGRADUATE EDUCATION

Prior to being selected by John Etchemendy to be vice provost, I worked with John Bravman as his senior associate vice provost. Bravman had his internal staff handling issues that affected the undergraduate experience. One of those was thinking about the needs of students coming from underresourced backgrounds and trying to create a bridge program that would help them transition. Another was looking at how advising was done for undergraduates and trying to fix that. One of the main projects we worked on was accreditation, meaning that we had to get the [accrediting] body—the Western Association of Schools and Colleges, WASC—to approve us for another ten years. And we wanted to make it, rather than just an exercise, into something that was going to help us further develop our undergraduate education.

During my second year of working with Bravman came the Study of Undergraduate Education at Stanford, SUES. I, along with History faculty member Jim Campbell, co-chaired the committee examining the undergraduate core requirements. At Stanford, those have changed every ten years or so.

The charge was to look at the first-year requirements and to decide what would become of the Introduction to Humanities, which had been in place for some time. It had run its course. And to look at those requirements also in relation to breadth. How does a student get breadth and depth at Stanford? We sought to look at this experience as holistically as possible, and this was new, a change from the past. As it existed before, the first-year requirement in all its permutations focused strictly on the humanities. How could we potentially expand that to the social sciences or even the sciences?

What we were trying to figure out was how to provide our students with a liberal arts foundation for their undergraduate education. We wanted this new first-year requirement to ground them in critical thinking, approaches to problem solving, and values like lifelong learning. There were certain key principles that we wanted to establish: education that was adaptable, education that encouraged creative confidence, and education that involved experiential learning, hands-on learning.

Priorities as Vice Provost for Undergraduate Education

I was named vice provost for undergraduate education in the summer of 2010. The Vice Provost's Office exists as a place to advocate for undergraduates, to work with faculty, staff, students, alumni—all stakeholders—on making undergraduate education the best it can be at Stanford. Part of the impetus at the inception of the vice provost position was the desire to bring our world-class faculty together with our incredible undergraduates. That was sort of groundbreaking to think about—to really invest the faculty in the process of undergraduate education and that sense of partnering with all the stakeholders to make sure that we have the best liberal arts experience within a great research institution. We have the best of both; that's what we're bringing together. We have Nobel Prize winners teaching introductory seminars to undergraduates, and that's very unique.

What should be understood about the VPUE is that it's the only entity on campus that touches all undergraduates. The VPUE works to assist our undergraduate students in fulfilling their Stanford journey and to help them articulate what they want and where they're going. Under the VPUE are major requirements and programs that undergraduates can take or are required to take, including the first-year requirements and Stanford Introductory Studies. There's also the Program in Writing and Rhetoric; every student has to take two writing courses, and those are offered through the Program in Writing and Rhetoric. In addition, there are signature initiatives and additive programs, like the Bing Overseas Study Program, which is within the purview of the VPUE, that we encourage students to take advantage of.

Studying abroad is a transformative experience. Nobody does undergraduate overseas studies the way we do, because we have ten of our own campuses overseas that students can apply to and enroll in for a quarter. We send a faculty member over there—a unique and important approach to undergraduate education more generally, but overseas studies specifically. The Overseas Study Program also manages other off-campus efforts such as Stanford in New York, a relatively new program we launched in 2015.

In addition to those entities, we also have responsibility for undergraduate advising and undergraduate research. Currently, we're able to give out some $6 million a year to departments, faculty, and students for undergraduate research. It's really helped to transform undergraduate education.

One of the areas of focus for VPUE has been that first year, which is a critical learning point for students and acclimating to Stanford. We have, at Stanford, become more diverse in terms of socioeconomic diversity. Up to 18 percent of our most recent incoming class are first generation, low income. They've often also come from underresourced high schools, and so there can be a gap, an unevenness, between the students who come from schools where they didn't have any AP courses and those whose high schools had upwards of thirteen AP courses that students could take. So, in 2012, we created the Leland Scholars program, which is a summer bridge program that helps students acclimate to Stanford and prepare for what they will face when they come to school in the fall.

Within this framework, we want every student to take advantage of what we call high-impact practices. These put students together in a small intellectual group with faculty, so they really have that live interchange with a faculty member. So undergraduate research certainly fits there, overseas studies fits there. Introductory Seminars is another way we do high impact; these are small seminar-style classes with esteemed faculty that freshmen and sophomores are strongly encouraged to take. And then we have offshoot programs, such as Sophomore College, which brings students together to take one class intensively in the

period before school starts in September. We want students
to have at least one of those experiences in their first two
years at Stanford.

Harry J. Elam Jr., Vice Provost for Undergraduate Education, right, chats with
freshman Robert Poole III, left, and his dad, Robert Poole Jr., during Move-In
Day in 2011.

Faculty Engagement

When I came into the role as vice provost and started to think
about what I wanted to achieve, one of the things the search
committee told me was that they were concerned about faculty
engagement with the VPUE. It seemed too bureaucratic and
not engaging enough in terms of faculty. I sought to impact
faculty engagement with the VPUE in a number of ways. I
activated what we call the Undergraduate Advisory Council,
UGAC, which includes faculty members from across the
campus. Before, the UGAC had been there to just talk about

undergraduate research and where grants were going, but I wanted this committee advising us on every decision coming out of the VPUE. That changed them and how we worked with UGAC and faculty as a result.

Also, the Bass University Fellows was previously an honorific that recognized some of our best faculty members for their contributions to undergraduate education. But it was just an award; I wanted the fellows to be part of the process as well. So, we have used them sort of as a board of trustees to sound out initiatives that potentially would change undergraduate education.

We started putting out a faculty newsletter that told faculty what was happening that they potentially could take advantage of, be it in terms of their teaching to undergraduates or other ways they could be involved in undergraduate education, such as advising. I created something at that point called Faculty College. It was a space where faculty could come together and nurture and incubate an idea for a course, a new program, or a new curriculum. It met four times a year. The faculty who were involved in it had homework that they would work on inside and outside of the Faculty College class sessions. Faculty really wanted that opportunity to speak to each other about teaching. There are many opportunities to speak to folks about your research, but this doesn't happen with teaching that much in an institution like Stanford. Faculty relished it.

So those are some of the things that we did to engage faculty differently. We also met twice a quarter with the directors of undergraduate studies of every department as a way of spreading information and thinking about what was happening collectively in undergraduate education.

Undergraduate Curriculum

One of the things that became clearer as I got into the role as vice provost was the need to think about the whole student, that so much learning takes place outside of the classroom as well as in it. How do you allow for that, provide for that, develop that? We wanted to adopt a more holistic approach—so that we're looking not just at undergraduate education, but at the entire undergraduate experience.

How do we find a system that has a more capacious view of liberal arts education? How do we create something that's going to inform other classes and activities that students are engaged in? That was the task: to give students a grounding in something that they could apply in other contexts and think about in other contexts. And so, that was one of our goals: that students would actually come to Stanford for that first-year requirement instead of in spite of it.

We implemented two different requirements. One was the first-year requirement where students would take a course that looked at an idea, a problem, a question of historic or contemporary import, and answer the question, "How does thinking matter in relationship to that?" Correspondingly, that first-year program was called Thinking Matters. Then, in addition to that, there were the general education breadth requirements that required every student to take a certain number of designated courses from certain areas—for example, a course on engaging diversity, something in applied quantitative reasoning. Other categories were aesthetic and interpretive inquiry, ethical reasoning, formal reasoning, creative expression, social inquiry, and scientific method and analysis.

Courses had to be approved to count for those particular core requirements, which we called Ways of Thinking/Ways of Doing. In some cases, the oversight committee would turn a course down because they wanted more not only in terms of content, but also the oversight committee was concerned with how you teach that content. That was an adjustment that was very different for some faculty.

With the core courses, it wasn't so much about content as methodology. It was about learning and putting the students' learning first. So, let's say I'm teaching a course on American drama. If I was teaching it the old way and it was about content, I'd say, "Well, they've got to read these ten plays from this period. These are ten of the most important plays." Now, if I'm teaching it from this idea of learning and learning objectives, then I'm asking questions, like: "What do I want them to learn through reading these plays?" I want them to learn how to approach a play critically and engage in ways that open up what the author is trying to accomplish. So, if that's a goal, how do I get at that goal or learning objective? It's a different approach than thinking, "Okay, they've got to read fifteen plays, and they'll go chronologically, and at the end I'll give them an exam." So that's the idea with putting student learning as the key objective. And it's still, I think, a great idea.

Advising

Another thing that was really important was growing our advising and structuring advising differently than it had been. The advising experience became one that we honed and refined. Advising is something that is easily criticized. Advisors are trying to give the right advice, but sometimes students don't know what to expect of an advisor relationship. Now, a student's first advisor—their nonmajor advisor—is someone who is a paid professional. We wanted advisors to be people who knew the curriculum, and Stanford's curriculum is vast. The faculty advisors couldn't be expected to know all of that, whereas the advisors that we were hiring could and should know the different possibilities for majors and be able to ask questions and suggest where students might go.

At first it was a hodgepodge. We had some advisors who were faculty and were not paid for it, and some who were part of the new system. The orientation for that hodgepodge system was never good enough. We focused on getting it to a point where we could think about the training of advisors and what we wanted them to do to help students develop and make choices. We wanted advisors to coach students to not be strictly tunnel vision in what they saw, not pick a course for the wrong reason—because it was supposed to be an easy credit grade or something like that. We built up the number of professional advisors to get to a good ratio. We also embedded advisors in programs that wanted them. For example, an advisor embedded in the Department of Computer Science worked with computer science students in particular. We tried to pick advisors who had expertise in certain areas so that when giving advice they would have the experience from their background. But they still had to know the whole curriculum.

Adaptability—Emphasizing Internships and Career Possibilities

We had to adapt to the changing environment in and around all that was happening outside the university—the growth of technology, students more interested in school as a means to an end rather than an end to itself—so, a practical bent and focus of students. The switch at Stanford that we were seeing was the growth of students interested in technology and computer science. In 2008, 2009, 2010, after the fall of the stock market, we really started to see that growth, to a point where we saw some 43 percent of our students majoring in engineering and some 40 percent of those as computer science majors. That's one thing that impacted my thinking about the need for experiential learning.

Adaptability was one of the things that came out of the SUES report, having students be able to take what they learned in the classroom and apply it to something out in the field. What's become increasingly important at Stanford, as I think at every institution, is internships and internships that take advantage of different areas, be they industry or nonprofits. In terms of nonprofit work, the Haas Center for Public Service was really important to encouraging internships and work with community organizations.[113]

We also tried to create a robust experience at the career guidance center and with employers who came to the campus. At Stanford we had such strong and amazing students that finding employers who wanted to come to the campus to meet them was not difficult. But also, we wanted to encourage students to think differently about careers. The Haas Center introduced students to nonprofit careers and partnered with agencies to offer community-engaged learning experiences. In the arts, we taught a course, Art Is My Occupation. It looked at the idea that you didn't have to be a performer per se or an artist. There are other arts careers that you could look to.

So, showing students different possibilities for career options, having experiential courses in which they had to use those skills, and also expanding what the career center did to promote these goals. When education costs as much as it does, people want to know there's a value added in getting that degree and that there's a job at the other end.

Bringing things within our office at the VPUE was one way to centralize certain things, but it's impossible to centralize internships because of their number and diversity. There are so many different internships and summer grants that you can get at Stanford. If anything, we tried to ensure they would have the same pay scale so that if you wanted to do X over the summer versus Y, you wouldn't be deciding because of money. And we wanted to make it so that students from underresourced back-grounds could do the same thing so there was equity and access within it.

Diversity and OpenXChange

One of the places that many others and I felt was critical for the university to evolve further was the area of diversity and inclusion. Around 2014, across the country and most specifically at Stanford, students felt that the administration was not listening to them. Students wanted to see change during that time, and they were holding the university accountable. The president and provost recognized we needed to do more to improve the campus climate. I pitched John and John on a program that became OpenX-Change, which was looking at, in this increasingly polarized world, how could we create conversations? How could we create programming across differences and get students to think about diversity in ways that could have an impact not only on the campus but on the greater society? Some of the programming was very successful. Some of it had an afterlife as a result.

But OpenXChange did a number of things, including creating opportunities for students to participate in designing the programming. We told student groups that they had to get with somebody from a very different group to bring this together. So, we supported Jewish and Muslim student organizations working on a joint project, for example, around Syrian migration. That was something that we did in the last years of John's time at Stanford.

John Hennessy cared about the issue of diversity and continued to seek ways to increase diversity at Stanford. This, however, remains an ongoing concern in need of collective intervention and attention.

Over the tenure of John Hennessy's presidency, faculty diversity really didn't change that much, and the administration's diversity certainly didn't change. In terms of the Executive Cabinet, I think I was it for diversity. New ideas and strategies are needed here to achieve the kind of inclusive environment that Stanford can be.

REFLECTIONS ON JOHN HENNESSY AND WORKING WITH THE LEADERSHIP TEAM

When I became vice provost, one of the things that I really learned from and enjoyed was the meetings at the president's house of the Executive Cabinet. The deans of the different schools, the vice provost for undergraduate education, the vice provost for graduate education, and the vice provost and dean of research were in on those meetings.

The style was that you had everyone sitting around the table, discussing the critical issues facing each school or unit and the university as a whole. What made these meetings so unique was how John and John encouraged everyone to work and think together. Thus, I had the deans collaborating with me in planning the Thinking Matters requirement and having faculty from the various graduate schools teaching undergraduates in this program. In those meetings the structure was that John and John—John Hennessy more so—would talk about things that had happened that week that were important. Then we'd go round the table, and everybody would give information or a report—something that they wanted worked on or wanted others to know about in terms of their unit. Here's where communication was really important. Working in those cabinet meetings to talk about undergraduate education regularly with the deans was exciting and unique.

And what was amazing—even though the deans were the masters of their own universes—was how John Hennessy commanded the room. Everybody knew that one of the things that separated us and made Stanford successful in ways that are different from someplace like Harvard was that it wasn't the philosophy of: "You're a tub on your own bottom." But: "We work together for the good of the whole university." Still, John Hennessy was able to encourage collaboration and used the cabinet to test out bold new ideas. The mood was often electric, and it was orchestrated by John. It was hard work, but he also made it fun.

When I came to Stanford and would attend campus-wide meetings thirty years ago, Harvard invariably came up, and Stanford, I thought, had "Harvard envy." Now it's just the opposite, and it has been for some time. Harvard is very envious of things that we have achieved here at Stanford.

What was really interesting was that John was looking for something big at the end of his tenure. He always said, "Big ideas lead to big donations." And that idea eventually became the Knight-Hennessy Scholars. There were incredible conversations about that. What an amazing job of fundraising, too, to get it off the ground—close to a billion dollars. Watching his approach, he was someone who would ask questions of the Executive Cabinet, and people would give their opinions, but he wasn't looking for consensus. Rather, he was looking to how these ideas worked with what he was trying to accomplish and something he could draw from. He wasn't oblivious in any way to what people were saying, but he was thinking about how that fit within what he was trying to structure.

I don't know that John Hennessy was thinking consciously about legacy, but he has created an indelible legacy and changed Stanford for the better and his accomplishments have informed all of higher education.

CHAPTER 16

PATRICIA GUMPORT

Vice Provost for Graduate Education
and Postdoctoral Affairs (2006–2019)

Patti Gumport, professor of education and director of the Stanford Institute for Higher Education Research, served as Stanford's vice provost for Graduate Education and Postdoctoral Affairs for thirteen years. A sociologist of higher education and an expert on the dynamics of academic change, she has been a faculty member in the Graduate School of Education since 1989. Gumport also earned her master's and PhD degrees in sociology and education from Stanford.

Coming into the Vice Provost Role

I was a graduate student at Stanford in the 1980s. I was a postdoc and assistant professor at UCLA, and then I came back to join our faculty in 1989. That's important, because my experience as a graduate student and then as a faculty member affected my decision to take up this offer to serve as vice provost. As a sociologist of higher education, I focus on higher education leadership, academic change and the forces that facilitate and inhibit it, and the relationship between higher education and society.

I have a long track record of service within the university, serving on academic planning committees, the Faculty Senate, and more. John Etchemendy selected me to serve on the provost's budget group, which I did for about fifteen years. Some way into that, he invited me over to his home and said, "You must know why you're here." I said, "I have no idea." And he said, "I want you to serve as the first vice provost for graduate education." There was no job description, and I didn't fully appreciate what his offer entailed.

The recommendation to establish this position and office came from the Commission on Graduate Education that John Hennessy had convened, which completed a report in 2005. This report reflected a far-reaching analysis with hundreds of people involved, and they wanted to know, "How could we build on Stanford's strengths and yet rethink our practices in graduate education and address the systemic challenges?" As you can imagine, the commission offered plenty of recommendations for addressing challenges in a place of this complexity and scale. Their overarching goal was to ensure that graduate students had the best possible educational experience. But that's complicated, because graduate education is highly decentralized. That was their point: "We want to have a visible person and new office, VPGE, dedicated to graduate education—to foster collaboration across the seven schools, to facilitate problem solving, and to inspire innovation."

The charge was to be bold and ambitious and take risks—a very John Hennessy imperative, right? The VPGE would become a member of the Executive Cabinet with the president and provost and the deans, along with the two other academic vice provosts for research and for undergraduate education. That was essential because the Executive Cabinet was a place for us to develop a deepened understanding of the challenges facing the university and then work to identify our opportunities and priorities. The initial three years that I had agreed to serve soon became five years, and five became ten, and then it was three more years for the leadership transition. It was such an honor to have been given this responsibility, and I loved serving in this role.

EARLY DAYS

I started as vice provost in the fall of 2006 because there was planning to do, and then I opened the new office in January of 2007, and gradually I hired staff. At the outset I took a comprehensive look at the scope and the opportunity, even though I also benefited greatly from the commission's report. I think my first observation—this was so important—was that graduate education had been central to the university's mission and reputation since its founding. John Hennessy and John Etchemendy and the leadership team for the university were very invested and supportive of it. Obviously, graduate education was already excellent. We had top-ranked programs across all our schools, and we attracted outstanding students from all over the world. One-third of our graduate enrollment was international. So it was great in and of itself.

But in making the case that graduate education needed our attention collectively and then advocating for the problem solving around it, what I realized was that graduate students also helped us attract and retain the best faculty in the world. They'd come here to work with our students, especially PhD students, who would help do path-breaking research. It was vital to call that out. And graduate students instruct, mentor, and advise undergrads, so they directly contribute to the quality of undergraduate education. People didn't talk much about that. That was my first revelation in launching the new office, that it'd be helpful strategically to point out the interdependence of excellence in graduate education with excellence in each of the university's missions.

Much of the university-wide media coverage back then was around undergraduate education. For example, you'd see the enthusiastic focus at the beginning of each fall quarter, "We're welcoming the freshman class" and lots of descriptors about the profile. There were twice the number of people who were also coming in as new graduate students, but it didn't get much university-wide attention. That would change of course over the next decade. And it felt very affirming whenever I heard John and John speak publicly about Stanford's excellence in graduate education as well as the opportunity to raise more endowed fellowships, including the new Stanford Interdisciplinary Graduate Fellowships.

So I thought deeply about the role of graduate education in the university. It's been such a major force in Stanford's rise and preeminence nationally and internationally that I needed to talk with people about this as well as what the enormous scale and complexity of graduate education has meant for Stanford. The latter was the second thing to unpack analytically and politically in its challenges, which set the stage for identifying priorities.

EXPANDING WHAT'S POSSIBLE IN GRADUATE EDUCATION

The academic issues were certainly not simple, so it wasn't a matter of saying, "Okay, here are the top three priorities, let's deal with them and check them off as resolved." There were complex interdependencies—doing anything in this role was going to require extensive collaboration across the entire university as well as sustained attention.

I sought to build trust and relationships. I spent much of my time—from the beginning—convening, listening, establishing shared understandings, and articulating those back to everyone, then collaborating on our problem solving and our opportunity finding. This required a lot of humility, a lot of learning. I loved it. It also required a lot of optimism, especially in the face of people who felt frustrated or unhappy. In fact, there was so much optimism in my approach, I had a tagline for the new office called "Expanding What's Possible in Graduate Education." It became not just a tagline, but a touchstone for everyone to know why we were convening, why we were coming together.

So where to begin in this highly decentralized place? Graduate education is very local. Programs and departments decide how many people to admit, what the requirements are, how to support them through their degrees, and all of that. With such local autonomy, I would ask folks to consider, "What's the potential for a university-wide perspective?" And that's where the convening and collaborating came in.

Just to put some numbers on it, graduate students were more than half the enrollment. We had over 9,400 graduate students in master's, professional, and PhD programs; over a dozen types of degrees; and a few hundred graduate programs. I needed to figure out with my colleagues just what our priority areas would be, how to align with the deans of the seven schools, and how we could do this in a university-wide way. And then also how to dive deeply into some of the academic fields that had different needs and bring resources to those areas and their leaders. While we benefited from the recommendations of the commission, we were hampered by a lack of institutional data. We had basic trend data on enrollment and degrees granted, but much more was needed to give insight into admissions, funding, degree completion, career and employment outcomes, and more—both in the aggregate as well as by program.

GRADUATE STUDENT FUNDING
AND AFFORDABILITY

We dove into several priority areas that emerged as most urgent. In sync with the dedicated efforts of John Hennessy's leadership team, we launched an array of fellowships and programmatic initiatives to foster interdisciplinary learning, research, and collaboration as well as address the barriers. Beyond that, several priorities came to the fore as specific to graduate education. I can't mention them all here, but I'll point to a few that spanned more than a decade. The first was graduate student funding. It was the most complex area for us to understand—and I continued to work on this my entire time. When you have that many students in that range of programs with local understandings, practices, and decision-making authority, it is a monumental undertaking to find out what are the needs, what are the trends, what are all the sources of support, what is the impact on faculty research grants, and so on. We worried about fluctuations in external funding alongside endowed fellowships. We needed to develop models to work through alternative scenarios and contingencies.

This wasn't just a financial issue for the university; it was also an affordability issue and a quality-of-life issue for the students. What you realize very quickly is that if people don't have funding to meet their basic needs, they can't have a good educational experience.

When I began as VPGE in 2007, these affordability challenges were simmering. Well into the next decade they were boiling in the university discourse, which was a good thing because this needed collective deliberation and action. Even though we annually set a minimum floor for salaries for RA-ships, TA-ships, and fellowships, students who were funded made very different amounts. What had long been variation in funding practices and vague worries over sources of support became intolerable uncertainties and unacceptable inequities from some students' perspectives. Students helped us understand how their needs varied with life circumstances and where there were persistent daily challenges—especially those that posed significant obstacles to their graduate education. We held town halls to talk together about this and other significant student stressors, including mental health challenges.

We had a lot to learn about funding practices across graduate programs in the seven schools. Many staff worked tirelessly over several years to compile and analyze funding data and then develop a much-needed planning tool. Tim Warner and Dana Shelley in the budget office, Karen Cooper in financial aid, Suzi Weersing and Sally Gressens in the schools, Corrie Potter in institutional research, and Pat Cook and Rebecca Jantzen in VPGE were among those who worked steadily on this. Although progress was underway, this set of challenges occupied much of my time and attention. Some challenges—both for the university and for the students—were also discussed at peer universities and nationally, especially as graduate students in private universities began to organize for collective bargaining status.

Prioritizing Graduate Student Housing

Housing was a major piece of all this. You can imagine, a single student living on campus had different needs than a student supporting their growing family, including international students whose spouses were not permitted to work given visa restrictions. On-campus rental rates were subsidized to be less than off campus, but they varied and there just wasn't enough on-campus housing, despite new buildings in the prior two decades.

I got to problem solve with a number of people throughout the university—leaders and staff in offices like Residential and Dining Enterprises; Land, Buildings, and Real Estate; and of course the Budget Office to figure out how we could build more on-campus housing. This resulted in the largest student housing complex yet for Stanford; it added space for 2,400 students and cost over a billion dollars. The Escondido Village Graduate Residences opened just two years ago, in 2020. This was an amazing solution to the needs—a tremendous increase in on-campus housing with subsidies to keep their expenses lower.

The housing initiative was very strategic and highly iterative. To make the case, I worked initially with Tim Warner, the vice provost for budget and auxiliaries management, and Shirley Everett, the senior associate vice provost who directed residential and dining enterprises. We were limited by the lack of available data—so we scrambled to put numbers together—numbers of students in different types of housing for varying amounts of time, all cross-walked with enrollments by degree type and academic program. I remember Tim, Shirley, and I doing a presentation to the Executive Cabinet—in 2014 as I recall—so that the deans and president and provost and other vice provosts understood what the challenges were here. There was a defining moment when people said, "This is the right thing to do. We have to build more housing."

Tim and Shirley were key to moving this forward with the provost and president, along with Bob Reidy who helped everyone understand how we could do this. But the "how" was different from the "why." The "why" was a strategic necessity and the right thing to do, because many students were unduly stressed, and it was compromising the quality of our graduate education as well as our ability to recruit. Then it became the "how" and the "what" and the "how much" and "how to pay for it" and "how to build it." It involved complicated modeling and planning by these dedicated leaders and their staff who figured out the funding and the design, and then managed the building project as well as all the communications with constituencies internal and external to Stanford. I just on occasion reminded people about the why and the urgency, and expressed our deep appreciation for their tremendous work. In fact, the needs were so pressing that the university had secured housing off campus, spending several million dollars annually to subsidize rent for thousands of graduate students until the new housing was built. This was all so impressive—one of the heaviest lifts I've seen Stanford do.

Advancing Diversity in Graduate Education

The scale, complexity, and decentralized nature of the university was always going to shape the nature of the challenges in graduate education and how we would make our way to address them. Advancing diversity is no exception, and it became a prominent set of priorities.

Diversity, which came to be called "diversity and inclusion" in that era, was first about diversifying our enrollment—principally, our graduate student enrollment, which meant recruitment and admissions, which is highly decentralized—and then supporting the success of students from all sorts of backgrounds and life experiences, which also entails enhancing their experiences of the university community once they're here.

Much of the talk when I started was still pipeline: "Diversify the pipeline." "It's a 'leaky' pipeline, especially for underrepresented minorities and women in STEM fields." That was the discourse at the time. Also, although we knew we wanted to define diversity broadly, the data—to the extent there were any—were limited to basic demographic categories of race, ethnicity, gender, and nationality. There was so much we needed to know. Of course, we now understand a lot more about diverse life experiences and identities and all the difference that makes.

In conversation with people, I learned more about this—to make the case that diversity was required for excellence in the university and after graduation. In the previous era, the framing was unfortunately "equity versus excellence." We reframed that to "diversity is *required* for excellence." It's essential in education and research, in our university, and in fulfilling our mission to prepare future faculty and leaders in all sectors, and for the advancement of knowledge and innovation at a global scale.

The other thing about "diversity is essential to excellence" is a social justice agenda. We wanted to provide opportunities for students who hadn't yet benefited from education like that offered at Stanford. And the third piece was faculty diversity. We were never going to move the needle on student diversity unless we could diversify our faculty. The initial talk about pipeline gave us some traction, but it wasn't nearly enough.

How I worked into the mix was, first of all, understanding and helping to create that shared sense making. It's so important for leaders to ask and reflect back: What is the nature of the problem? What are the challenges that we're facing here? And then, where do we have leverage to do something? So that was my other role: to find critical junctures in graduate education where we had some real leverage to advance diversity. Among our initiatives, I developed two fellowship programs that became signature programs for Stanford, and it turns out some peer universities wanted to emulate them.

The first was called EDGE, Enhancing Diversity in Graduate Education. It started on a very small scale by Karen Cook, vice provost for faculty development and diversity, and I was able to get resources to scale it up across our schools. This was a fellowship program for doctoral students who were offered admission to graduate programs at Stanford. We offered the EDGE fellowship to admitted students who would bring diversity to their fields of study. Diversity considerations included low-income and first-generation college student backgrounds, race, ethnicity, and gender. We also began to consider LGBTQ identities—which intersected with these other dimensions. Students got extra funding resources for professional development and research, peer mentoring, and faculty mentoring, as well as experiences to foster a sense of belonging in our community. Led by Chris Gonzalez Clarke, EDGE became very visible and exciting, and it continues to thrive.

The other big initiative was even bolder. Here's where I could invoke the commission's call to: "Be bold, be ambitious, and take risks." I wanted to develop a multiyear fellowship program for PhD students who could diversify the professoriate nationally. This became two years of full fellowship funding for advanced doctoral students who would gain knowledge, skills, and confidence, so they'd be prepared for academic careers and could hit the ground running. The program is called DARE, which stands for Diversifying Academia, Recruiting Excellence. It was established in 2008, so we're now in our fourteenth year.

I designed DARE as a fellowship program with Chris Golde, who was an associate vice provost in my office. Among other areas, Chris brought expertise from a national initiative on preparing future faculty. That informed her yearlong course for DARE Fellows to learn about the variety of faculty roles and responsibilities in higher education. The course also deepened fellows' connections with each other so they'd become a cohort of colleagues for support. We hired Anika Green who became the program's director and has since been an enduring source of compassion, support, and inspiration.

Initially, it took a lot to persuade the provost and folks that we should invest in this initiative because it's very expensive. I shopped it around to the deans, vice provosts, and department chairs. A key factor for leverage to get DARE launched was that we grounded the rationale, design, and evaluation plan in robust research findings. We had national data and Stanford data on PhDs who became faculty, and we learned about their experiences related to their diversity. Here again, we conceived of diversity as multidimensional.

One of the things we did in the beginning with DARE was to encourage fellows to consider how their diverse backgrounds and identities may be an asset, a tremendous source of strength. That did a lot to increase people's confidence—inviting them to consider how their life experiences can inform their aspirations and distinctive contributions as faculty, that they could have a place and a career in academia if they wanted that.

After the two-year fellowship, as our graduates got visibility, people began to know DARE Fellows, and national attention made them more competitive. Now there are well over 200 DARE alumni, many of them pursuing very rewarding and successful faculty careers, with some even receiving early awards for their scholarship, and also for their teaching and service.

Of course, many advanced doctoral students are concerned about changes in the academic labor market. At colleges and universities of all types, there are fewer tenure-track positions. Some graduating fellows are interested in what have become known as "alt-ac" ["alternative to academic"] positions. And some PhD graduates work in other sectors, which is fine. We invest in them, and we want them to thrive. Still I do hope many will have fulfilling academic careers, which will help ensure the future vitality of higher education.

Vice Provost of Graduate Education Patricia Gumport speaks at the Graduate Recruitment and Diversity Day (GRAD Day) reception in 2013. Under Gumport's leadership, VPGE launched initiatives to enrich students' academic experiences by advancing diversity, preparing leaders, and positioning Stanford at the forefront of innovation in graduate education.

REFRAMING ADVISING AS A RELATIONSHIP

In their efforts to find excellent faculty advisors, graduate students reported some struggles. This is especially consequential for PhD students because when the advising relationship goes well, it is amazing; it launches your whole career, your sense of possibility and your goals, and it may extend over decades.

Personally, I've been extremely fortunate to stay connected with my own dissertation chair, and I too have advisees I'm still in touch with thirty years later.

As I learned more about our students' "uneven" advising experiences, I wanted us to reframe it. Among the powers of the vice provost's office, we can convene, we can listen, we can cultivate shared understandings, and we can reframe. And this was a classic example of being able to reframe. When I listened to people talk about advising, it often sounded like it was a lottery. They either won the lottery or they lost big time. There wasn't much agency in that for students, and there's an inherent power imbalance.

So, we shifted this discourse to talk about advising relationships. This was critically significant because in a relationship, both parties have responsibility for communicating, setting expectations, and so on. There was a lot of leverage in reframing that discourse, including running workshops with students on: How do you communicate? How do you set expectations with a faculty member? And then holding corresponding workshops with faculty, asking: How can we do advising more effectively and efficiently? How can we work with students to set expectations? Both sides enhance the relationship by being more explicit, making agreements, talking together about progress, and so on.

Beyond supporting the development of advising relationships, we found students could benefit from spending time outside their department, getting access to resources for their professional development, their skills, their career preparation. Departments varied widely in terms of how much they would provide this locally, so we decided to invest in graduate professional development that was open to students across the university. The creativity of Stanford staff members, including Helen Doyle, Caitlyn Craft, and Blanca Virrey in VPGE, enabled us to be ahead of a national sea change of universities investing centrally in these resources.

We wanted both students and faculty to see how students benefit from time to reflect, to self-assess, and locate resources to meet their needs—from communication skills and teaching to leadership skills, personal development, and career resources. Faculty started to see, "We have things for students tailored to our program, but there's also value when students do this centrally. There's information and networking they can do outside our program." So part of this change was to get faculty on board. This aligned well with the cross-disciplinary and interdisciplinary collaboration we all sought to foster—while also enhancing students' experience of community within the university. All of this was complementary to improving advising relationships.

SUPPORTING POSTDOCS

At any given time, I had between twelve and fifteen issues in graduate education that I was working on with my staff and collaborators around the university. A significant set of issues also emerged for postdocs. Postdoctoral growth had been substantial. Since 2000, it grew 75 percent—up to 2,300 postdocs. About 60 percent were in the School of Medicine. That makes sense, given the nature of advanced training in the biosciences and medical fields. This also reflected a proportional decline due to increases in the number of postdocs in fields all across the university. Talk about something occurring without central planning—hiring postdocs was a great example of unplanned growth.

Obviously, postdocs have needs. They're hired by individual faculty, but there are significant institutional consequences for hiring. Imagine—we have 2,300 people getting advanced training while also contributing actively to faculty research and enhancing Stanford's reputation. Postdocs and their challenges needed visibility and resources. There was an office of post-doctoral affairs, but it needed more support. I got to work with the director of that office, first Rania Sanford and then Sofie Kleppner.

I stepped up because, in addition to setting minimum salaries for the graduate students, I was responsible for recom-mending annual increases to minimum salaries for the postdocs. Affordability challenges became widespread, as the cost of living in this area had increased dramatically, no subsidized housing, and many had families. Most postdocs were funded externally, so increasing postdoc salaries put pressure on faculty research grants. Those faculty were in a conflicted position: "I know my postdocs need more money to live, but it's creating a huge strain on my research budget." You see, in addition to covering the rising costs of research itself, the grants provide funding that supports the people—grad students, postdocs, staff, some faculty salaries—alongside substantial indirect costs if the funding source was a federal agency.

Working with people around the university to create this shared understanding, we were able to build consensus and increase the minimum salary from $44,310 to $50,000 in 2015, and then just three years later from $53,406 to $60,000. You can imagine, times 2,300, the financial impact of these unanticipated increases, especially on multiyear grant budgets and national training grants that had lower starting salaries. We needed to provide some funding to support faculty to make that transition. Again, it wasn't just a strategic necessity for us to attract postdocs and give them enough resources to have a decent quality of life so they could do this fantastic work, but it was also the right thing to do. Postdocs became such a significant part of my role that we added it to my title.

I remember speaking at the Faculty Senate in 2017, I think it was the first time postdocs had been on the Faculty Senate agenda, and that felt like a defining moment institutionally. I began the presentation by asking, "How many of you were a postdoc?" And nearly every one, myself included, in the room raised their hands. We had a few postdoc leaders who spoke, as well as some faculty mentors and funders of postdocs talking about the significance of postdocs and supporting this critical stage of their development, and how they were managing the challenges. Much like expanding what's possible in graduate education, I aimed to infuse the same spirit into postdoctoral training.

LEADERSHIP APPROACH

One of the most significant things about my leadership approach was relationships. To do any of this, it had to be highly collaborative. From the outset it was about establishing trust and listening—a lot of humility, listening to get an understanding, to develop a shared understanding, and doing that sensemaking together. That had to happen first in every one of these areas. There was a tremendous amount to learn; every day I was learning, and we all learned together. It was essential for people to be heard because their challenges take shape and have different salience for different individuals. So, together we prioritized needs and opportunities; we went back and forth between local realities and what we could do centrally. None of this would have been possible without the amazing staff members in my office and the people who collaborated with us across the university—all with the support of the university's leaders at every level, right up to John and John.

You know, much was going well in graduate education. I've talked here about the areas where we sought to improve. But it was because so much was going well that I knew we could devote time to these systemic challenges. And people were happy to do that because they could see how essential it was for our students. There was a growing movement to have a more holistic appreciation for students' experiences. You can't just separate out their education; you have to support the whole person, organically, daily, for people to feel valued and be okay. There's a lot of soul-searching that happens in graduate education, and our students helped us learn how to support their well-being alongside their educational experiences and success.

All of this was so highly collaborative. How to advocate effectively, I think that was a big lesson learned. I was always refining my skills. I was always very clear that this was not about me; I was just a channel. If I framed things as in the service of the whole, which I believed, we didn't get into conflicting and competing interests as much. And I found it inspiring to envision our work as investing in the future—not only the future of the university and the future for these particular students, but also the future of higher education, the society, and the world. Among these students are the intellectual pioneers, the change agents, the human beings who will determine the quality of life and accomplishments of future generations. In graduate education, we always have this opportunity for profound influence.

RELATIONSHIP WITH JOHN ETCHEMENDY

My relationship with John Etchemendy was foundational; it deepened and developed. John was amazing. I used to tell him that I didn't think I'd have a boss when I became a faculty member. He would laugh at that. But he persuaded me to do this. I was a very happy faculty member: I had grants, I had students, I had courses. I was working nationally and internationally and consulting. When you take a faculty member and say, "I want you to be a vice provost," that's a huge shift. He said, "You're going to love this. You get to establish a new office. It's a big pivot point for the university, a tremendous need. It's going to be exciting. You get to practice what you teach and study." So, he sold me on it, and then he spent the next several years telling me, "I told you so. I knew you'd love it." He was right of course!

He was such an excellent thought partner. Our frequent conversations helped me chart our path forward. We went back and forth deliberating a lot. For example, with the funding I sought for DARE, he said, "Why should I support this? It's expensive. It's going to diversify the professoriate nationally;

what's it going to do for us?" He challenged me to think even more deeply and critically. It was a great working relationship. He supported all that I was able to do in this leadership role. At the end of my term, he said that I led "with my heart and my mind," which I found very affirming.

Reflections on Administrative Service

I got to work alongside truly exceptional university leaders—John and John and the dedicated members of their leadership team. I think we all knew how special this era was. John Hennessy was such an inspiring leader, not only for Stanford but for higher education writ large. Among the many qualities I always appreciated about him, three stood out—his brilliance, his candor, and his conviction to tackle problems directly. This fit perfectly with John Etchemendy's same attributes... After John and John stepped down, I supported the next provost and president in that leadership transition for three years. I was happy to do it; they're great people. Then my successor, I helped in that transition. Again, we got a great person.

I just saw this as a once-in-a-lifetime chance to serve and a tremendous opportunity to collaborate. I knew I had some analytical, substantive knowledge to bring from my field. And I thought I could do it in a unique way—that was highly collaborative and invited us to envision all that was possible. Plus, I had a heartfelt commitment in that I didn't want students to suffer in ways I did as a graduate student. That was a driver for me. I knew we could do better institutionally.

As I completed my term as vice provost, I was honored with the Kenneth M. Cuthbertson Award for distinguished service. This meant the world to me, of course. Yet I knew it was for our collective accomplishments. I was fortunate to collaborate daily with many faculty leaders across the university, including those serving as deans, vice provosts, and associate vice provosts. Among them, John Boothroyd stands out for his contributions, from his role on the Commission on Graduate Education to serving as associate vice provost in VPGE throughout my term as vice provost. Together, we charted a path forward propelled by a vision for institutional change in which the realities aligned more closely with our ideals. We recognized that genuine transformation occurs by invitation rather than by mandate, and that cultivating trust is central to generating both optimism and leverage for change throughout the university.

When you do this type of service, you get an opportunity to work with people in ways that you don't as a faculty member. Not only with the university leadership, but with faculty, students, and staff—including the dedicated people in VPGE and university-wide. Stanford has about 15,000 staff, many working here for decades. I often spoke about how they were central to fulfilling our mission. They are such dedicated people who don't get the spotlight like the faculty do.

It's a big decision to step up and do this kind of service; you can't concurrently do everything from your faculty role. I taught a few courses while vice provost; it was challenging because I have a very high standard for my teaching. At this point in my career, I've resumed my faculty responsibilities, and I'm happily engaged in teaching, advising, and research—which is all very fulfilling. I work primarily with graduate students, and I can see people benefiting from some of the institutional changes we made as well as some initiatives we developed and supported through the vice provost's office. I see the instantiation of them in this next generation of graduate students—enhancing their educational experiences, helping them feel part of the larger university community, and supporting them to imagine and prepare for what's next. So that too makes me even happier to have served.

CHAPTER 17

ANN ARVIN

Vice Provost and Dean of Research
(2006–2018)

Ann Arvin is the Lucile Salter Packard Professor of Pediatrics and professor of microbiology and immunology at Stanford, where she has been a faculty member since 1978. She served as the associate dean of research from 2001 to 2006 before becoming the vice provost and dean of research in 2006.

Roles at Stanford

I was on the faculty in the School of Medicine my whole career. I had exposure to the "main campus," as it's sometimes called, because I was on the Faculty Senate and different university-wide committees. Then I was asked to be associate dean of research at the university level. In that role, I was responsible to the vice provost and dean of research. This is a position held by one person. The "vice provost" part of the title refers to administrative oversight, and the "dean of research" part refers to being the cognizant dean for the interdisciplinary university-wide centers and institutes.

As associate dean, I oversaw research-related administrative units, working with the senior staff who direct research compliance, environmental health and safety, technology licensing, and others from 2000 until 2006, when I took the vice provost and dean of research job. It's an unusual organizational structure because at many universities you would be either the equivalent of the vice provost, or you would be the dean of research, not the combination. There was discussion about whether that really was the right way to do it. I think it was, but it was a big job that required the work of a highly experienced team within the office to accomplish.

Part of the job is to work closely with your counterparts at other research universities on shared issues. We had regular meetings, typically three times a year. This is a common practice for leaders at U.S. research universities. The presidents meet, the provosts meet, the vice provosts for graduate studies meet as well as administrative directors of major units because the institutions are often encountering the same problems.

The Structure of Interdisciplinary Programs at Stanford

Part of why it was more straightforward for Stanford to adapt to creating strong interdisciplinary programs goes way back to 1982 when the university Faculty Senate decided they would have a policy around establishing interdisciplinary centers, institutes, and labs. Most of the initial ones were in the natural sciences (chemistry, physics, etc.) and in policy studies (international policy, economic policy). Part of that Senate policy from 1982 was to designate the dean of research as the cognizant dean for those university-wide entities. That's really important because as a cognizant dean, you're working at the same level as the school deans, and that is not a common organization.

Most universities had a structure where the interdisciplinary institutes were within a school, or maybe between two schools. But we, for all this time, had a structure to support cross-school entities. We didn't have to go to the schools and say, "We're going to reinvent this place, and don't worry, it's all going to be fine." We didn't have to do that because we had a model and a process in place. The original centers, labs, and institutes were the foundation. In the early days, these involved physicists, chemists, electrical engineers, material scientists, and mathematicians, or faculty from economics, political science, international studies, and other disciplines related to public policy.

The Senate policy for establishing interdisciplinary institutes had explicit criteria that were set out: What are the reasons for creating a university-wide entity? Do we see a long-term need for a program like this? Do we see interest among faculty from different schools in whatever the problems are that this interdisciplinary institute would be set up to deal with? Do we see student interest? Do we see faculty from several different schools that would come together in this program? As it turns out, the organizational structure for interdisciplinary institutes, laboratories, and centers is very transportable across sectors. A social sciences–oriented interdisciplinary institute doesn't function that differently from Bio-X. The template is the same, if you will.

If these were the criteria for setting up institutes, my thinking was that these should be the same criteria for phasing out institutes. One thing that you learn in studying this kind of a structure within universities is you've got to be able to sunset them. For example, if an institute evolves to be of interest only to faculty from one school, then the school dean can decide whether to support it as a school center. As custodian of the general funds that are allocated to the university-wide institutes, it's important for the dean of research to be able to justify this central support.

EXPANDING INTERDISCIPLINARITY AT STANFORD

So, we had a core group of institutes, labs, and centers that had been in place for many years. Many of the newer inter-disciplinary institutes emerged from the Stanford Challenge fundraising campaign. The Stanford Challenge document focused on generating momentum for research and education around several themes. One theme was international studies; there was an initiative on energy and the environment; others on the arts and education. Those initiatives gave John the resources to create new institutes as one way to achieve the Stanford Challenge goals. We would not have been able to accomplish these goals without donor interest. Fortunately, many people understood what we were trying to do and the value of research and teaching at the interfaces of disciplines. John went all over the country and the world raising resources to build new programs around the themes of the Stanford Challenge. Once that money was raised—which if I'm not mistaken, was around $1 billion— the president had funds to launch new university-wide programs.

Around 2000, the first new institute, Bio-X, was created across the Schools of Medicine, Humanities and Sciences, and Engineering. So that was the beginning of the new wave. Shortly after that, we created the Precourt Institute for Energy and the Woods Institute for the Environment. The Institute for International Studies was expanded to become the Freeman Spogli Institute, and the Center on Longevity was created. On the social sciences side, the Center for Advanced Study in the Behavioral Sciences (CASBS) had a distinguished history as a separate entity located on Stanford land on the hill above campus. As its earlier model became challenging to support, CASBS became a Stanford interdisciplinary center. Most recently, the Neurosciences Institute and ChEM-H were established, creating a variety of programs that involve faculty from all of the seven schools. When I stepped down, we had eighteen interdisciplinary centers and institutes.[114]

The Clark Center was built deliberately to house interdisciplinary research that became Bio-X, meaning that there would be faculty whose appointments were in the School of Medicine, the School of Engineering, and natural sciences departments in the School of Humanities and Sciences working side by side. As I understand, there was a considerable amount of hesitancy about people moving into the Clark Center because they thought, "What is this? Is this going to be some place where I will want my lab to be, as opposed to having my departmentally assigned lab up and down a hallway with all of my departmental colleagues?" So that created an interesting dynamic, with people saying, "I'm going," then, "No, maybe not," and then, "Yes."

The Clark Center was already up and running when I started as vice provost and dean of research. The first thing that I had to do was to find a new director for Bio-X, which was Carla Shatz, who was my colleague from years ago. We always laugh—finally, we had our "old girls' network."

Another key thing that John and John decided to do with "start-up money" from the Stanford Challenge and other sources was to allocate faculty billets to these new programs. I think how Stanford handles faculty appointments for university-wide interdisciplinary entities is very important. Every faculty member has a primary departmental appointment. So, it's not that you're creating institutes and centers through a process different from regular faculty appointments. Because they allocated the billets and some resources, the directors of the institutes were in a position to partner with the departments to recruit faculty interested in the work of the institute and whose appointment also benefited the department's teaching and research missions.

There was a very big concern about how new assistant professors recruited with a shared billet would fare when it came time for reappointments and promotions. How would you recognize individual contributions in a program where the whole goal is collaboration? That was a big worry at the beginning, but experience shows it hasn't really been a problem for those junior faculty. They have as good a track record of promotion to tenure as other junior faculty. I think it's because most academics now recognize that the kind of science that we're doing simply cannot be done, for the most part, by one researcher with their own small group of students. Working at the intersections of disciplines and with collaborators who have complementary expertise is important in very many cases. Certainly, a student can still do basic chemistry, get a PhD in chemistry, and never go anywhere near ChEM-H. Fine. But there is a recognition that we have a lot of opportunities to do research that wouldn't be done well if there weren't two, three, or many faculty members and their trainees working together.

The other benefit about the way Stanford's policy for interdisciplinary labs, centers, and institutes works is that since the faculty already have a home department, they can just say, "I want to be a fellow of this institute." The faculty affiliated with the institute say, "Okay, what is it about your research that fits with the institute's goals?" If the two align, the institute faculty decide, "Fine, you will be appointed as a fellow." Later if the faculty member's work goes in a different direction, it's not a problem because they have their departmental appointment. They don't have to be part of the institute anymore.

Funding Interdisciplinarity

Like other U.S. research universities, Stanford's funds come either from research grants, tuition, or philanthropy. The president's budget includes money that can be allocated for new initiatives, often used as one-time, start-up money. The provost has general funds that are meant to support all of the day-to-day operations of the university and faculty recruitment and retention. The provost allocates general funds after review and recommendations by the provost's budget committee. Every year, as the vice provost and dean of research, I had to make requests to the Budget Group for programmatic needs, as did the school deans and other leaders who oversee all of the major university operations.

The goal for the new institutes was to use the start-up money in such a way that we created a foundation to transition to the provost's money for operating costs. The directors and I had to really keep an eye on spending the initial support and how we were pulling in new resources, because the President's Office was very clear that new institutes and centers were not going to be funded in perpetuity. Over the longer term, the expectation was that faculty would get outside grants and that the institute faculty would engage with donors interested in the work of the institutes for help in endowing research and education programs and, in some cases, buildings and other infrastructure. To meet this challenge, it was always important for faculty to be able to communicate effectively about how their research addresses larger problems and aims to have long-term impact.

In this context, another really good thing about our centers and institutes is that, as we established them, we created advisory boards for each one. Those advisory boards involved people who had a major philanthropic interest in funding the education and research programs at Stanford. They were made up of like-minded people who shared the institute's goals and had relevant expertise from other sectors outside the university, including related foundations, NGOs, and industry. In other words, people who could come in from the outside and give us a perspective beyond our ivory tower here. That was one of the major unforeseen benefits of our interdisciplinary institute structure that I didn't anticipate.

The other thing that really made this organizational structure work *inside* the university was the pilot project money. The requests for proposals were set up so that the faculty applicants had to find a colleague they wanted to collaborate with on the project, and that colleague needed to be from another discipline coming at the problem from another perspective. Pilot projects typically were allocated two years of funds. In many cases, that money translated into the collaborators getting outside grants. The fact that people could come together and generate initial data to use for an NIH or NSF grant is very easy to show with the data tracking that we've done. The pilot projects allowed people to have a track record of working together, and their joint applications could show that they had postdocs or graduate students who were already involved in the project. In fact, as I told John Hennessy, we learned that we did not need to have given out any money, because just by writing the proposal for the pilot project money, they had already formed a working relationship and had come up with the ideas that they wanted to pursue. They were successful in getting extramural money whether or not they received the pilot project money. Providing the pilot project funding was—as John Hennessy called it—"moving the cat food around." Giving faculty and their trainees a reason to come together to write a proposal, that was really a key outcome.

The Senate policy doesn't provide for tuition funds to flow to interdisciplinary institutes and centers. These funds are handled by the departments, which made things easier in terms of defining the role of institutes. It's also appropriate because degree granting is the departments' responsibility. In our structure, interdisciplinarity doesn't mean that faculty should abandon their disciplines or their departmental homes. There may be a rationale to move to having diplomas that list both a department and an institute in some cases, but my perspective is that it's not critical because the students are going out into the world having been trained to participate in interdisciplinary research.

Looking back, the Stanford Challenge set the stage for a new era of interdisciplinary research not just by raising resources but by the themes that articulate where these approaches were important. That's when we really got our momentum and really started to expand opportunities. The achievements of the institutes are reflected by their ongoing successes in raising money to support their programs through faculty grants and philanthropic engagement.

MANAGING GRANTS AND INDUSTRY-SPONSORED RESEARCH

The chief financial officer of the university is responsible for the financial management and oversight of money that is received when faculty applications to extramural funders—whether from federal, foundation, or industry sources—are successful. The head of the Office of Sponsored Research reports to the vice provost and dean of research and to the chief financial officer jointly. There are major financial compliance and audit requirements that come with any federal funding that must be tracked by this office. There are other nonfinancial requirements related to grants management, such as adherence to policies on the responsible conduct of research and regulations for research involving human subjects and animals, that are overseen by the senior staff of the vice provost and dean of research.

Sixty-five percent of Stanford's external funding for research comes from NIH, and their funding plateaued during my tenure. The National Science Foundation funds that support other fields were also limited. In this funding environment, faculty were submitting more and more grant applications but the amount of money coming in was the same. Our faculty are highly competitive, yet the funding rates for grants went down to as low as 7 percent in many fields. This is likely to be an ongoing problem for universities because the federal agencies are by far the primary source of research funds regardless of the field.

Another job of the vice provost is overseeing industry-sponsored research. An important requirement is to be sure that industry contracts do not have terms that are contrary to the Faculty Senate policy on openness in research policy. The companies have to agree that the work is going to be published and that they do not have the ability to approve or disapprove the papers that are written. A review to make sure proprietary information is not disclosed is allowed, but contracts can't give companies the right to say, "Oh, no, you can't report those results."

Explaining the policy on openness and research to faculty as well as potential funders is an important responsibility of the vice provost. Faculty might not be concerned about publication of particular data, but it is necessary to maintain openness in research as a defining principle of academic research and for compliance with federal regulations.

Managing Facilities and Establishing a New Attitude toward Shared Facilities

The vice provost and dean of research at Stanford manages a large amount of real estate, added to most recently by ChEM-H and the Wu Tsai Neurosciences Institute. Each of the institutes has a senior director whose responsibility it is to manage the budget for operations and maintenance of their assigned space.

Managing shared facilities is another job of the vice provost and dean of research, such as the facility that supports nanosciences research and others that are used by faculty from multiple schools. The importance of shared facilities has increased dramatically as science has changed. In the past, the concept of shared facilities was "everybody just chips in to buy a microscope and pay the maintenance contract." That cannot work anymore, not when the microscope is a cryo-electron microscope that costs $6 million. The faculty do contribute towards the expense of using the instruments, but the problem is achieving sustained funding on this basis. If you raise the fees for using the microscope high enough to cover the full cost, then very few faculty can afford to use it, and their individual costs go even higher. It was very important to have some general funds to support shared facilities. Depending on what is offered by a shared facility, a certain amount of the general funds budget every year is expected to be allocated more or less in perpetuity as long as the resource is needed in order to ensure continuity of access to state-of-the-art instruments.

In establishing shared facilities, it was essential to work closely with the faculty who knew what was required for the science. Bringing the senior faculty with the relevant interests and expertise together as working groups was an effective approach. Jokingly, it went, "Okay, who around here needs to be involved in planning a high-performance research computing center? You, you, you. Are you interested? Let's figure it out. And, are you going to help tell the president that we need $40 million?"

Furthermore, shared facilities need to have research scientists to manage them. They are also centers of education, so the senior scientists who run shared facilities have to be supported in their role as teachers as well as service providers. In addition to maintaining their own scientific knowledge, their time is spent helping the graduate students learn how to use the instruments, generate the data, and analyze their results.

In addition, we have SLAC National Accelerator Laboratory right up the road. The long history of the Stanford-SLAC relationship gave us the basis for building a much stronger connection, which is very valuable because we had more and more different kinds of scientists who were greatly advantaged by access to SLAC facilities and to research funding for projects together with SLAC scientists. We were able to create several institutes that bridge between Stanford and SLAC. It was also possible to build new facilities there, like the High-Performance Research Computing Center and the Stanford-SLAC Cryo-Electron Microscopy Center.

The Stanford Research Computing Center (SRCC) located at SLAC National Accelerator Laboratory, one of the shared facilities supported by the Vice Provost and Dean of Research to advance research at Stanford.

MANAGING TECHNOLOGY LICENSING AND REGULATORY COMPLIANCE

Another role of the vice provost and dean of research is to work with the director of the Office of Technology Licensing, which files patents for Stanford researchers and handles licensing of intellectual property to interested companies, in many cases to those started by faculty. In my view, this activity is directly in support of Stanford's mission to "transfer knowledge for the public good" because companies can do the work that is often needed to translate discoveries into benefits for society. In the U.S., the federal government grants universities the right to license intellectual property that results from federally funded research under the Bayh-Dole regulation. The government expects that we do due diligence and offer licenses to an outside entity that has the capacity to take the discovery and turn it into useful products.

In practice, patents in the engineering sector tend to be licensed by large companies whereas in the biosciences, most licenses are awarded to start-up companies. Many university biomedical discoveries are early stage and need further development of the technology to create drugs or other therapies.

This process requires working with the faculty so that their technology is transferred successfully, often by having people from the Stanford lab teach the company scientists about the technique. But after that is accomplished, it is necessary for the faculty to separate their research at Stanford from the company's work. Overseeing policies and procedures to keep that separation in order to avoid inappropriate use of Stanford resources and to avoid personal financial conflicts of interest is an important role for the vice provost and dean of research in partnership with the school deans.

The Office of Technology Licensing creates visibility for Stanford discoveries through general releases of information about new intellectual property and announcements directed to companies in the sector. The technology licensing associates at OTL have a particular focus and expertise to communicate with companies that would be potentially interested.

Finally, working with counterparts at peer institutions and national organizations of research universities on research policies and to communicate effectively with the federal agencies about research regulations is a key role for the vice provost and dean of research at Stanford. My experience included serving on committees of the National Academy of Sciences that prepared reports on *Fostering Integrity in Research* and on *Federal Research Regulations and Reporting Requirements: A New Framework for Research Universities in the 21st Century*. Our goal was to reduce the burden of administrative tasks, such as by triggering certification of compliance requirements when a grant was awarded, instead of at the time of submission, given that only 10–15 percent of proposals are actually funded, so that faculty spend their time on research rather than unnecessary paperwork.

CHAPTER 18

CARLA SHATZ

Director, Stanford Bio-X (2007–Present)

Carla Shatz is the director of Stanford Bio-X, which is a pioneering interdisciplinary biosciences institute bringing together biomedical life science researchers, clinicians, engineers, physicists, and computational scientists to unlock the secrets of the human body. Prior to joining Stanford as a professor of biology and neurobiology, she was the chair of neurobiology at Harvard Medical School.

The Origins of Bio-X

Bio-X started years ago with a small group of faculty. Many people claim they had the idea. But the most common story is that it started in 1998 with Steven Chu in Physics and Jim Spudich in Structural Biology doing some really beautiful biophysical experiments to study the contractility of muscle. In the late 1990s, they realized that this collaboration between a physicist and a cell biologist was extremely potent, exciting, and effective. They started to discuss a mechanism to actually bring scientists from different disciplines together to collaborate. Lucy Shapiro, Channing Robertson, Charles Kruger, and Dick Zare joined their enthusiasm for creating opportunities for interdisciplinary research collaborations as members of a faculty steering committee. Even today, you run into somebody from a different lab, you start talking, and you have a great idea. You want to do an experiment together. But experiments are expensive, or you don't have the equipment you need. How do you take a great idea that requires collaboration and make it work?[115]

The way you do it is money. You have to have some resources that allow for ideas to be tested in even the simplest ways. So they went to the president—I believe it was Gerhard Casper at the time—and asked him if he could create a little pot of money for seed grants that would support interdisciplinary collaborations. My understanding is that in the year 2000, a small pot of money—and I mean small, maybe a few hundred thousand dollars—was created, and there was an invitation to submit ideas for seed grants that had to be interdisciplinary. They already were thinking, "Wouldn't it be great if you had someone from the Medical School and someone from the School of Engineering, or someone from the Medical School and someone from Physics, or someone from Biology and someone from the School of Engineering collaborating?"

They were smart in awarding the first set of grants. There were just a few of them given out, but it was enough money so that you could launch something. The first one was $75,000 for two years—$150K—which was enough money in 2000 to fund a postdoc or a graduate student to work between labs. When John Hennessy became president, he continued to make a commitment. Both Casper and Hennessy took their own presidential money and used it to jump-start this idea. Of course, there was a competition for the seed grants. As time went on, we got more money. By around 2004, we could fund twenty seed grants. John Hennessy committed to giving $3 million every two years for research. You could not pay a faculty salary, but you could fund a graduate student salary or a postdoc.

Then a really amazing thing happened. Jim Clark, who was a former professor at Stanford, a successful tech entrepreneur, and a friend of John Hennessy, decided to make a big gift.[116] It was enough to have a building named after him. This was announced in 1999. Giving the building to a department would have been the standard thing to do, but Hennessy, who was provost at the time, and Jim Spudich and these faculty that had already been collaborating made the argument that the building should actually be a home for this new idea of interdisciplinary collaboration.

Many universities claim that they're inventing interdisciplinary research in the sphere of life sciences and biomedicine and that they thought it up. One good example is MIT. They claim that they've invented this concept called Convergence, and they actually brought together people at a workshop at the National Academy of Sciences in 2013 to show everybody what they've been doing.[117] I went to a meeting, and it was actually extremely annoying, because they claimed to have invented all this stuff that we have been doing since 1998. A lot of places are trying to claim the brand that not only already existed, but also really catalyzed change at Stanford. Other places are just now discovering real catalyzed change.

Becoming the Director of Bio-X

I was chair of Neurobiology at Harvard Medical School, which was a real honor. No woman had ever done that before. Around 2006, Harvard was exploring ideas for some really interesting programs across the university. We had a faculty committee, and we started to study what other universities were doing in this vein. We were asked to think about very creative ideas for a new campus for Harvard across the river, right next to the Business School. I was on that committee, and somebody said, "Carla, you know the guys at Stanford. Why don't you call them up and ask what this Bio-X thing is all about?"

So, I called Matt Scott, whom I knew very well, and we spent probably four hours on the phone.[118] I thought it was unbelievable when I heard what they were trying to do and what they'd accomplished. Then he said, "Well, you wouldn't be interested in being director of Bio-X, would you?" I said, "Well, I don't know. That's amazing!" And he said, "I'm tired.

I've worked on it so hard, and I'd like to go back to the lab. We have a search; we're thinking about a new director."

I got a phone call from John Hennessy a couple of days later, and then I came out to look at it, and I just got so excited about it. This is what we'd been trying to do at Harvard. I'd been trying to do it for four years, to create something for neuroscience across the university. I couldn't get anywhere; nobody wanted to do it. Everybody said they had everything they needed already. It was really not good, very siloed. And then I came out here and John Hennessy said, "We have this wonderful thing, but I really want you to figure out what it is exactly and how I can tell the story and fundraise." He wanted me to help him raise money so he didn't have to keep giving money to this program. He wanted to have it stand on its own. I said, "Look, if I can figure out how this could work, and what stories we could tell to explain this crazy idea of interdisciplinary collaboration, would you allow me access to some of the very important and significant philan-thropic donors at Stanford?" I'd learned at Harvard Medical School that you can have the best idea in the world, but if you don't have access to people, you'll get $1,000 here and there, and you're never going to do anything. John was great; he said, "Yes."

I came in 2007. Between 2003 and 2007, Bio-X had grown organically with this idea of collaborative science between biology and medicine, engineering, physics, and chemistry. The X represents interdisciplinarity. They were bringing various faculty into the building who were from different parts of campus—both wet labs working on living things, and dry labs focused on computational, mathematical, and theoretical components that were essential to not only studying life, but also modeling it.

When I came, I spent a number of years figuring out how to "brand" Bio-X and how to tell the story. Donors were interested, but they didn't understand. They would ask, "What is Bio-X? What does it do? What is it producing?" The original mission statement of Bio-X was very scientific. It didn't reach out to explain why we were bringing together all these interdisciplinary themes. Essentially, Bio-X faculty invent new things in the sphere of biomedical and life science research with funding from our programs, bringing to bear disciplines ranging from engineering and computer science all the way to clinical research. But we fund ideas early before faculty can write grants that would attract external money. Assessments of Bio-X by Professor Dan McFarland, and our own tracking of how Bio-X seed grants have been leveraged, indicate that every dollar that President Hennessy invested in Bio-X grants has generated over ten times the amount in subsequent external funding![119]

The idea is really that human health and biology is too complex to be solved by any one discipline, and the only way to understand the complexity of life, health, and disease is to take advantage of every discipline—which includes all of the major computational approaches—and also to invent new disciplines and new tools. That is the goal. We're looking for themes that support the mission statement, and the ideas are driven by faculty and students, not by directors of programs. If you have some good new crazy idea, but it involves collaboration and you have no way of getting it launched, that's what we want to see.

THE BIO-X BUILDING:
THE JAMES H. CLARK CENTER

I like to make a joke: I call the building Noah's Cl'ark because the idea was to have this building be a home for people from disciplines all over the university and be a place where they could interact. The idea was that the first people who would come into the building would be from different fields—engineering, chemistry, physics. Actually, Steve Chu was in this building before he went off to be secretary of energy. Dick Zare's lab is in this building. Jim Spudich's lab is still in this building, even though he's away launching another company. People from the Biology Department, Cardiovascular Surgery, Developmental Biology, and neuroscientists came into the building, and they started to build this home for interdisciplinary collaboration.

Originally, nobody wanted to move. A lot of people didn't want to move because they were worried that this was some weird experiment that wouldn't work, and they'd be stuck in this building. The first few people who moved in were really pioneers in that way. Now, we have this long waiting list, and the building is packed full. I think it was designed for something like forty-two labs, and we now have forty-eight labs, which is wonderful. Researchers actually agree to downsize their labs to come into this building.

It's an open lab design. There are no walls between labs; people run into each other. That's the way the building was designed. Instead of moving a bunch of departments into this building, it became the home for some new experiments. This was a major breakthrough in the way a university would think about what to do with a building. This was unique in America.

Matt Scott was intimately involved in designing the building and this notion of open lab. The architect was very famous—Sir Norman Foster.[120] At the time, people were starting to design these industrial-style buildings by not covering the ceiling and allowing the pipes and infrastructure to be visible. It was very exciting architecturally at the time. The idea was that you could put lab benches anywhere and then theoretically, because of the open lab design, you could move them around. Of course, once you got them plumbed and wired in, it could cost a fortune to move them. Nevertheless, the lab benches are on wheels. They had crazy great ideas.

The building opened in 2003. I don't know of anywhere else in the world where interdisciplinarity started that early. The design of the building at the time was also revolutionary. Basically, the labs flow into each other. To come to my lab, you have to walk through somebody else's lab, and that fosters amazing synergies. Our researchers go back and forth. We share equipment. It's very efficient. Once you start having open lab designs, everybody has a different mentality. If somebody needs something, they'll send an email out to the whole building, for instance, "Do you happen to have sodium chloride?" There's this very nice shared mentality. There are all these different fields, so some weird reagent that nobody in your department would ever think of buying, somebody in this building might actually have. Those kinds of synergies are great. Many other people who are designing new buildings have learned lessons from us. The fundamental idea of creating open labs is a very popular idea now.

Jim Spudich, Matt Scott, and Steven Chu actually established criteria for who could come into the building, which stand in very good stead today. There has to be a proven record of collaboration, openness, and generosity. The dean or department chairs cannot just shove somebody in. You have to get support, not just from your department chair, but support that shows that people recognize you as someone who goes beyond your own discipline. That's the fundamental requirement. Letters of support really should be coming from people in a different school—that's the best—but certainly different departments. And then, you have to explain not what the building can do for you, but what you can do for our Bio-X community.

Proposals used to go to the director of Bio-X and the Executive Committee, but I decided when I came that that wasn't good enough. We needed to have an internal faculty group because the faculty in the building were concerned that decisions were being made without their participation. So, I created something we call the Clark Center Faculty Working Group. Every application for lab space is presented to our internal working group of ten to twelve faculty members in this building who are very senior—people like Steven Chu, Bill Newsome—a very diverse group who also understand what Bio-X is.[121] That group basically is advisory, but I've never gone forward with any application that hasn't had major support from it.

When I came as the director, they hadn't thought about a way *out* of the building once it was full. So I had to actually institute a process for taking back space in the Clark Center. The first thing I did was talk to this faculty working group. We thought about the criteria that would enable us to recover space and also a process for how to do it—a space recovery plan for cases where faculty members have space, but there's nothing going on and they have very few students. Our criteria require very active research, and the center of your research has to be here in the Clark Center. You can be very active, but if all of your work and collaborations are at some other university, why should you have precious lab space in the Clark Center?

Last, but not least, is whether or not you have any funding. We realized that the first thing deans would say is, "Well, get rid of that person because they don't have a grant." We thought that wasn't right. If someone is still teaching students, is still collaborating, is still really active, is creating an environment that's still part of what we would consider the mission of Bio-X, why should we throw them out? We felt that as long as they continue to try to get funding over a certain amount of time—not months, but years—they should still be here if they are actually contributing to our community in some way. In the end, grants are important, but they aren't the first criterion. The only spaces that we've actually recovered have been from very inactive labs, but, still, it's a very painful process.

EARLY CHALLENGES WITH BIO-X

People really enjoyed the collaborative interactions, so even by the time I arrived, this was a very popular place to be. But it wasn't clear how long it could last, for several reasons. First, there was a lack of funding to continue programs that had been started, including the Bio-X seed grants and the Bio-X PhD Bowes Fellowships. Second, the faculty in this building come from different schools—primarily Engineering, Humanities and Sciences, and the Medical School. So, the question was:

How do you provide governance for a building and a program that isn't sitting in one school?

There had already been some precedent for this because a number of institutes had been created at Stanford—independent labs, mostly in physics and applied sciences. But the idea for this institute, Bio-X, was to create a governance committee of the director and the cognizant deans, all of us essentially reporting to the vice provost and dean of research so that no one dean could take over the program or the building. Bio-X also has a Leadership Council which has about thirty faculty members from all over the university. Our Leadership Council is amazing; it's as diverse as our programs are. The Leadership Council actually helps us select seed grants that are coming from all over, with all kinds of crazy ideas.

Space is what it's all about, so there has always been a struggle to create and maintain a reasonable distribution of faculty in this building who represent biomedical and life sciences. That challenge started at the very beginning: Who was going to come in, and if they were all going to be from the Medical School, why didn't the Medical School own the building and apply medical school metrics to running the building? The Bio-X program and this building had to negotiate a new budget arrangement that would make it more immune to the vagaries of any individual dean who might want to own the program and the building. It was apparently difficult to do but Dr. Heideh Fattaey, the executive director of Bio-X, in collaboration with Charles Kruger, then the dean of research, worked things out a year or two before I came, and it was brilliantly done.[122] There was a formula so that different parts of the university would agree to pay their share of the budget to run and staff the building. That share would be the same every year.

MAJOR PROGRAMS AND ACCOMPLISHMENTS

We have three programs: the seed grant program, which was the founding program, a Bio-X fellowship program, and a summer undergraduate program. We don't have a PhD program; we give fellowships to PhD students in different programs who want to have mentors from different schools or other programs. For example, someone in mechanical engineering might want to work on neuroscience, and they might want a mentor who's a neuroscientist and a mentor who's a mechanical engineer. We didn't just want to give people money and have them go away and do their thing. We wanted them to report back and share. So, we started symposia and poster sessions that would require anybody who gets money from us to present a poster once or twice a year and also give a talk or presentation so that our community could grow and people could find out what other people were doing.

We have stories of success from the fellowship program, and those are really, really amazing stories. PhD students who do interdisciplinary fellowships immediately get jobs. A lot of them are going into the biotech industry. Others are still in their MD/PhD programs or are doing postdocs. Some of them go right into faculty positions. Former Bio-X fellows are on the faculty at Caltech, at MIT; some have gone into bioengineering departments, others have gone into just standard basic science departments, and some have gone into medical school departments, so it's diverse.

Then we added a summer undergraduate fellowship program. Undergrads started to hear about us. One sent me a lovely email asking, "How do I major in Bio-X?" Of course, you can't major in Bio-X, but I thought it was a wonderful question to ask. The undergrads were clearly very interested in participating in the interdisciplinary experiment that was going on. In 2007, we created a formal program to give undergrads from any field a ten-week intensive real lab experience in the summer.

The seed grants have also been successful. We ask people who received them, "For every dollar we gave you, how much money did you get back in external grant award funding?" For the first eight rounds, we put in about $28 million and we got back over $280 million. When John Hennessy saw that number, it provided him with a good rationale for continuing his funding of the Bio-X seed grants.

Bio-X and the Clark Center have also acted as an incubator for new departments and institutes. The first area that had its home in the Clark Center was Bioengineering, which did not exist previously at Stanford. It was put into this building; it had a home here to grow, and the presence of this new department also cross-fertilized interactions with other faculty in the building. Bioengineering hired very different kinds of people. They weren't just from the engineering side of the university, which is typical of most bioengineering departments; the department included people from biology, clinicians, and people who trained in computer science. I consider Bioengineering to be the first "offspring" of this whole effort to do interdisciplinary work. It grew so well and became so successful that it now has its own department and its own buildings in the Science and Engineering Quad.

Another really good example is the discovery and promulgation of optogenetics, an amazing new technique for activating cellular processes. When you look at the world, you see because your retina has nerve cells that can capture light and convert it to an electrical signal. Karl Deisseroth, one of the inventors of optogenetics, realized, "I could just genetically express rhodopsin, the molecule that captures light, in any other cell, and hook it up to something to do work in the cell, and then shine light and just have the cell make insulin, for example." His first two grants from the National Institutes of Health were turned down, but Bio-X gave him seed grants to start to develop this method. He developed that concept here in the Clark Center. Then, we built the Optogenetics Innovation Lab that could train people from all over the world, including Stanford students and faculty, to use that technique. We jumped on top of a technology that we knew would benefit everyone, and we helped develop it and teach it.

Stephen Quake was another seed grant beneficiary.[123] He invented these amazing microfluidics devices in the Clark Center. He built a foundry that is still available for people to come from all over the world to learn how to make them. It was his idea to create a resource that could be not only developed in his own lab but also shared and taught. The idea was you invent it, and then you develop it, and then you teach it before it's even something you can buy off the shelf.

Professor of Bioengineering Stephen Quake was a beneficiary of a Bio-X seed grant, which aided his research on microfluidic chips and led to the opening of the Stanford Microfluidics Foundry at the Clark Center. Quake (second from left) is pictured here with Foundry Director Jessica Melin, Medical School Dean Phil Pizzo, and School of Engineering Dean Jim Plummer at the facility's opening in January 2006.

Stanford President John Hennessy (left), entrepreneur Jim Clark, and Bio-X Director Carla Shatz at the tenth anniversary celebration of the James H. Clark Center and Bio-X in 2013.

The most recent thing we've done is to help in the initiative to build a cryo-electron microscopy resource here at Stanford and to build strong bridges with SLAC. A cryo-electron microscope is a tool used by structural biologists to study the structure of molecules along with X-ray crystallography. Bio-X helped recruit and house three major cryo-electron microscopists, including one who is now heading the SLAC program and using high energy physics and cryo-electron microscopy to study the structure of molecules. All of these scientists wanted their labs to be located in the Clark Center so they could recruit students and act as magnets for interactions with SLAC and cryoEM. Then we encouraged them to teach workshops and make our community aware of this amazing resource. So again, these scientists come in, they build the technique, and then they teach it.

We've just started to do it again with brain organogenesis. A faculty member was being recruited away from Stanford, and we wanted to keep him. We created a beautiful research lab for him and the opportunity for him to be a part of this interdisciplinary community. In the spirit of Bio-X, he decided not only to create a place to make brain organoids but also to hold workshops for students. They come and learn how to take skin cells and turn them into nerve cells and grow them into tiny human brains. Pretty amazing, right?

These innovation labs stem from a very simple concept. If someone at Stanford invents something, and it's clear that researchers want to learn how to use that method or technique or instrumentation before they can buy it off the shelf, we try to help by creating resources that would allow copies to be made or by providing teaching opportunities. They're now calling them "sandboxes."

We've also done it for neuroscience. Bio-X created a significant fund of money that the neuroscientists could use to begin to fund big ideas in neuroscience, including some programs focused on the brain-machine interface. The first neuroscience grants used a combination of Bio-X gift money and presidential money from John Hennessy. In 2008, we created a program called NeuroVentures, which was an effort to take the Bio-X approach of interdisciplinarity to move neuroscience out of the Medical School and bring it to the broader representation of faculty across the university including the School of Engineering and the Department of Biology. We asked Bill Newsome to run it. It was created under the Bio-X umbrella, and the goal was to create resources that would allow the neuroscience community to build beyond clinical neuroscience.[124]

This early Bio-X NeuroVentures effort then grew into the concept of a Neuroscience Institute at Stanford that reaches all across the university. We didn't have that before, and we had no resources that would have allowed basic scientists or even engineers to participate in studying the brain. Now we have 400–500 faculty who belong to the Wu Tsai Neuroscience Institute. We incubated it here in the Clark Center, and in 2020, faculty moved into the gorgeous new Wu Tsai Neuroscience Building.

I'm always looking out for what is cool and exciting that could be a new area of research. My role involves two things: one is to be a talent scout and look at all these new ideas that are popping up, and the other is to talk to my colleagues and have my finger on the pulse of discovery at Stanford. I only know small parts of what's going on here, so I do the best I can. For example, when I wanted to use cryo-electron microscopy, I thought, "We need to leapfrog from having nothing to being the best in the world. We can't just build capacity slowly; this needs to be a big deal." Marc Tessier-Lavigne was key in actually providing funds to get those hugely expensive instruments, and Bio-X made a key contribution by working with our faculty to recruit and house these wonderful scientists.

Looking Ahead to the Future

Currently, the program has over 900 faculty throughout the university. Bio-X has created a horizontal web of intellectual interactions across disciplines, across the vertical towers of the schools and departments. It has created a formal new dimension to the way an academic institution works that has grown organically from support from the seed grants, the graduate fellowships, and partly from the mentality of the founders. Bio-X has created a foundation for translation, and a mindset to work in this collaborative way, which has led to many discoveries.

My pledge to John was that he wouldn't have to keep giving money for Bio-X from presidential funds. Ultimately, we were able to convince wonderful donors to make gifts to underwrite these interdisciplinary experiments. Then we could actually have students and faculty show up and tell their stories about the collaborations and about the discoveries. That has led to our being able to fully endow the seed grant program.

In 2013, we thought we would have a big tenth anniversary party to talk about some of these success stories regarding faculty seed grants. We were going to have some of our Bio-X PhD fellows tell their stories and run a big symposium to celebrate this kind of interdisciplinary science. And then we thought, "We'll invite John Hennessy. We'll ask him to come and interview some of the Bio-X PhD fellowship students. He is so good at getting people talking, and they can tell their stories about how their PhD fellowships allowed them to do novel interdisciplinary work."

We also invited Jim Clark, the donor for the Clark Center. John came and conducted these wonderful interviews. At the end, I asked Jim if he would make a comment to wrap up the afternoon's symposium before dinner. Jim got up and said, "Wow, I have never seen my money used in a more creative, better way. I'm going to give you another $60 million."[125] John Hennessy was sitting right next to me, and he practically fell off his chair. It was just amazing to see how excited Jim was by our progress report from the students and faculty who had benefited from Bio-X programs. Jim's additional gift was used in part to help Bio-X create an endowed fund for the Bio-X Seed Grant program, and also to help launch two new interdisciplinary initiatives: the Wu Tsai Neuroscience Institute and ChEM-H.

When Bio-X was conceived, we believed it would also allow new start-up companies to form and result in substantial new patents. Although that did happen—quite a number of companies have been founded, almost 100 patents have been filed, and so on—Bio-X actually created new fundamental knowledge because it brought so many people together from different disciplines. People like to talk about the intellectual capital that we've built. That's something very unique and unexpected, and I think it has put Stanford faculty and students in an extremely competitive position to get external grants from the NIH.

But much of the created knowledge is dormant or latent in terms of translation because even if you get to the NIH grant stage, it's still very difficult to jump across the "valley of death"—to get the amount of funding that would really allow you to make a drug or bring a new technology to market. We've all known this to be a problem, and it's getting worse because most companies are so risk averse now. They used to invest in some of these seed grants, but they don't do it anymore.

I recently served on the design team for the Innovative Medicines Accelerator.[126] Although it is not a Bio-X initiative, I don't think the concept really could exist without the Bio-X idea that we can do something quite unique that will actually speed the way to more rapid translation. The idea is to create another resource that would take all of this discovery and give it an opportunity to make a difference.

CHAPTER 19

JEFFREY KOSEFF

Founding Co-Director, Stanford Woods Institute
for the Environment (2005–Present)

Jeffrey Koseff is a founding co-director of the Stanford Woods Institute for the Environment and a professor of civil and environmental engineering with expertise in the interdisciplinary domain of environmental fluid mechanics. He has spent his entire academic career at Stanford, where he earned both of his graduate degrees—an MS in 1978 and a PhD in 1983.

Establishing the Woods Institute

If you want to think about where the whole thing started, it was probably in the early 1990s. There were a number of us in different departments at the university who were thinking about climate change—which was not something that people talked about a lot back then—and how it was manifestly a very interdisciplinary challenge. That is, solutions would not yield from the knowledge provided by individual disciplines.

That conversation was heightened a little bit by our recruiting of Stephen Schneider from NCAR, the National Center for Atmospheric Research. He had written a book called *Global Warming*, and so a group of us decided to create this regular seminar where we would basically start out by everybody telling everybody else what we did in the area.[127] It was held every second Thursday, and it just took on a life of its own. People heard about it and asked if they could come. When visitors came, they were invited, so this whole thing expanded to one of the more popular seminar series on campus. People put everything else aside at that time, and they made it a priority. It was amazing. It was known as the environmental interdisciplinary seminar.

So, that went on for a few years, and out of that emerged a sort of activism. We said: "It's all very well us getting together. It's all very well us chatting. What are we going to do about it?" We wanted to create some entity at Stanford that would formalize this structure that had manifested itself through the seminar. And so we went to the provost at the time, Condoleezza Rice. To be honest with you, I don't think she was looking for something big, but she didn't want to blow us off because there were a lot of senior people in that group, including the former university president Don Kennedy, Paul Ehrlich,[128] and others—some pretty famous people. So, she said, "All right, we'll form this Provost Committee on the Environment." It formed and then nothing really happened. It was chaired by a few people, but it did nothing more than what we were already doing separately.

But, a few of us persisted with it, and we used it as a platform to start developing the ideas for what we wanted to see long-term at Stanford, which essentially was something bigger than we already had, something approaching maybe a school for the environment or some kind of larger entity where we could formally participate together—maybe get funding, hire new people, etc. However, that idea sort of stayed in limbo; I don't think there was an appetite for it at Stanford at the time. That changed, though, in 2000 when John Hennessy became the president.

John Hennessy and I met each other when we were both department chairs in the School of Engineering. I got to know him through weekly meetings of the School of Engineering Executive Committee. When he became the dean in 1996, I started selling him on the concept of environmental engineering and how it was an important part of Stanford University's legacy, and we needed to really invest in it. I was the department chair of Civil and Environmental Engineering, and John was incredibly supportive in helping to raise funds for the renovation of labs and also to hire some key new faculty. He understood the whole set of environmental issues. I think he believed in it. So, when he became president of the university and he was looking for a way to create his legacy, he very quickly gravitated to: "We have to take the university out of the ivory tower. We have to have an impact on the world. We have to be socially relevant." This was an interesting time for American universities, which were getting pounded by public perception that faculty didn't really care about undergraduate education. There were all kinds of reasons out there for sort of recentering the discussion and focusing it in a way that emphasized that universities were still relevant to social change.

He wanted to create some big new initiatives and embarked upon a process for identifying them. It was sort of grassroots but nimble and fast. Because we had already established the Provost Committee and had been thinking along those lines, we were able to articulate very quickly and very clearly what we wanted, and we put forward this whole concept of an environmental initiative.

He said, "Yes, that sounds absolutely correct." It took two or three years to get everything going, but in 2003 he announced the environmental initiative in the Faculty Senate. An environmental institute would become the centerpiece that would drive the work of this initiative forward, and the initiative would focus on finding solutions to our global environmental challenges. He purposefully chose an institute and not a school—an institute that would integrate and draw its faculty and participants from across all seven schools, but would focus primarily on solutions, on policy-oriented research. That was what he wanted to do, and that's what we wanted to do, and that's how it started.

In 2004, Pamela A. Matson, Dean of the School of Earth Sciences, Jeffrey Koseff, professor of civil and environmental engineering, and Barton H. Thompson, professor of law, discuss plans for interdisciplinary environmental research that will be conducted through the new Stanford Institute for the Environment.

The concept of a school was not dismissed because it was not a good idea. The concept of a school was set aside back then for a number of reasons, a lot of them pragmatic (difficulty of starting a new school) and not deeply philosophical. I don't think there was the kind of money available that was necessary for a new school. We thought we should perhaps do something that was less permanent until we had some data to figure out how successful this would all be. We wanted to be able to include faculty from all seven schools in a very nimble way, and perhaps we'd form teams to address a certain problem that could then disappear after their useful lifetime—no harm, no foul. The institute structure would allow that to happen. You wouldn't have to move people out of their home departments or schools; you wouldn't have to break affiliations. You could add a new affiliation and you'd be a fellow at the institute, but you weren't leaving your own department. That was critical. Another argument was that we couldn't possibly put all the faculty that were interested in working on the environment in one school. It was just not going to happen. Plus, faculty were coming from all these different schools with different cultures and different ways of doing things. Just overcoming all of those things was difficult.

We looked at a couple of other schools of the environment that did exist at the time, and we decided that they were performing below their potential and that perhaps it was the structure of the school that was an impediment. We wanted something more nimble, and so the institute idea really took hold. The idea would be that you'd have an institute of all seven schools and that faculty could be appointed jointly in the institute and in their departments. The institute would raise additional resources and funds that it would distribute in a way that promoted this new activity, which was solutions-oriented research, not blue-sky research. And so that's what was done.

At one point, the selling point was that we needed to create a big tent and put all our environmental assets in it, so that when you looked at Stanford from the outside, you saw this sort of monolith of environmental activity, and it was simple for you to plug in and engage. That was not a bad motivation. But very quickly, we were challenged to write a business plan for this institute, for fundraising. That's another whole thing that never was done before. What do I know about business plans and things? We had to write a strategic business plan explaining why we should exist and what we were going to do. And, it was very, very apparent very soon that simply creating a big tent for assembling all of the environmental assets was not the reason to form an environmental institute. It's not strategic. What's new? What's different? The philanthropy part of it was very, very important in terms of driving the change. We had people who were potential donors who were saying: "Show me your business plan. How are you going to make a difference?" So, philanthropy in many ways was changing at the same time as we were doing this. Donors' attitudes were shifting from "Here is $10 million. You're Stanford University. I trust you. I'm a friend. I'm an alumnus. I want to support you," to "Show me how my money is going to make a difference." So, we were really challenged in that way. We had to articulate what was new and different and unique about what we were doing.

Potential investors would ask questions like, "So how are you going to change the world?"

We would respond: "Well, we're going to bring faculty together from different disciplines, and they're going to look at these problems using multiple lenses and approaches."

"Okay, great, big deal, and then what?"

"Well, they're going to work with external stakeholders to define the problems and in a sense co-create the solution space that you want to create."

"Okay, that sounds really good, that's different, right? How are you planning on doing that?"

"Well, we'll need funds to do that."

"So, what kind of funds would you like?"

"Well, we'd like seed funds. We're calling it 'Environmental Ventures Projects.'[129] We'll act as a venture capitalist entity investing in big ideas that will do exactly that, and that's what we want your money for."

"Okay, great. I'll buy that. I'll give you money for that."

And they did.

EARLY OUTPUTS OF
THE WOODS INSTITUTE

So, the Environmental Ventures Projects was exactly that. You could look at it on multiple levels. It was a way of investing in interdisciplinary research. It was a way of creating new partnerships and collaborations. It had a social element to it. It had an organizational element to it. It was the way we truly built a community that wasn't just people saying "hi" to one another, but deeply sharing ideas and influencing each other's thinking in terms of how they went about what they did. Ultimately, it was quite profound in that sense. If you ask people, "What do you think the biggest success of the Woods Institute is?" they'll point to the Environmental Ventures program. I think it fundamentally changed everything.

The first round of investment was in 2004. At around a million dollars a year, that's approximately $15 to $16 million, and it's probably generated another $40 to $50 million of research money. This was funded through seed funds, which had to be highly focused and not discretionary. We got pretty sophisticated. Towards the end of my tenure, researchers needed to submit a theory of change with their proposals: "This is how this research will change this issue, and this is who we'll work with, and this is who's going to benefit from the results." It was very much focused on the translational part, the engagement part. Getting that knowledge into the hands of people who could best use it to make a difference in the world.

Funding for each project was up to $200,000, philanthropically raised, and then that begat other programs. After about eight or nine years of this, we had forty to fifty projects that we had funded. We sat down and we said, "Okay, let's analyze. Has any of this work made a damn bit of difference? Given our goals, it's not enough just to create new knowledge. I mean, that's what we do ordinarily. It's not the business of the Woods Institute. So what do we do?" So, we sat down with each of the projects and got five people together and said, "Right, let's be really honest." We developed a seven-point analytical scale that didn't exist before. We just came up with it. A value of one meant "nothing came out of this project," which is possible. I mean, everybody has probably had research projects where it just didn't work and nothing came out of it, not even a good paper, right? A value of two was probably "some papers." All the way up to seven, which was "your idea, your research was developed; it was adopted; and here are the measurable outcomes of that. Here's the good that came out of it." We had some projects like that. In Maputo, Mozambique, they completely redid the way they distributed water—they basically adopted illegal water hook-ups into the system. They legalized them and solved the big water distribution problem. Valentina Zuin's PhD thesis became Mozambique's water policy before it was published![130]

How many sevens did we have? Not too many. Where did most of the projects fall? At three or four, which means, "Yeah, there's something really good. Maybe it was tested at the bench scale, and it was quite successful, but it never got beyond that." Why didn't it get beyond that? Because of this whole "valley of death."

So we said, "We need to help our researchers across the 'valley of death.'" So, we came up with something called REIP—Realizing Environmental Impact Projects—which would be follow-on projects. You didn't have to have an EVP [Environmental Ventures Project] to get a REIP, but if you had an EVP you could apply for a REIP. If you had an idea that you had demonstrated at some "bench scale" success, you could apply for the REIP to help you move it into the next phase. That meant connecting you with stakeholders and the people who potentially could be your partners. The EVP and the REIP are two hallmark programs of the Woods Institute. They continue to this day.[131]

University Relations

There's a fellow in the School of Education, Dan McFarland, who uses these "spider diagrams" to look at how things change, and so he did some early work with the Woods Institute to see if any of these programs actually changed the way people collaborated at the university. There's definitely a change that occurred in how people view interdisciplinarity.

The whole way we evaluate people for tenure and promotion has changed to reflect this collaboration. It used to be that when you were hired, you were hired for your own individual excellence. You were expected to come in, to write research proposals, to bring in funding, to hire graduate students, to do fundamental research that you published in the best journals. At the time of tenure, you got twelve to fourteen letters from people around the world that said, "You are among the top two or three people in the world. You've influenced fields. You've created new lines of research. You've made a difference." And, if your teaching was okay, then everything was cool. It wasn't going to make a huge difference. Mentoring graduate students was expected, and as long as you weren't mistreating them you were fine. Then along came this change, where suddenly it's not you and a grad student writing a paper; it's you and another faculty member and another faculty member and maybe a grad student or two writing papers in a team. The world's muddled now. What was your contribution? So, initially there was that effort to try and dig out what your contribution was, but eventually I think people realized that that's just not a good way to go. I think ultimately, if you're associated in a serious way with a team or teams that ultimately have produced high impact work, your chances of getting tenure are going to be very good. So, it's not just your individual excellence anymore, it's your ability to create excellence around you and be part of excellence. Not to say that the whole university is like that, as there are still parts where they're still a little bit more traditional, but it's changing.

People felt threatened by this interdisciplinary model in terms of where the decision-making power was located. There was a lot of tension between the institute directors and the deans of the schools in terms of where the decision-making authority was. A lot of students gravitated towards interdisciplinarity. We were teaching classes in the institute, but we started to think, maybe we need some degree program that reflects this interdisciplinarity. Who's going to award a degree: the institute or the school? What school would it go in if it's interdisciplinary? In the end, guess who won? The deans and the traditional power structure. They said, "We can have these interdisciplinary degrees in the environment and sustainability and energy, but they're going to be awarded by schools." And we said, "But it doesn't make sense because the faculty participating in teaching these are from all over the place."

To this day, E-IPER, the Emmett Interdisciplinary Program in Environment and Resources, is probably one of the hardest PhD programs to get into at Stanford University. There are probably fifteen or eighteen applicants for every person accepted. It's very difficult. It's designed to allow students to explore the interface between science and policy in the environment and sustainability realm. It mandates that you have not just an advisor, but an advising team that is manifestly interdisciplinary. It's directed by a young faculty member who was hired by the Woods Institute when she was still an assistant professor, Nicole Ardoin, who's in the Graduate School of Education, joint with the Woods Institute. She's in the Graduate School of Education, and guess where this degree is located? In the School of Earth. Why is it in the School of Earth? Because it had to be in a school, and it was decided that it was the closest to focusing on the environment, so they put it there. Does it make sense to have it there? No! Students are confused. They say, "I have very little affinity to the School of Earth. Why is this program in the School of Earth?" These are some of the problems that we haven't fully solved. I suspect a new school of sustainability or environment might be the only way to truly solve that, where you get a congruency between the purpose of the degree and the faculty that are teaching it. This is a big issue.[132]

There were a bunch of students who came and said, "We identify with what Woods is trying to do. An interdisciplinary entity that transcends schools and disciplines, that's what we want to be." If somebody says, "What's your home unit on campus?" many of the students would like to say the Woods Institute, but they can't because we don't have students. So now they say E-IPER. They won't say E-IPER in the School of Earth, they'll say E-IPER. Whereas if you ask a student in Civil and Environmental Engineering, "Where are you at Stanford?" they'll say, "I'm in Civil and Environmental Engineering." They won't necessarily say, "I'm in the Environmental Engineering Program," or "I'm in this lab." So, it's an interesting way of identifying. I don't think it's going to change very soon, but that tension will continue because the university rule is now that degrees have to be awarded by schools and not by these interdisciplinary entities themselves. Not even co-awarded. We even went at one point and said, "What if we could do a joint Woods/School of Earth awarding of a degree?" and the answer was, "No, you can't." To me, that's one of the dragons we never were able to slay, and we slew a lot, let me tell you, to get where we got.

When the Woods Institute was founded, there was one entity on campus—the Institute for International Studies, which later became the Freeman Spogli Institute for International Studies—which was allowed, even though it wasn't a school, to appoint people to the Academic Council, not as professors, but as fellows or senior fellows of that institute. A policy center exception was granted to them. Typically, these people had been active in policy. They had specialized knowledge that was deemed to be useful to the purpose of the institute. They were some pretty high-powered people who might have had a stint in government and even been a secretary or an under-secretary or something like that. So, they were allowed to be appointed. Some of them had advanced degrees, but they were mostly divorced from contact with students. They didn't teach, really. They just were there to do policy research. So, we came along and said, "We want to be able to appoint faculty to the Academic Council jointly with departments. We'll fund half, and the departments will fund half." The purpose was to strengthen that relationship between what we were doing and the departments that we were partnering with.

So, we were given eight billets—but no funding. Every time we wanted to fill a billet, we had to raise the funds. All the people who were being appointed in that one policy center (Freeman Spogli) were at the senior level. The administration said, "Of course, this is only for senior people, right?" And we said, "No, we'd like to be able to bring in junior people as well." Some of the people that were at the cutting edge of doing the kind of work we wanted were not senior people.

We prevailed. We became the second policy center on campus that was allowed to appoint faculty to the Academic Council, except our goal was not to appoint them 100 percent within the institute, but to appoint them jointly with depart-ments, and we did that. Over the years, we've appointed about fifteen faculty, and it's worked incredibly well. Every single one that we've hired at the junior level has been tenured; all the senior people have been effective leaders. The idea is that they're 50 percent in a department, 50 percent in the institute. They would teach a half load for the school, and then what would the other half be? In support of any interdisciplinary environment sustainability program on campus. They could choose. And, here's the beauty—when they put their set of classes together, given Stanford's very low "boundaries" between departments, it's not like: "Okay, in winter I'm teaching for the School of Earth and then in spring I'll teach at Woods." The classes were attractive to everyone, so you didn't ever feel like: "I'm wearing my Woods hat now or I'm wearing my school hat." The set of courses that were offered had this universal appeal.

But at the Woods Institute, we had a limited number of these formally joint appointments. We said, "We can't run the institute that way. We would like to appoint a set of senior fellows comprised of the existing faculty." So, I, for example, became a senior fellow in the Woods Institute at 0 percent time and 100 percent time in Civil and Environmental Engineering. This is why it worked so brilliantly. I don't know how we managed to do it, but we did it. Even though I was devoting a serious amount of time to the Woods Institute, especially as director, nobody from the School of Engineering ever went to the Woods Institute and said, "We want compensation for Jeff's time." They never have. So, 0 percent time just became a nominal way of doing it. My salary was still 100 percent time through the School of Engineering. These senior fellows created further links. We were able to create a significant group of faculty that came together and made the decisions together with the leadership of the institute about what we should be doing, where we should be going, what kind of programs we should have, what research we should focus on, and what faculty we should think about hiring going forward. So, we have sort of an onion. We have the inner core of the onion which comprises the jointly appointed faculty, then those like myself who still have 100 percent appointments in departments, and then we have less active affiliated faculty in the outer rings. That was a very, very powerful and meaningful outcome of this whole thing. Affiliated faculty would end up being over 200—close to 10 percent of the university.

There are now five or six policy centers on campus because they essentially copied the blueprint. While we were doing this, we were sitting with the Provost's Office and writing the language in the faculty policy handbook about how to do it!

DECISION MAKING WITHIN THE WOODS INSTITUTE

If you were appointed as a senior fellow in the Woods Institute, either by virtue of your formal joint appointment or by your invitation to be at 0 percent, you then were in a voting body where everybody had the same voting rights. Questions that came up were everything from, "What areas do we need to invest in that we're not invested in?" to "Where are the holes where we don't have the faculty strength to meet student demand or to address what we perceive to be the important areas of the future?" So, we organized the institute around programs or centers, which were subdivisions. We decided we just couldn't be this big, huge amorphous bunch; we had to put a little granularity into the organization. So, we created programs around the focal areas that we thought were really important. For example, we formed the Natural Capital Project,[133] the Center for Ocean Solutions, and three separate programs in water: Water in the West; Water, Health & Development; and the Global Freshwater Initiative. And then we formed the Center for Food Security and the Environment jointly with the Freeman Spogli Institute. Those programs required core faculty; often, faculty that we appointed jointly ran them. They had fund-raising needs, but the Woods core faculty provided ground-truthing and checks and balances on what we were doing. We needed that. We couldn't just be making the decisions ourselves; we needed a formal academic body to help make decisions.[134]

The issues were who we should hire and what we should be doing. For the Environmental Venture Projects, there was a big committee that made the decisions on that. We had leadership training programs for students, including one called RELP, the Rising Environmental Leadership Program.[135] We have a committee of faculty drawn from the senior fellows that oversees that. The institute's ongoing activities required people to dedicate time and effort. So, it was a very democratic thing in that sense.

Essentially, all those appointed 100 percent in their departments volunteered their time. We couldn't pay them anything, really. It was not like, "I'm going to give you $10,000 if you do this." They did it because of their belief in what we were doing. It really was remarkable in that you could get people's attention because of a fundamental belief that this was the right thing to do. Unfortunately, the flipside of that is that when you needed to kick someone's butt to do something, you didn't really have the authority or the right to do it. It's not like, "I'm paying your salary so go and do that!" We had staff, of course, and that's different. But the faculty had to be motivated through the sense that if they put in this time and effort, they would benefit in some way down the line from these programs that they were helping. The one thing we did was, if you ever got money from the EVP, then you had to be willing to review and be on the committee. That was fair. Probably one of the only leverages we really had was: "You got money; now you've got to serve."

FUNDING STRUCTURE FOR
THE WOODS INSTITUTE

The Center for Ocean Solutions was a $25 million gift that we raised from the Packard Foundation that became the core funding.[136] However, this did not allow for the faculty hires. For every faculty position, we raised a separate endowment: $5 million for a full position and $3 million for a half position, which would fund the positions in perpetuity.

We raised money for programs like E-IPER, which basically had a director and student fellowships, and those were around a million and a half each to endow. And then each of the programs would have fundraising needs. For Water in the West, we would go out and get fairly big grants to support their activities. There was a continuous fundraising effort around all of those activities. If you look at the consolidated budget of the Woods Institute now, in terms of the expenditures, it's about $22 million a year. The university was providing central support of about $1.2 million a year out of this.

There was competition over the donors. Let's say I'm out playing golf one day, and there's some person playing golf, and she says to me, "So, what do you do, Jeff?"

"Well, I direct the Woods Institute for the Environment."

"What does that do?"

And I tell her.

"That sounds fascinating." And then she might come back and say, "Is there a way I can do something to help?"

And if, at that point, I did not go to the central Office of Development at the university and check in, I would get my hands slapped. Because the idea was that you can't just negotiate a donation of your own. You have to have it managed by the Office of Development, because that person who was being very generous with you might be a key donor to some other program on campus that is going to get really upset with you if you're interfering. So, the bottom line is that it has to be coordinated.

When we were putting the institute together, we created a list of people, all the people we could think of that we knew were sympathetic or empathetic to this whole cause. And, then we had to give it to the Office of Development. They might have added some names, but ultimately, somebody sat there and said, "You can't talk to this one. You can't talk to this one." Why? "Because they're reserved for the big $50- to 100-million gifts." Or, "They're giving to some other program at Stanford, and we don't want to divert their attention." Fortunately, when we started this, we had access to some really supportive and generous donors like Jerry Yang, for example, and his wife, Akiko Yamazaki, who were the foundational donors for the Yang and Yamazaki Environment and Energy Building (Y2E2).

IMPACTS OF THE WOODS INSTITUTE

I think the institute has legitimized interdisciplinarity in a way that people realize it's serious scholarship. Twenty years ago, if you said, "I work in the interdisciplinary field of X, Y, and Z," interdisciplinary was a code for *soft*—fluffy, not rigorous. People had this negative connotation of it, even though it was totally unfair. So, we had to fight against that. Fortunately, we had a leader who was willing to let us try—John Hennessy. There was strong leadership there. We fought negative connotations of interdisciplinarity by saying, "Let us show you that this person will produce the kind of scholarship that is regarded as being rigorous but also high impact." It was, "Let us show you. Give us the chance to show you." And they did.

Fortunately, the initial hires we made were very high-quality people. I always tell students, getting the initial condition right is so important to getting the problem right. And man, the initial hires were really high-quality people. And, probably part of the reason we made such high-quality hires initially was because we knew the "proof was in the pudding" and we needed to prove ourselves.

Who were some of the people we hired? Jenna Davis came from MIT.[137] She was a young assistant professor in the general field of public health. She was in Civil and Environmental Engineering, but her training was in public health. Her interests were firmly in water supply and sanitation for the developing world. She was untenured but was pursuing an area of research that we felt was critically important to the future, because I mean, what could be more important than water? She won a search against some senior people; she was going to be great. The School of Engineering was the logical partner because half her appointment was going to be in Civil and Environmental Engineering. Convincing the dean of engineering to hire this person who's not an engineer, whose PhD was in public health, was like trying to overcome a double-whammy! Joint appointment and nonengineer? Eventually, we were able to persuade him that having people who are capable of evaluating the efficacy of water supply and sanitation systems from a nonengineering perspective—that is, from a policy perspective—is really valuable. We were persuasive, but they set a high bar and she cleared it. She's a full professor now. So, there's a good example.

I talked about Nicole Ardoin who runs the E-IPER program. She was I think the second or third person we hired, also untenured. She's an anthropologist from Yale, hired into the Graduate School of Education with a joint appointment in the Woods Institute. So, we bet on some very ostensibly risky appointments from the point of view of, high-quality, but nontraditional, people. Gradually you could change the narrative to say, "You see? You can succeed. You can hire young people in joint positions, and they'll succeed. They'll contribute both to the institute and to their departments. It's not an either/ or." So, that's the way you change the narrative. You change it initially through persuasive arguments but ultimately through "facts on the ground."

FUTURE DIRECTIONS FOR THE WOODS INSTITUTE AND STANFORD

There are parts of Woods that have succeeded more than others in terms of delivering that impact beyond the boundaries of the university. The Natural Capital Project is an excellent example. They have massive amounts going on in China and things like that. Clearly, they've been a leader in the world in terms of doing that kind of work, so that's worked really well. But, to be honest with you, Stanford's capacity to really engage the world in terms of getting our research deeply connected to solve global problems has not been realized to the point where we want it to be. We want to do more. And, so this is what we're talking about now at the university: How do we get there? What do we need to do in order to get there? Yes, we have had success stories, but can we do more? Absolutely. Because by and large, when it's happened it's happened very locally. It hasn't happened with the full weight of the university's resources behind it. It's not yet something that the university has committed as an institution to doing.

In Mozambique, global impact was achieved through the offices of Jenna Davis and through her connections to the World Bank, but it wasn't like Stanford was right there putting the full weight of its resources behind her, making it happen. No. It might take reorganizing the university—to have an office of global engagement, for example, that provides the infrastructure to all these teams that want to go and work in distributed ways around the world and truly make a difference. The engagement part has evolved to where it is no longer a case of me taking my knowledge and "throwing it over the fence" and hoping someone catches it on the other side and uses it. It's not even a matter of me throwing it over and more actively finding someone to actually give it to. It's a matter now of being able to go on location, co-create the solution path, and develop that knowledge together. That's what I think is next—that's the next frontier. We need to make a decision as a university if we want to do that.

Based on what Marc Tessier-Lavigne is saying, I would have to believe that's what he wants to see happen. So let's make it happen. It requires a massive investment in resources and people. And here's maybe one of the hardest parts: it requires a fundamental rethink about how we hire, promote, and reward, not just faculty, but academic staff who support that. We don't have all the right academic or staff hiring lines in place in order to be able to deliver on this. You can't just expect university tenure-line faculty to be doing the kind of translational or engagement work that they're not experts in. We might have to have a different kind of faculty, like professors of practice, who are valued and rewarded and have a career path as well. We might have to change the structure of the professoriate or the Academic Council in order to be able to do that. You're not going to win cricket games by having ten opening batsmen, right? We've got to think about building a team like a cricket team. You value all talents. That's essentially what we need to do.

THOUGHTS ON JOHN HENNESSY'S
LEADERSHIP

I don't say this lightly, but there are not that many people in the world in academic leadership who could have succeeded the way John Hennessy did. It took a pretty special set of talents, I think, because not everybody would be up for what he did. He gave people space. He gave you responsibility. He gave you opportunity. It was built on trust, but he was not afraid to shut it down and to move on. He was the right person for that time, and I'm not sure how many other "right people" were around then. Look at all the universities in the United States, and how many have done what we did? Not that many. So, it points out the uniqueness of his leadership in putting responsibility in the hands of people and giving them a chance to succeed.

In all the time that we did that, we had one conversation that I would say was really hard. He kicked my butt because he wasn't happy with the progress we'd made in fundraising. And he was right. I didn't take it personally. He was absolutely right. Other than that, we might have disagreed on issues, but I always felt I went into a conversation with John Hennessy with a fighting chance of convincing him of my point of view if we didn't see eye to eye at first. To me, that's all you can ask for. Too many leaders just don't have that capacity. He did, and I think Stanford benefited from it. Don't for a minute think that John didn't have a pretty good notion of what he wanted to get done, but he was willing to be persuaded and change course if necessary.

CHAPTER 20

RANDY LIVINGSTON

Vice President for Business Affairs, Chief
Financial Officer, and University Liaison
for Stanford Medicine (2001–Present)

Randy Livingston oversees many of the administrative organizations that provide support for Stanford's academic mission, including Financial Management Services, University IT, the Office of Research Administration, the Office of the Chief Risk Officer, and Improvement, Analytics, and Innovation Services. He also serves on the boards of Stanford Health Care, Lucile Packard Children's Hospital, and Stanford Management Company. Prior to joining Stanford in 2001, Livingston spent sixteen years working in Silicon Valley in a variety of finance and marketing leadership roles and six years with McKinsey & Company as a management consultant.

I was a student here, an undergraduate and then later an MBA student in the Business School. As an undergraduate, I had the opportunity to work on one of the first large interdisciplinary research projects at Stanford, looking at alternatives to petroleum energy. It was at the time of the first great oil crisis, when the Yom Kippur War triggered the formation of OPEC and a dramatic rise in the price of oil. There was a widespread belief that there was only twenty to thirty years' supply of petroleum left. As a result, Stanford created what was possibly its first interdisciplinary institute, the Institute for Energy Studies. It was the precursor to a lot of what John Hennessy focused on later. I ended up being the co-editor of the final report and through that process worked very closely with about a half-dozen different faculty members. I came to appreciate what an idyllic life faculty members at Stanford have.

After completing my undergraduate degree at Stanford, I was a sanitation engineer for a couple of years working on trans-forming municipal waste into fuel gas. I returned to Stanford for my MBA, then worked at McKinsey for six years doing management consulting. I worked in Silicon Valley for sixteen years for a wide range of young technology and life science companies in a variety of different roles—marketing, corporate development, finance, general business operations—and had kind of forgotten about this wistful thinking as an undergraduate about how great life at Stanford would be.

Returning to Stanford as CFO

In the summer of 2000, I was at the movie theater with my wife. After the movie ended, she went to the ladies' room. I was waiting outside and ran into an individual who I'd worked with in one of these Silicon Valley companies who had just taken a job at the Business School as chief operating officer. I congratulated him and said, "I always thought how wonderful it would be to be a faculty member or go back to Stanford." He said, "Funny you should say that because Stanford has started to search for a new CFO. Would you mind if I put your name in the hat?" So, it was truly that chance encounter at the movie theater that led to my return to Stanford.

I started here March 15, 2001. John Hennessy had just become president at the beginning of September 2000.

One of the first things that struck me is the sense of time at Stanford. I had worked for a number of young companies where their entire life cycles might play out over a two- or three-year period. The first week I was here, I got an email from the Provost's Office in March, saying, "The provost needs to urgently have a meeting with the people on this list. What's your availability in the third week of May?" That said everything I needed to know about urgency in a higher ed environment. In the world I'd come from, urgent would be, "Can we meet now?" The idea that urgency would still be six or eight weeks out was really a revelation.

I had taken a couple of companies through IPOs and worked at some public companies where there's so much attention to quarterly earnings and quarterly results. Whether you made your numbers or not had a radical impact on the valuation of the company. At Stanford, nobody really cared what our actual results were. It would take us three months to close the books. The end of our fiscal year was August 31, yet it was mid-December before we completed our financial reports, and it would be rare if there was one news article about it. People were not interested. So, that was quite different as well. I think our annual university budget was about $2 billion. Today it's over $6 billion.

I had mostly worked with very small companies. I had never managed a team of more than 100 people, and my team at Stanford was 800 or 900 when I joined. I think one of the other striking differences was the age of the workforce. At the last Silicon Valley company I worked for, I was like the grandfather, even though I was in my midforties. I was the oldest person in the company. When I came to Stanford, I think I was younger than all my direct reports. So, that was culturally a bit of a shock as well.

I think another really striking difference was the turnover of the workforce. Great companies like GE or Hewlett-Packard or IBM developed their people by giving them many different experiences. At IBM or GE, an up-and-coming executive would be moved every eighteen months to two years. IBM infamously stood for "I've Been Moved." On average, people only changed roles at Stanford every ten years, and many people had been in the same role twenty years, thirty years—not only in the same organization, but literally the same job. Early on, when I would talk to different units about talent development, I would say, "If you've been in your job for more than five years and you're interested in advancing your career, you should be looking at doing something different, even if you're moving laterally."

For many staff, their primary loyalty was to their department within Stanford; this was particularly true in the academic departments. If they were in the Biology Department, they would feel like that's their world. The department chair would say, "Oh, I could never lose that person because the department revolves around that individual." So, one of my goals has been to get both the leadership of Stanford and the individuals to say, "No, my world is Stanford," and to really encourage more movement across units. A lot of my people have moved out of Business Affairs into leadership roles in other parts of Stanford, and I encourage and celebrate that.

FOCUS ON TALENT DEVELOPMENT

One of the things I have put a lot of focus on is talent development. I observed that all of the senior people we were appointing in the early period of Hennessy's regime were being hired from the outside. It was very strange to me that we were not promoting people from within. I was connecting the dots and saying, "We haven't done a very good job of developing people internally with the breadth of experiences and skills that make them ready to take on this more senior role." So, we started encouraging people to do more, take on different roles, move around.

In the early to mid-2000s, we decided that it would be fruitful to try to put together some kind of training or advancement program. Through university HR, and with the support of John Hennessy and John Etchemendy, we created this program called the Leadership Academy. We were very fortunate that John Morgridge, the former chairman of Cisco, and Chuck Holloway agreed to co-lead it.[138] They further developed and led that program for the first ten years, and now Bob Joss has taken it over more recently.

Around the same time, we created a program within my organization called Leadership at Stanford. It targeted leaders one level down from the most senior level, and it was more focused on staff, whereas the Leadership Academy had been both academic and staff. The first year, I funded it out of my budget, but from the outset I said, "I don't just want this to be for people in my own organization." We invited people from other units at Stanford, and it was very successful. The demand was incredible. The program was organized by an outside facilitator, not by Stanford faculty. At the beginning, each participant would do a self-assessment and have a 360-degree performance review to identify some areas to work on. The participants would also be assigned a mentor, and then the group would meet monthly for about nine or ten months with different themes as to their development. It was successful, and university HR decided to turn it into a university program. I'm thrilled, but the downside is that my own organization now only gets to send one or two participants a year.

Within my Business Affairs organization, beginning about seven or eight years ago, we assigned my HR director and some of my senior staff members to a broader talent development program internally. Formal training is a very small component of what makes people effective leaders. Far more important are the mentorship and feedback that people get along the way and the breadth of experiences they are exposed to. So, we aimed to create a talent development program focused on that. So far, this has largely been contained within Business Affairs, although I would love to see it extend more broadly to other parts of Stanford. We have roughly forty participants in the program at any given time. They stay in the program for two to three years. Interestingly, both the mentors and the mentees get a lot out of that, because helping someone else develop actually forces the mentors to recognize what's important in that process, to become more effective at developing people. That's an important component of being a leader.

We also created different rotational programs where people could rotate into different roles, either part-time or full-time, for a limited period of time. At my senior staff meetings, we invite two or three of the talent development participants to sit in, so they actually can see what happens at a senior management level. Participants in the program can shadow an executive over the course of a day or two, just to see what they do. All the different mechanisms are aimed at exposure and mentorship. We get the program participants to take over actually managing different components of the program, so that they gain responsibility for some of their own and their colleagues' development. That's been a very important component.

We have had some really tremendous successes. People who have emerged from that program have taken on more senior roles. The head of my finance team was one of the earliest talent development participants, widely recognized as a high-potential individual. Last year, when her predecessor retired, she was promoted into that role. Another individual who had been in the program was chief administrative officer for my organization, responsible for all the budgeting, facilities, HR, and so forth. Those are a couple of great successes, but it's not 100 percent. When we hired a new chief information officer, we ended up picking an outsider, but at least we had more viable internal candidates.

Randy Livingston, vice president for business affairs and chief financial officer, speaks about faculty and staff benefits at a meeting of the Faculty Senate in February 2011.

APPROACHES TO THE FINANCIAL CRISES
OF THE 2000S

When I came in, the dotcom bubble was bursting, so that led to a mini financial crisis. Stanford had seen tremendous growth in the value of its endowment, largely driven by venture capital investments and returns that peaked in 2000 just before I arrived. In 2001 through 2003, the investment markets really cratered.

Stanford's investments are managed by a division of the university called Stanford Management Company. It's not literally a separate company, but, when I arrived, it operated as if it was. It had offices up on Sand Hill Road, about three or four miles from campus. The CEO of Stanford Management Company reported to his board, not to the president of the university, and acted with a great deal of autonomy. It operates as what we call a "fund of funds." Stanford does not invest directly in individual companies or securities; rather, it invests in managers who manage portfolios of public equity investments, venture capital investments, traditional private equity investments, and so forth.

One of the big issues in managing a portfolio is that typically, the more risk you take, the greater the volatility of the returns. Stanford had been very successful in its portfolio of venture capital investments, even though it was a relatively small part of the portfolio. The venture returns in the late 1990s were ten to twenty times, so even if you invested 5 percent of the portfolio, suddenly that became, I think at the end of 2000, 40 percent of the value of the portfolio. Very early in 2001 when I arrived, there was wide recognition that the values of the venture portfolio were greatly overstated, that as a result of the dotcom bubble bursting, these things were going to completely crater. There was a lot of discussion as to what the risk profile should be going forward. John Hennessy and I both had ex officio seats on the Stanford Management Company board. Most board members were outside investment professionals. John very strongly took the view that we want to lean into the risk, that in the long run, the returns are so important to the growth and health of the university that we could deal with the volatility in the short run.

John's attitude about volatility and risk was even more reinforced coming out of the 2008–2009 financial crisis when the merged pool—the integrated endowment investment portfolio—lost about 27 percent of its value over the course of a year. Just before the impact of the global financial crisis really hit us, the annual payout on the endowment was 25 percent of our consolidated operating revenue, so it was a huge part of funding all aspects of everything we do. As things cratered at the end of 2008 and early 2009, we were in the midst of the budget process for fiscal year 2010. Normally, when we have short-term volatility in the returns on the endowment, we apply what's called a smoothing formula to buffer the effects and have a more stable payout on the endowment. When we were watching the endowment decline so steeply, the big question was, "Do we continue to apply the smoothing formula, or do we depart from it?" John Hennessy, in one of his greatest moments as a leader, said, "This is a systemic change and resetting of values in the marketplace; we should view this as permanent, and we should reset our budget as quickly as we can to the new level of the endowment value."

The nature of universities is such that it's very, very hard to eliminate any programs and their associated expenses; university budgets in general are incremental. The core budget process is based on the presumption that you continue to fund everything you did last year plus inflation. The annual budget debate is, "What are you going to add on top of that?" A financial downturn creates the excuse or the opportunity to do some pruning. The decision was made in the FY10 budget cycle to reduce the endowment payout by 25 percent over two years. We cut general funds allocations by 15 percent, and we forced every budget unit to say, "All right, we've got to go through a major cost-cutting exercise. Let's get it over with." Everybody on campus understood that we were in the midst of a giant global recession; there was urgency, and nobody was questioning the need to do this. That enabled us to have a salary freeze for a year. In a sign of incredible leadership, the president and provost announced they were going to take a 10 percent salary reduction, and other senior leadership, a 5 percent salary reduction. It was much easier to have everybody else on campus accept no pay increases when the top people were taking 10 percent decreases. We also laid off about 500 people. That was very tough, but it gave us the opportunity to identify the least productive positions or individuals and say, "We can survive without them."

Notwithstanding the magnitude of those cuts, I don't think we missed a beat. I think the organization coming out of the 2009 crisis was, if anything, far more efficient, far more productive. The next several years were fantastic years for Stanford. Taking a high-risk, high-return approach to our investment portfolio creates volatility in the operating budget, which occasionally gives us the opportunity to do some healthy pruning. I think we were ahead of many of our peers who said, "It's going to take us some time to figure out how we're going to get costs down, so let's do it over two or three years." They moved much more slowly. When you're pruning, it's a lot easier to prune abruptly than to prune slowly. I think we were regarded by our peers as a role model, and I think it was in large part due to both John Hennessy's and John Etchemendy's strong leadership during that time period.

The recovery was actually relatively quick. From 2010 through 2014, the returns on the merged pool were very good. We did lean into the risk, so we were heavily invested in things like private equity. We had significant regrowth in payout on the endowment, so we had a lot of new resources that had not yet been designated. That gave us a lot of budget freedom and flexibility that allowed us, apart from philanthropy, to make big investments in some interdisciplinary initiatives, to help fund a lot of the capital projects on campus. We ended up with new incremental resources that could be invested in new initiatives and strategic priorities versus the things we had pruned away. The higher returns themselves are helpful, but the volatility is helpful to us as well.

CHALLENGES WITH ENTERPRISE SYSTEMS

The largest part of my organization is central IT. When I arrived in 2001, we had already made commitments to implement new ERP [enterprise resource planning] systems for all of our core student administration, HR, and finance. We had selected PeopleSoft for our student administrative systems and HR, and Oracle for finances. The student implementation went relatively smoothly. HR and payroll were implemented and went live at the beginning of fiscal year 2002: September 1, 2001. The first payroll we ran in the new system, there were huge numbers of errors. I got called before the Faculty Senate; faculty wanted to know who was responsible and what we were going to do to hold them accountable. I had to apologize and commit that we were going to get it fixed. We did eventually get the payroll fixed, but it was a huge embarrassment.

We were supposed to do the rollout of Oracle financials in summer of 2002. It could only go live during the transition from one fiscal year to another because a midyear transition would have upset too many different things. Three weeks before the transition, the team and the user base said, "I don't think we're ready." I had to go to John Hennessy and say, "We're postponing this a year. The additional project cost is going to be about $35 million, so I need you to figure out how to set aside another $35 million to allocate to this and bridge us over another year," which he agreed to do.

We got to the summer of 2003. It still was not rock solid, and the team at that point said, "We know there are some things that still need to be fixed, but we think it's good enough. The best way to fix the software is to put it out there, get people using it, identify all the bugs. We have the capacity to fix things really quickly, so we'll put it out there." I was very naïve. We put it out there, and it was a disaster. I got called before the Faculty Senate again. They wanted to know, "Who's responsible for this system and this implementation? How are we going to hold that person accountable?" The Faculty Senate formed a subcommittee to figure out why we had done such a bad job and what we were going to do to fix it. Unfortunately, it took us several years before we got that system operationally smooth and functional.

In higher education, the world of research grants is a dimension that doesn't fit under the normal model of a corporate accounting system. Normally, you roll things up by organizational unit, and then you have line items like tuition and research dollars and so on. That's the structure of the general ledger and chart of accounts. When you have to do all of that for a research project that crosses organizations, things get complicated.

Oracle had created a module called grants accounting to address this, but we were their first customer, so it was very buggy. We had tremendously overestimated user readiness to adapt to the new system. The prior system was mainframe based; it had been in use for probably twenty years. All the finance people across the university were accustomed to all its vagaries and challenges. With Oracle, we were moving to a client-server architecture and system, and users had to learn a whole new chart of accounts as well as a whole new way of interfacing with the system. The reporting was horrible. We had almost no reporting when it rolled out, so people were blind. It ended up taking a long time and many changes of personnel in the IT area to finally get a team in there that could get it fixed and operationally smooth. John Hennessy and John Etchemendy had my back. They continued to provide the funding and support, and we did eventually get it fixed.

A couple of lessons I've learned are we need to have a broad vision and plan; we need to have a lot of patience in getting it accomplished; and we need to avoid a "big bang"—so don't try and change everything at once. And invest much more heavily in what we call "campus readiness," which is really training and bringing along the users and recognizing how difficult it is for them to adapt to new practices.

MANAGING COMPLEXITIES ASSOCIATED WITH THE MEDICAL ENTERPRISE

The medical enterprise is composed of three parts. We have the School of Medicine, Stanford Health Care (the adult hospital and healthcare system), and the Lucile Packard Children's

Hospital. The two hospitals are separate 501(c)(3)s; they're subsidiaries that have their own boards, their own management teams, but we consolidate their financials when we put out the university financial reports. Including the hospitals, it's actually now about $12 or $13 billion in total revenue. It's further complicated because while the two hospitals employ the nurses and the technical staff and operate the hospitals, the physicians for the most part are School of Medicine faculty members. So, funds flow from the hospitals to the school to compensate the faculty for physician services. Over time, a big part of the university budget reflects those clinical revenues flowing over to the School of Medicine.

Another complication is that the School of Medicine is what we call in Stanford parlance a "formula unit"—a more financially independent school. The School of Medicine and the Graduate School of Business collect their own revenue, and they're responsible for their own expenses. They pay a tax to the university for the central services we provide to them, but that's expected to be cost-neutral. Because of that, the School of Medicine has operated with a degree of financial autonomy and independence from the rest of the university, unlike the rest of the schools.

John Hennessy tended to largely ignore the medical enterprise. He would often not speak well of them in senior staff meetings. There was no one at his staff meetings representing the medical clinical enterprise. The School of Medicine dean reported to the provost and was part of Executive Cabinet meetings but not part of the president's senior staff meetings.

Part of my role from the get-go was to attend hospital board meetings as the liaison from the president's office and the Board of Trustees, but I didn't really have much of an official role. Clinical revenues had been growing at about 12 percent a year for twenty years, whereas the rest of Stanford's revenues had grown about 6 percent a year. Last year, of the $12 billion in consolidated revenue, clinical revenues were 57 percent, about $7 billion. The healthcare enterprises are gargantuan and also represent a disproportionate amount of risk. Even though the hospitals are separate entities that issue their own debt, and legally the liabilities are separate, because of how intertwined the hospitals are with the School of Medicine, there's this very tight financial interrelationship. So, if the hospitals were to go down, it could be catastrophic for the university.

There have been three CEOs of Stanford Health Care during my time. The second one was very, very ambitious and started dramatically expanding Stanford Health Care's activities, opening up clinics. We acquired another in-patient hospital in the East Bay, and the trustees started asking, "How does this relate to our academic mission? And what's the incremental risk?" About four or five years ago, the trustees started wanting more purview. I was the point person to pull that together, working closely with the leadership of the School of Medicine and the two hospitals, trying to assess the risk and put together information for the trustees. When Marc Tessier-Lavigne came in, he created a more formal role for me as university liaison for Stanford Medicine. As part of that, I sit on the boards of Stanford Health Care and Lucile Packard Children's Hospital and meet regularly with the dean and the two CEOs to help forge better collaboration and cooperation, and monitor their activities on behalf of the president and the board.

The value of clinical activities to the university is around the research dimension. If we take Stanford's sponsored research portfolio, and exclude SLAC, about two-thirds of our activity is in the School of Medicine. And even what's outside of the School of Medicine—say in engineering, chemistry, biology, physics—I would guess that at least a third of that is related to medical applications. Even though we've built this great reputation for computer science and IT, the vast majority of research today is in the life sciences. Having close integration with the clinical enterprise is a huge benefit to the research enterprise. There's a growing amount of research in clinical trials, and faculty investigators want to have access to tissue samples, blood samples, cell samples, and to be talking to physicians who are actually practicing. Medical students have a place to do their rotations, residencies, internships, and so forth—so that's an obvious given. But other departments benefit, too—in Management Science and Engineering, there's a whole body of activity around making hospitals more efficient, and so there are students and faculty whose research and internships are being done at the hospitals.

From a financial standpoint, the clinical enterprise is very helpful, because the funds flow from the hospitals to the School of Medicine, which, in addition to compensating the faculty for their physician practices, also subsidizes research and education. One other benefit is regional reputation. We have great challenges with the surrounding community because of the traffic and the cost of housing. Many people view Stanford as, on the one hand, this great economic engine that's created the wealth of Silicon Valley, but also the evil empire that keeps growing and increasing traffic and congestion in the area. But, by and large, there's an incredibly favorable view of Stanford Health Care and Lucile Packard Children's Hospital, because when people get cancer or have a preemie baby or serious heart disease, this is where they want to be treated. So, it's definitely enhancing our reputation in the region in a favorable way, notwithstanding the fact that the hospitals themselves contribute enormously to traffic and congestion.

The question that gets asked all the time is: To satisfy the need for research and education, how big does the clinical enterprise need to be? Nobody has satisfactorily answered that. The current leadership is focused on partnerships versus owning and building stuff everywhere. But, notwithstanding more constrained expansion, clinical activity and revenues are continuing to boom.

IMPLEMENTING RISK MANAGEMENT PRACTICES

One of the other units under my watch is now called the Office of the Chief Risk Officer. When I came in, the Risk Management Department was largely responsible for property, liability, and workers' compensation insurance. What was emerging in the early 2000s was this notion of enterprise risk management. Leaders of any kind of complex enterprise, both at the board or the senior management level, should be continually asking: What are the major enterprise risks? Do you have appropriate mitigation plans? Are there things you can do to protect yourself? In the mid-2000s we started promoting this idea of enterprise risk management, both with the university cabinet and with the Board of Trustees. That has matured tremendously where I think we would be widely viewed within higher education as having the most robust enterprise risk management program. I give most of the credit to Rick Moyer, who now is the chief risk officer of the university. Traditional insurance risk management, privacy, compliance, information security, and internal audit are all part of that office now.

We have identified about twenty-five different enterprise risks. An example of an enterprise risk for us is an earthquake. In the worst-case scenarios, it could be $4.3 billion in property damage and other costs to the university. Another enterprise risk is investment volatility. We could have a very dramatic bear market. For example, in the 2009 financial crisis, our endowment lost about $4 billion of value almost overnight. Information security is another example. As opposed to these infrequent, very high value risks, information security breaches are a constant irritation; we're continually surprised by the different dimensions of that risk. The clinical enterprise is another enterprise risk. If we end up with Medicare-for-all, that would be calamitous for our health system because it would dramatically reduce reimbursement levels. Sexual misconduct is another constant and serious enterprise risk.

Risk management went from being something that indi-vidual units might occasionally have thought about to where now, at each university cabinet meeting, we highlight one or two of the risks. We've assigned senior executives to be respon-sible for overseeing each one of the enterprise risks, as well as leading the cabinet-trustee discussions. It allows us to have an intelligent discussion of, "Are we comfortable with the risk? Should we be doing more in that area?" and so forth.

Implementing New Work Arrangements to Address Local Challenges

Beginning in the early 2000s, senior leadership recognized that we were reaching the limits of potential expansion on the historic campus, not because of constraints on land, but because of our ability to absorb the traffic. We started looking at sites where we could house an administrative campus, and in 2004 ended up purchasing forty acres of land in Redwood City that had been the headquarters for the technology companies Ampex and Excite@Home. At the same time, Stanford Health Care acquired four buildings across the street and built outpatient clinics there.

John Hennessy signed off on a plan to move forward fairly expeditiously with building an administrative campus. Then the great financial crisis hit, and everything got put on hold. So, it actually took ten years before we reengaged with the project and fifteen years before we finally moved in, but we finally did in 2019.

When we started thinking about Redwood City, we also embraced what we called "work anywhere," which is the concept that where we're physically located should not impact our work. That also led to starting to embrace the notion of telecommuting. Parts of my organization have been way out in front of most of Stanford in supporting the idea that people could work from home if they had an appropriate home office, or the idea of satellite locations around the Bay Area. I've got people that commute over two hours each way every day. It's unimaginable for me that employees devote three-and-a-half, four, or five hours of their day, with the uncertainty that comes with those long commutes, that if there's an accident it can suddenly become twice that. The reason people commute, by and large, is because they can't afford a house nearby; housing prices are ridiculous. So, the impact on morale and productivity even from allowing them one or two days of their work week to avoid that commute is just enormous. Even before the move to Redwood City, some teams were telecommuting three days a week.

Because of that, we were very strong advocates for collaboration tools. In Redwood City, we've invested heavily in very good video conferencing in all the conference rooms, and we advocated upgrading the campus conference rooms, so they have that capability as well. We've invested heavily in tools like Slack, Jabber, and Zoom. Some units, like the Office of Research Administration, which deals with research proposals and grants and all the research compliance, are completely comfortable working remotely.

It's put us in an incredibly strong position with the COVID-19 situation that's unfolding, because working at a distance comes very naturally. We haven't missed a beat; we had a staff meeting this morning with ten people on Zoom and ten people in the conference room. I think in the next few years, we will start having more remote workers. That will be one of the solutions to dealing with the high Bay Area housing costs.

CHAPTER 21

BOB REIDY

Vice President of Land, Buildings, and Real Estate (1997–Present)

In addition to developing and implementing Stanford's $4.1 billion capital plan, Bob Reidy manages $5.9 billion in commercial real estate, as well as campus utilities, grounds, parking and transportation, and operations and maintenance for almost 300 buildings with over nine million square feet of space on Stanford's 8,180-acre campus. He oversees a $213 million operating budget and over 500 employees. Since 2000, his division has constructed seven million square feet of new academic and commercial space and 5,200 units of housing at a total cost of $7.5 billion.

Starting at Land and Buildings

I was recruited to come here under the Real Estate Group, which was part of the Stanford Management Company. It manages investment properties in which Stanford has significant holdings. The value today is about $6 billion; when I started it was about $1.5 billion of just real estate value. The income generated from those commercial properties supports general funds, which are valuable because they're discretionary, and the provost can do what they want with them.

The commercial properties are all proximate to the academic campus and a portion of the original 8,200 acres. I was recruited to come and take over some projects that they were having some troubles with. At the time, I was a partner in a small company. I was doing a project in Puerto Rico, one in San Diego; I had engineers and contractors all over the country, and it was just like, "I can't do this anymore." I came to Stanford because I could be home; I had three little kids. They recruited me, and I thought I'd stay five years. I've been here almost twenty-two years.

Long story short, I was recruited to Real Estate, managed some projects for them, and met a wonderful person who basically had the job that I have now, Curtis Feeny.[139] He's a tremendous person and a mentor of mine. He made it possible for me to take on the academic side of Land and Buildings. I was on the commercial real estate side, and two years into that commitment, there was complete chaos on the academic side. There were three different groups that made up Land and Buildings; all three didn't work constructively. One very strong individual, highly political, would essentially leverage his relationship with leadership and faculty to get the outcome that he thought was appropriate. In my opinion, it was almost counter to the university's mission.

I think John Hennessy very early on learned that was the case. He charged me to write up a position paper on what I would do to fix things. The position paper basically said you've got to have one leader over that three-bucket organization. He said, "Well, Bob, it can't get any worse." He basically handed me the keys. I thought, "Wait a minute, is that a vote of confidence or is that just desperation?"

CHANGING THE CULTURE AT LAND AND BUILDINGS

When I took over the Land and Buildings academic portfolio, there were project delays and lawsuits. The faculty didn't trust the people managing the projects. They would say one thing and do another. It was just a mess, a complete mess. One of the first things I did was sit down with some people that I thought were very talented but had no structure, no support, no leadership per se. We did a mission-vision-values exercise. I wanted to ground them in the notion that we're here for a higher purpose—the purpose of the academic enterprise, to support them and provide a service so they could have confidence that they could continue to do their work. I went through this exercise and brought some people along that I thought were very talented. I wanted to make them feel accountable for their own actions and to participate in putting forward a guide or a set of process controls that they could own.

While I was doing that, John Etchemendy and John Hennessy were in early discussions with the faculty, doing outreach on where they wanted to go, the academic priorities. In parallel, we were doing these activities, and it just so happened that when John and John finished their exercise, I'd made some headway. We'd negotiated all the bad deals away, and I had repositioned people in the organization. I made it clear they were going to be accountable, and we were going to be open, honest, and transparent, and that fundamentally, we were going to make informed decisions. So that was the baseline to start from.

One of the first initiatives that John put forth was Bio-X, which was an attempt to co-locate multiple scientists from different disciplines in one building, engaged in solving complex problems that required a variety of scientific expertise. They had selected an architect prior to changes that I was trying to instill in my group. I came into the building formulation process at the halfway point, and it was very clear that the world-renowned architect was going to want to make the decisions about where to spend money. But he didn't realize that it wasn't his money to spend.

We butted heads a little bit, but we got through that and came up with this process controls document that aligns decision making with the appropriate persons and a communications matrix that made it clear who was responsible for what decisions. Roles and responsibilities are clear, and you're accountable for that role and that responsibility. Stay in your lane. Don't go outside your lane. We want to listen to you. We'll be transparent. But, at the same time, if you're a faculty member, and you want to go in a direction that you have no expertise in, that's inappropriate. Our job is to provide the faculty member with a set of decisions to move forward. That's what we set up at Bio-X.

We formed a very small subcommittee of one representative from each academic discipline. Five of them came together around a table and talked about priorities and trade-offs. It was a big mystery as to what was going to happen. There was a lot of conflict, but in the end, by the time we had opened the doors, everybody was so excited about the opportunity to do cross-disciplinary research. The notion was that these teams are going to change—they're always going to change, change, change. Looking back, I don't know if that's exactly what's happened there. They do change teams around, but it was the process of coming together and working towards a vision of this cross-disciplinary research that brought them really close together, and then good things came from that.

CONTROLLING COSTS

In concert with this process controls piece, which was vital, we needed to show the faculty that they could have confidence in what we thought things would cost. We felt it was important to set expectations early on spending limits, but we needed to establish credibility about how you establish a limit on a project. What we did was build a database of other similar projects from around the United States. We still have this database today. The rule is: "University X, if you want the data, you must contribute data. We're not going to charge you for it. We'll manage it. We'll administer it. We just want the data, and we want the data in a certain way." So, we built this database of projects—whether it's wet labs, dry labs, housing, office buildings, teaching facilities, etc.—and we used that information to set the limits.

John Hennessy said, "I want us to be at the fiftieth percentile of that database set." We argued. I said, "John, it's really difficult to hit the fiftieth percentile when you have stone buildings," and "We really care about the sense of place," etc. John pushed us: "I want you to be at the fiftieth percentile." Lo and behold, we got to about the seventieth or seventy-fifth percentile. If we had set it at seventy, we would've been at the ninetieth percentile. He knew that. He had the vision. He understood. And he was so supportive of us. Faculty have a tendency to go around staff people like us and try to get to the president or the provost to reverse decisions, but the president and the provost really supported us.

The database is not a cost estimating tool. It's just an order of magnitude that can be used to reasonably argue what a project should cost. Then we had credibility to say, "We're going to manage to this limit." Every project exceeds the limit as you progress through the design process, and we utilize specific control points along the timeline to stop and formulate a list of trade-offs that empower the faculty subcommittee to make informed choices in concert with the early cost limits. Our job is to establish the limit and then provide decision-making options for faculty so that they can handle the prioritization and the trade-offs. The limit that you set has got to be reasonable so that the end product enables faculty to do their work.

When I first arrived, individual project managers had no authority. So, as we developed our database, our process controls, and communication matrix, we made sure that among the many participants in a project, the project manager had decision-making authority on certain aspects of the project, and the faculty had decision authority over programmatic aspects, as opposed to aesthetics or structural facets of the project. We were building a culture of supporting the project managers, training them, giving them confidence that they could perform their duties, and that we would protect them. When people came to them and said, "You can't do this. You must do it this way," we said, "No. Time out. We are balancing many priorities, many wants and needs under a limit, so we're going to make trade-offs and prioritize our decisions."

I really believe that you should bring a team together very early on—architect and contractor at the same time—so you can make informed cost choices. I'm not a big believer in hard bidding all these things against twelve different contractors to get the best price. To me, this is a relationship business. You have to have experience in building relationships with contractors and architects. You get them in early, and you make them accountable to the project to deliver. That was very successful, and I think that gave the project managers a qualified resource to counter any inquiries or challenges.

I think a lot of universities—especially public universities—are bound by state law to use the lowest bid possible. What happens is you go out to bid and the bids come back very low because contractors know that there are loopholes and they're going to ask for change orders. We don't take that approach. Fortunately, we've built a very competent team. They know what things cost and how the market changes. Right now, the market is on fire. Costs have escalated quite a bit, but we're still managing to these limits, and the trade-offs and choices are getting harder and harder. The seventieth percentile is where we're targeting. We still have challenges. Every project goes over budget every single step of the way, and you've got to bring it back to the cost limit you established.

Another factor in the decision-making pathway is the Board of Trustees. The trustee committee of Land and Buildings plays a vital role in creating a gateway. If there is tremendous internal pressure to spend more, the board is there to help me say no. The board understands that these early limits are important to manage, and they must be reasonable. I use that board process, these stepwise approvals as you go through a project delivery, to reaffirm the importance of managing to a limit.

Securing Funding

Another thing that I had my CFO put forward is a funding plan and a funding agreement. The funding plan is a very simple two- or three-page letter that outlines the funding mix at the early stages of the project. It's not often that you have all the capital identified at the early stages of the project. The funding plan identifies the specific amounts for each of the three funding sources: debt, reserves, and gifts. Those three buckets of funding opportunities are put in a funding plan very early on. There might be a donor that gives $100 million or $40 million or whatever over a five-year window or a ten-year window, so there's some backstopping funding. But before we start construction, we must have a signed funding agreement from a donor, an obligation from the school to service any debt, and some notion of reserves if they're going to put that forward. We can't start construction until we have an agreement signed by me, the provost, the dean leadership, and the budget officer.

The other thing that was important to do was to have the major donors participate in the planning process. The beauty of it was that these particular people didn't want to interfere or be too directive, but they wanted to help us and be engaged. They helped John determine how to position projects to the donor community and how to sell the whole package. Four or five of these fundamental partners would come, and we'd share our views and our vision and where we're headed.

The faculty typically were not in the partner meetings. It was really John Hennessy, John Etchemendy, and these fundamental partners. They'd invite us in to make presentations and have a discussion. By then, I'd delivered a number of buildings, so they had some confidence in me. I think a lot of universities are critical of people who do what I do because they don't have a lot of confidence. And they don't have a lot of confidence because the people who do what I do don't have the necessary tools, processes, and support that are needed to be successful.

NOTABLE PROJECTS

If you look around the campus, we've basically touched every school. I'll just highlight some unique projects.

Graduate School of Business
The Graduate School of Business is a collection of six buildings; it's a campus. It's quite spectacular, in my humble opinion. I like it very much. For two years, we tried to cobble together a plan to renovate some of the old GSB buildings and add a new one. It just was not working. So, we took this big step to build an entirely

new campus, here in the central campus, and a donor was excited about an entirely new campus within the larger campus.

We started working on this concept, and then all of a sudden, the great recession hit. We had basically negotiated all the deals, we had a GMP [guaranteed maximum price] and we had started. Everybody was panicking. There had been a 35 percent correction within weeks, and many of the companies in the Valley were stopping capital expenditures. I said, "We have a choice to make. We can stop or we can move forward." I thought that we should try and renegotiate the deals, because for contractors, having a job at a reduced number is better than not having a job.

So that's what we did; we went back and renegotiated all the deals. Remember what I said earlier: it's a relationship business. I basically said, "I'm here for you in these difficult times. I expect you to be there for me when I have difficult times." And it worked. We saved over $20 million renegotiating those deals and that felt really good. The contractors came out okay. They didn't make a lot of money—they probably just broke even. What they wanted to do was to keep their people employed.

Science and Engineering Quad

Another big highlight I would say is the Science and Engineering Quad (SEQ). That was unique, because John had the vision to put together a series of fundamental partners, donors, that were interested in engineering, but beyond engineering, they were interested and passionate about the university in and of itself. John allowed us at Land and Buildings to think big and come up with a four-building plan, essentially to extend the quadrangles.

Frederick Law Olmsted's original plan for the university had a series of quads.[140] There was the central quad with the Oval and the big ceremonial entry, but he also envisioned that the quads would extend east–west. It didn't turn out that way. What is now the Science and Engineering Quad was a collection of haphazard physics buildings and very low density. John gave us the opportunity to think bigger about it. We went back to the original Olmsted plan and designed a quad, essentially copying what Olmsted had set out to do. I think that's why John likes it. Not just because it's engineering, but because we were returning to the founding principles of the institution. The first building we did was Y2E2, and that was forward thinking and a leader in sustainable design. I think John was very proud of that.

Arts District

John's advocacy for the arts district was one example that I found to be very refreshing. Here is an engineer, a business-person, a really driving, enthusiastic individual, and he turns to the arts. I didn't expect that and was so pleased that he did. He made a big difference in getting that arts district off the ground; he spent a lot of time on that.

We were fortunate enough to have donors in Peter Bing and Burt McMurtry, who wanted to do a world-class concert hall and a replacement building for art history and art making. Today I look at the Bing Concert Hall and the McMurtry art history/art making building as two examples of buildings and aesthetics that really challenged us and went counter to our standard approach to design. If you think about the arts, why shouldn't they challenge the norms? The Bing Concert Hall is this elongated oval that I can argue fits with the surrounding architecture, but it's not a stone building that's a rectangle or a square. The McMurtry Building is a good example of contemporary architecture with irregular forms, metal materials, and very porous openings to connect to the exterior. It sits next to the Cantor Art Museum, one of the earliest buildings on the campus, a very regular form, made of stone and concrete with a monumental entrance.

Another building that was located in the arts district was the Anderson Collection building. This building was designed and built specifically for a collection of mid-century modern art donated to the university by the Anderson family. It is a tremendous collection and one that further cemented the arts district as a destination.

Ultimately, we were able to build a collection of three additional buildings located in close proximity that then felt like a place unique to our culture and environment. A true district.

The Bing Concert Hall, pictured here at dusk in 2013, was one of three new arts bulldings constructed at Stanford during John Hennessy's presidency.

Stanford benefactor Peter Bing speaking at the opening night of Bing Concert Hall in 2013.

School of Medicine and Hospitals

The children's hospital, the adult hospital, and the School of Medicine all reside on the western side of Campus Drive. There's a physical divide there. There was also a bit of a management divide. The two hospitals are wholly owned subsidiaries of the institution; however, they have their own boards. Sometimes it's challenging. They prioritize research and medicine, which is fantastic, and they happen to be conveniently located near engineering and the basic sciences, which is fantastic, too. The Medical School is in a location where all that collaboration can occur.

The hospitals are providing services, and they're a business. They want to optimize around their decisions, which sometimes are counter to what we think is appropriate. I'm carefully saying that there are tensions. They are different organizations and have different objectives. That's always been difficult, but Phil Pizzo was a good leader. He brought people together, and we built a number of buildings for Phil and his team. The great thing about the medical center is the buildings are quite dense, which I appreciate. We're not wasting space.

Big challenges occurred from 2009 to 2011 when we had to go to the city of Palo Alto, where the hospitals reside, for approvals. Most of the campus resides in a different jurisdiction, unincorporated Santa Clara County, even though you'd think it would be the same. These town-gown relationship issues are always challenging. We have a long history. We needed to get approval for 1.3 million square feet of new additional buildings. Individual jurisdictions look at Stanford as one big Stanford, not separate entities. So, we had to essentially tell the hospitals that my organization had to manage the approvals through the city of Palo Alto.

It was difficult, because I believe in data-driven decisions. If I can prove I'm right, then you should agree with me and we should move forward. Guess what? This is local, local politics. It's very challenging. It took three years to get that approved and a lot of battle scars along the way. The good news is, they were able to build their hospitals, and they opened them in November 2019.

Energy Delivery System

One of the most interesting, challenging, and inspiring things that we accomplished—and now it's somewhat controversial—is we transformed our energy delivery system. It cost $500 million. The problem statement was: What do you do with an aging plant that's coming to the end of its useful life? At the time, we hired a new person in my group to come up with a plan but also to think about climate change, greenhouse gases, and how we could improve our position as a leader in reducing our carbon footprint. He came back with a proposal to essentially abandon the existing central energy plant and build a new one on the western part of campus. It's called a heat recovery system, and it recovers the rejected heat and puts it back into the building systems as needed.

John and I had some very interesting meetings about this. The business case was we would save money over a forty-year period—the life of the facility—by a significant amount, as opposed to replacing the existing plant with the same type of technology. We went with a different type of system because we could make the economic argument.

It was very difficult, because it was a significant capital investment, and we had a couple of faculty members who didn't think it was going to work. You have these renowned thermodynamic engineers/faculty members at one of the best institutions in the country arguing against our approach and my people. It was a tough road, but we got through it. We convinced John that we were on the right path. So, we invested $500 million. We built this system, and we've reduced our greenhouse gases tremendously. That, coupled with developing two solar arrays in the California desert, will drop our GHGs [greenhouse gases] next year by 82 percent from the peak in 2011. It's huge. We've surpassed every policymaker's target to reduce greenhouse gases, and we're really proud of that.

That said, in the summer of 2019, we had these extreme weather events. We had ten days when we couldn't provide sufficient chilled water capacity, so some researchers lost some research. That was a significant issue. When we made the business case, we talked about N+1 redundancy, and we decided—John included—that we were not going to buy extra chilled water capacity. We were going to move forward with what we had. We've always curtailed in the summer. We've always been down a few days a year; it's not a big deal.

Well, new leadership comes in, and the faculty can't accept any curtailment. So, now we're going to spend another $80 million to get additional chilled water capacity. The system works exactly how it's supposed to. It's just we've had these weird weather events, really humid nights. If I could redo one decision, I would've put some extra capacity in very early on, and the economic case would still be beneficial compared to business as usual, but not as beneficial. Anyway, that particular system and that particular implementation is one of the proudest things I've ever been associated with. It was tremendous.

New Campuses

Second campuses I view as very, very difficult because the faculty want to be at ground zero. We have faculty who are leading in their fields, and they want to be here. I find it hard to believe we can actually open up a second campus unless it has a defined scope with a defined set of outcomes, which we did for New York.

My understanding was that Michael Bloomberg came to John Hennessy and said, "We want Stanford to open up a facility in New York City. New York has the brightest minds in finance, great in the arts, but lacking technology." John got excited; he's from New York. We started to think about it, started to pursue it. It became a competition with a $100 million incentive. While John was working with the faculty to do this, the general counsel and I were trying to negotiate a deal with New York City to get this $100 million incentive. It was a drop in the bucket. I estimated $2 billion to do what we wanted to do and negotiate a ground lease with them. Plus, the $100 million had so many strings attached to it, we were never going to get it.

Through that very difficult process, it became extremely clear that we were going to be considered just another tenant in their city. They just didn't understand that we were taking this huge risk to our brand and taking a risk with our faculty. And the campus would have been on Roosevelt Island; you're kind of isolated out there. So, the general counsel and I reported back to say, "This just doesn't feel right." After working with the faculty, I think John realized that this may not be the best outcome for Stanford. So, we came to the same decision not to pursue the New York campus from different angles.

I just finished a big Redwood City campus that I worked on for thirteen years under John. That's another huge accomplishment, because when I first started here, we had two million square feet approved, but the politics were really difficult. We recognized that we needed a pressure relief valve, so I started working on acquiring land. I acquired land seven miles away in Redwood City in 2005, and it was 2019 before we could move into the campus. We moved 2,700 people, all administrative functions, off the core campus so we can dedicate the core campus lands to pure academics. I think that's something that we'll do more of, I hope.

Future Challenges

The challenges we face are housing stock and a housing crisis—pricing is crazy—and transportation systems, which are really a mess because there's been so much rapid job growth from the tech companies. Those two things are very concerning. The third and most important one is getting approval to grow. We just exited a five-year general use permit process—three years of it a public process—where we couldn't get the deal done. There was no way we were going to get a favorable outcome. So, like New York, we exited. We did everything humanly possible, but it's politics. The cards were stacked against us in this environment where we're viewed as a very rich university with lots of resources and where there's a political minefield. They don't want to support the growth of the university because there's too much growth in the area overall.

I'm hopeful that in the next five to seven years we'll be able to get something done. In the meantime, we're going to use this time to become more efficient on campus because we only have 200,000 square feet of allowed growth. So, we're going to start thinking creatively about how we better manage the space that we do have.

Reflections on John Hennessy and Leadership

The leader of the university is so very important to many different constituencies: the faculty, the students—undergrad and grad students, PhDs, postdocs—as well as two hospitals and the community. You've got to be a very special person. Quite frankly, I don't know how university leaders do it. It's 24/7; it never stops. I would never do it.

I think John came at a perfect time. He was a really strong leader. He drove you pretty hard, but you knew where you stood. I like that style. I could be open and transparent with him, and he was open and direct with me. I think we were a good team. He's a little intimidating; he's so smart. But I respect him, and I've learned a lot from him.

Etchemendy was tremendous, too. They were a great team. They were very different people, and they were a great team together. There's something there with John and John that I hope people can capture somehow in the future. It's not just about John Hennessy or John Etchemendy, but that team. It was a great time.

My observation over the years—and I think it's unique to Stanford—is that if a faculty member had a really good idea and they could get John and John excited about it, they would support it. There were five pillars established by John and John early on. I think the faculty recognized that they could gain support if they were in one of those five buckets. We're a pretty distributed university, not a lot of command and control centrally. These creative, smart faculty members would be working on a research project, come up with something really interesting, and move it up the chain. It's ground up, I guess I would call it.

As a leader in Land and Buildings, when you're designing and delivering a product that everybody feels and touches and comes in contact with, you need to be aware of what the environment is around you. You need to be aware, but you cannot be subject to the whims of individuals. You've got to be able to have confidence to tell the story of why it fits. Why is it important that we're doing these things? I think confidence is so important. You've got to build confidence incrementally, and you've got to build your team.

I've hired some really good people, and I've inherited really good people. I view my job as supporting them and giving them a long rope to go do what they need to do. I'm not saying it's the perfect way to do it; it's just what I do, and it seems to work out pretty well. These people are creative; they're motivated; they want to do good work. I've been very fortunate to have really good people around me, and I think John has benefited from having good people around him.

APPENDIX

TABLE A1. STANFORD STUDENT POPULATION (2000 VS. 2016)

STUDENTS	ALL SCHOOLS/ UNITS	EARTH	EDUCATION	ENGINEERING	GSB	H&S	LAW	MEDICINE
UNDER-GRADS	6,554 (2000) 7,032 (2016)							
GRADUATES[1]	6,753 (2000) 7,931 (2016)	203 (2000) 278 (2016)	280 (2000) 265 (2016)	2,657 (2000) 3,089 (2016)	853 (2000) 989 (2016)	1,510 (2000) 1,663 (2016)	550 (2000) 650 (2016)	700 (2000) 924 (2016)
TGR[2]	947 (2000) 1,373 (2016)	21 (2000) 78 (2016)	48 (2000) 47 (2016)	308 (2000) 434 (2016)	13 (2000) 23 (2016)	448 (2000) 623 (2016)	35 (2000) 18 (2016)	73 (2000) 150 (2016)
POSTDOC-TORAL SCHOLARS[3]	1,281 (2000) 2,297 (2016)	14 (2000) 67 (2016)	5 (2000) 19 (2016)	61 (2000) 364 (2016)		179 (2000) 435 (2016)		1,022 (2000) 1,355 (2016)
GRAD NON-MATRICU-LATED[4]	664 (2000) 1,003 (2016)	3 (2016)	4 (2016)	520 (2000) 655 (2016)	9 (2016)	18 (2000) 80 (2016)	1 (2000) 6 (2016)	125 (2000) 168 (2016)
MISC/OTHER	29 (2000) 2 (2016)							
TOTAL	16,228 (2000) 19,638 (2016)							

Sources: Stanford Population Report, 2000 (FY2001); Stanford Population Report, 2016 (FY2017) – Stanford Office of Institutional Research and Decision Support.
1 Graduate totals for 2016 include 73 Master of Liberal Arts students in Stanford Continuing Studies.
2 TGR (terminal graduate registration) typically designates PhD students who have finished their coursework and are working on their dissertations. Totals for 2000 include one student categorized as Other.
3 Post-doc totals for 2016 include 57 postdoctoral scholars at the SLAC National Accelerator Laboratory.
4 Grad non-matriculated totals for 2016 include 78 students and visiting researchers categorized as Other.

TABLE A2. STANFORD ENDOWMENT MARKET VALUE (2000 VS. 2016)

	ENDOWMENT MARKET VALUE (IN THOUSANDS)	MERGED POOL ANNUAL NOMINAL RATE OF RETURN	MERGED POOL ANNUAL REAL RATE OF RETURN
2000/01	8,249,551	-7.3%	-9.6%
2001/02	7,612,769	-2.6%	-3.7%
2002/03	8,613,805	8.8%	7.2%
2003/04	9,922,041	18.0%	15.4%
2004/05	12,205,035	19.5%	17.0%
2005/06	14,084,676	19.5%	16.2%
2006/07	17,164,836	23.4%	20.7%
2007/08	17,214,373	6.2%	4.0%
2008/09	12,619,094	-25.9%	-27.1%
2009/10	13,851,115	14.4%	13.4%
2010/11	16,502,606	22.4%	20.0%
2011/12	17,035,804	1.0%	-0.7%
2012/13	18,688,868	12.2%	10.8%
2013/14	21,446,006	16.8%	15.2%
2014/15	22,222,957	7.0%	6.0%
2015/16	22,398,130	-0.4%	-1.6%

Sources: Endowment Market Value and Merged Pool Rate of Return (2000/01 through 2014/15), Stanford University Budget Plan 2016/17; Endowment Market Value and Merged Pool Rate of Return (2001/02 through 2015/16), Stanford University Budget Plan 2017/18

NOTES

Introduction

1. The A. M. Turing Award is an annual prize given by the Association for Computing Machinery for contributions of lasting and major technical importance to the computer field. It is generally recognized as the highest distinction in computer science, or the "Nobel Prize of Computing."
2. See Tables A1 and A2 in the Appendix for more details.
3. Stanford ChEM-H brings together chemists, engineers, biologists, and clinicians to understand life at a molecular level and apply that knowledge to improving human health.
4. Gerhard Casper served as the ninth president of Stanford University, from 1992 to 2000. He is the Bing Professor in Undergraduate Education, Emeritus at Stanford University.
5. Bio-X is Stanford's pioneering interdisciplinary biosciences institute, bringing together biomedical and life science researchers, clinicians, engineers, physicists, and computational scientists to unlock the secrets of the human body.

Chapter 1: John Hennessy

6. Steven Chu is the William R. Kenan Jr. Professor of Physics and professor of molecular and cellular physiology at Stanford University. He served as U.S. secretary of energy (2009–2013) under President Barack Obama. He won the 1997 Nobel Prize in Physics for his work on the cooling and trapping of atoms with laser light.
7. The Campaign for Undergraduate Education (2001–2006) raised over $1.1 billion to fund undergraduate education programs at Stanford University.
8. Condoleezza Rice joined the Stanford faculty in political science in 1981; she served as the university's provost from 1993 to 1999. She was the

national security advisor (2001–2005) and secretary of state of the United States (2005–2009) under President George W. Bush. She is currently a senior fellow on public policy and the director of the Hoover Institution.

9.   Martha Marsh served as president and CEO of Stanford Hospital & Clinics from 2002 to 2010. Prior to joining Stanford, Marsh served in hospital leadership positions at University of California Davis Medical Center, University of Pennsylvania Health System, and Dartmouth-Hitchcock Medical Center.

10. With its cancer center designations, the National Cancer Institute recognizes cancer centers that meet "rigorous standards for transdisciplinary, state-of-the-art research focused on developing new and better approaches to preventing, diagnosing, and treating cancer." The Stanford Cancer Institute (SCI) became an NCI Designated Cancer Center in 2007 and a Comprehensive Cancer Center in 2016.

11. Mariann Byerwalter served as chairman of the Board of Directors of Stanford Hospital & Clinics from 2006 to 2013. She also served three terms on the Stanford Board of Trustees between 1992 and 2012.

12. David Kennedy is the Donald J. McLachlan Professor of History, Emeritus at Stanford University and the former director of the Bill Lane Center for the American West. He won the 2000 Pulitzer Prize for History for his book, *Freedom from Fear: The American People in Depression and War, 1929–1945*.

Jack N. Rakove is the W. R. Coe Professor of History and American Studies and professor of political science at Stanford University, where he has taught since 1980. He won the 1997 Pulitzer Prize for History and the 1998 Cox Book Prize for his book *Original Meanings: Politics and Ideas in the Making of the Constitution*.

Chapter 2: John Etchemendy

13. The cat food model is an analogy about incentives. It suggests that while it is difficult to dictate the behavior of cats (or humans), one can influence their behavior to some degree by changing where the cat food (or some other incentive) is placed.

14. The Budget Group serves as an advisory committee to the provost and works to determine budget priorities as appropriate for the financial health of the university. It includes the provost, staff members from the University Budget Office, senior-level faculty, and executive staff from various university organizations.

15. Title IX is a federal civil rights law in the United States that was passed as part of the Education Amendments of 1972. Title IX stated that "No person in the United States shall, on the basis of sex, be excluded from participation in, be denied the benefits of, or be subjected to discrimination under any education program or activity receiving Federal financial assistance."

16. FERPA refers to the Family Educational Rights and Privacy Act (20 U.S.C. § 1232g; 34 CFR Part 99). This federal law protects the privacy of student education records.

Chapter 3: Jeff Wachtel

17. Isabelle Raubitschek, a scholar of classical Greek and Roman archaeology, was a lecturer and faculty member in the Departments of Art and Classics at Stanford from 1966 until her death in 1988.
18. Philip Zimbardo joined the faculty of the Department of Psychology in 1968.
19. Robin (Hamill) Kennedy is a Stanford alumna who served as the director of Real Estate, Land Use, and Transportation programs and as a member of the Office of Stanford's General Counsel. She and Donald Kennedy, Stanford's eighth president, married in 1987.
20. Marsh McCall is professor of classics, emeritus and has been a faculty member since 1976.
21. Donald Kennedy, a neurobiologist who joined the Stanford faculty in 1960, served as Stanford's eighth president from 1980 to 1992. From 1977 to 1979, he served as commissioner of the U.S. Food and Drug Administration. He was the editor in chief of *Science* from 2000 to 2008.
22. William J. Perry is the Michael and Barbara Berberian Professor Emeritus at Stanford and a senior fellow at the Freeman Spogli Institute and the Hoover Institution. He serves as director of the Preventive Defense Project at FSI's Center for International Security and Cooperation. He served as U.S. secretary of defense from 1994 to 1997 during the Clinton administration.
23 Karl Deisseroth is the D. H. Chen Professor of Bioengineering and of Psychiatry and Behavioral Sciences. He is a member of Bio-X and the Wu Tsai Neurosciences Institute.

    Marc Tessier-Lavigne, a world leader in the study of brain development and repair, became Stanford University's eleventh president in 2016. He served in senior leadership positions at Genentech, Inc. from 2003 to 2011 and as the president of the Rockefeller University from 2011 to 2016. From 2001 to 2005, he was a faculty member in the Stanford Department of Biological Sciences.
24. As a result of Stanford's technology licensing agreement with Google, the university received $15.7 million in 2004 and $336 million in 2005 when it liquidated its equity in the company.
25. Dmitry Medvedev served as president of Russia from 2008 to 2012 and prime minister from 2012 to 2020. David Miliband served as the UK's secretary of state for foreign and commonwealth affairs from 2007 to 2010.
26. Steve Jobs co-founded Apple Computer in 1976 and served as CEO from 1997 until 2011.

27. Located at Stanford University, the Hoover Institution is a public policy think tank promoting the principles of individual, economic, and political freedom. While it has its own board of overseers, its director reports jointly to the president and provost of the university. Donald Rumsfeld served as secretary of defense from 1975 to 1977 under President Gerald Ford and again from 2001 to 2006 under President George W. Bush.
28. The Anderson Collection is a gift of modern and contemporary art donated to Stanford University by Harry W. Anderson, Mary Margaret Anderson, and Mary Patricia Anderson Pence, the Bay Area family who acquired it over the course of five decades. The Bing Concert Hall was named after Stanford alumnus Peter Bing and his wife, Helen Bing. They donated $50 million to Stanford University to build a world-class concert hall that provides a premier venue for both artists and audiences on the Stanford campus.
29. James Rosse served as Stanford's eighth provost from 1984 to 1992.
30. Steve Denning and Roberta Bowman Denning provided a gift of $50 million to construct Denning House, a building that serves as the convening hub for Knight-Hennessy Scholars.

Chapter 4: Isaac Stein

31. The members of the presidential search committee that named John Hennessy as president were: trustees – Robert M. Bass, James R. Ukropina (chair); Roger A. Clay Jr.; Burton J. McMurtry; Denise M. O'Leary; Pamela A. Rymer; and Isaac Stein; faculty – John Etchemendy (deputy chair), Pamela Karlan, Jeffrey Koseff, Sharon Long, Lucy Shapiro, and Claude Steele; alumnus Warren Lyons; staff member Michael Hindery; and students Kristin Torres and Kaleb Michaud.
32. Dwight D. Eisenhower was president of the United States from 1953 to 1961. He was a five-star general and commanded the Allied Forces in Europe during World War II.
33. Robert M. Bass is an entrepreneur, investor, and philanthropist who served as chair of Stanford's Board of Trustees from 1996 to 2000 and as a member of the board for five terms spanning the years 1989 to 2018. He has also served as a director and chairman of the Stanford Management Company, the office that invests Stanford's endowment and other financial assets to provide long-term support to the university.
34. Michael Bloomberg was mayor of New York City from 2002 to 2013.

Chapter 5: Leslie Hume

35. Peter Stansky, an expert in the field of modern British history, is the Frances and Charles Field Professor of History, Emeritus.

36. The Michelle R. Clayman Institute for Gender Research empowers students and scholars by conducting and investing in intersectional gender research; mentoring students through fellowships and internships; and inspiring, translating, and amplifying gender scholarship. The institute was founded in 1974 as the Stanford Center for Research on Women (CROW).
37. John H. Scully is the former managing director and founding partner of SPO Partners. He served on the Stanford University Board of Trustees from 2000 to 2010.
38. Opened in 2015, the McMurtry Building houses the Department of Art & Art History, containing state-of-the-art studios, screening and gallery spaces, classrooms, and the Art and Architecture Library. Former chair of Stanford's Board of Trustees, Burt McMurtry and his wife, Deedee McMurtry, donated $30 million to fund its construction.
39. Jim Canales is president and trustee of the Barr Foundation. He served on the Board of Trustees from 2006 to 2015.

Chapter 6: Steve Denning

40. The Freeman Spogli Institute for International Studies is Stanford's premier research institute for the study of international affairs and is a hub for Stanford scholars who want to work across disciplines on research that has international impact. The Precourt Institute for Energy focuses on energy research and education, from basic science and technology to policy and business.
41. Christine Hazy is co-founder of the Sketch Foundation, which awards grants to charitable organizations that address compelling needs of children, youth, and families. She served as a trustee from 2008 to 2018. Linda Meier is an active fundraiser and community volunteer. She served as a trustee of Stanford University from 1984 to 1994. In 2001, she received the Degree of Uncommon Woman, the university's most prestigious award for alumni, for her manifold contributions to Stanford.
42. Chuck Feeney is a businessman and philanthropist who made his fortune launching duty-free shops in airports and achieved his lifelong goal of giving his fortune away, donating an estimated $8 billion to charities, foundations, and universities. Cornell announced Feeney's $350 million gift to support a tech campus in New York City in December 2011. Feeney, through his foundation Atlantic Philanthropies, was also a major donor to Stanford, supporting the Center for Clinical Sciences Research, the Stanford Cancer Center, and the Clark Center with multimillion-dollar gifts.
43. Philip H. Knight (MBA, 1962) is a philanthropist, American businessman, and co-founder of Nike Inc. He contributed $400 million for the Knight-Hennessy Scholars Program.
    Robert E. King (MBA 1960) and Dorothy J. King are investment

management experts and the co-founders of King Philanthropies. Their $100 million gift to the program funds scholars from less economically developed regions of the world and supports the King Global Leadership Program, a training curriculum in which all Knight-Hennessy Scholars participate.

44. SLAC is the acronym for the Stanford Linear Accelerator Center. In 2008, the lab changed its name to SLAC National Accelerator Laboratory.

Chapter 7: Jim Plummer

45. After receiving his PhD from Stanford, Jim Gibbons joined the Engineering faculty in 1957. He served as the Frederick Emmons Terman Dean of Engineering from 1984 to 1996.

46. Eric Roberts, the Charles Simonyi Professor of Engineering, Emeritus, joined the Stanford faculty in 1990. He was the associate chair and director of undergraduate studies for the Department of Computer Science from 1990 to 2002 and senior associate dean of the School of Engineering from 2001 to 2003. Mehran Sahami is the James and Ellenor Chesebrough Professor in the School of Engineering and Professor (Teaching) in the Department of Computer Science. He has served as associate chair for education in the department since 2007.

47. David Kelley is the David W. Whittier Professor in Mechanical Engineering. His work is rooted in the Design Thinking methodology, which begins with assessing user needs and involves taking an iterative prototyping and storytelling approach to developing solutions.

48. The d.school is the commonly used parlance for the Hasso Plattner Institute of Design. Despite its nickname, it is not a separate school but is situated administratively within the School of Engineering.

49. Hasso Plattner, co-founder of SAP, donated $35 million to establish the d.school.

50. Thomas Byers has been a professor in the School of Engineering since 1995 and is the faculty director of the Stanford Technology Ventures Program.

51. The Offices of the President and Provost are located in Building 10.

Chapter 8: Bob Joss

52. Robert L. Joss commenced a banking career at Wells Fargo in 1971, rising to vice chairman in 1986. He became the CEO of Westpac Bank in Australia in 1993.

53. The Wharton School is the business school at the University of Pennsylvania.

54. The Biodesign Innovation course was launched in 2002 by Paul Yock, a faculty member in Medicine and Mechanical Engineering, and Josh Ma-

kower of the School of Medicine. GSB faculty involvement followed soon after.

55. Lecturers at GSB are nonacademic teaching staff who have industry experience and are contracted to teach.

56. J. E. Wallace Sterling was the president of Stanford University from 1948 to 1968 and Stanford's chancellor from 1968 to 1985.

57. The "Higher Education for Business" report, commonly known as the Gordon-Howell Report, was published in 1959. Written by economists James Edwin Howell and Robert Aaron Gordon, it was highly critical of existing standards in business education.

58. Ernest C. Arbuckle was dean of Stanford Graduate School of Business from 1958 to 1968, when it rose to prominence as one of the best business schools in the United States. He left Stanford to serve as chairman of Wells Fargo from 1968 to 1977.

59. Ezra Solomon, a key figure in the modern understanding of financial management, came to Stanford in 1961. He was the founding director of the International Center for the Advancement of Management Education (ICAME) and a professor of finance until his death in 2003. George Leland Bach joined the GSB faculty as a professor of economics and public policy in 1966. The first dean of Carnegie Mellon's Graduate School of Industrial Management, he is considered one of the outstanding influential figures in the evolution of American business education. A founding faculty member of Carnegie Mellon's Graduate School of Industrial Management, organizational theorist James G. March joined the Stanford faculty in 1970. A pioneer in the field of organizational behavior, Harold J. (Hal) Leavitt joined the Stanford faculty in 1966. Alex Bavelas, a psychosociologist who played a central role in formalizing network theory in the academic field of management, also joined the GSB faculty in the 1960s.

60. D. H. Gruenfeld, *Acting with Power: Why We Are More Powerful Than We Believe*, 1st ed. (New York: Currency, 2019.)

61. John W. Gardner served as the secretary of the Department of Health, Education, and Welfare in the Johnson administration and played an important role in implementing social reforms such as Medicare. He was a staunch advocate for civic engagement and public service. Gardner served on the Stanford Board of Trustees from 1968 to 1982, and, in 1989, he joined the Stanford faculty as the Miriam and Peter Haas Centennial Professor in Public Service. He taught a leadership course at the GSB toward the end of his life.

Chapter 9: Phil Pizzo

62. The Li Ka Shing Center for Learning and Knowledge brings together cutting-edge medicine, modern education, and advanced technology to help aspiring doctors practice life-saving skills in the safety of realistic simulations.

63. The phrase "operate on their own bottoms" or a "a tub on its own bottom" is a commonly used phrase at Stanford. It refers to the fact that some schools are meant to operate independently in terms of finances.

64. Jennifer Cochran is Shriram Chair of the Department of Bioengineering, professor of bioengineering and, by courtesy, chemical engineering. In her research, she employs interdisciplinary approaches in chemistry, engineering, and biophysics to study complex biological systems and develop new tools for basic science and biomedical applications.

65. Li Ka Shing is a philanthropist who made his fortune as a business magnate in Hong Kong.

66. The Stanford Byers Center for Biodesign is an institute dedicated to educating and empowering health technology innovators and leading the transition to a value-driven innovation ecosystem.

    SPARK is an institute that provides access to specialized knowledge and technical expertise regarding drug and diagnostic development, dedicated core laboratory facilities, and sources of funding to support translational efforts.

67. The Stanford Cancer Institute is dedicated to translating Stanford discoveries into individualized cancer care.

    The Stanford Institute for Stem Cell Biology and Regenerative Medicine is devoted to exploring how stem cells are created, the mechanisms by which they are regulated, and how they devolve into specialized cells, with the ultimate goal of translating this knowledge into new medical therapies.

    The California Institute for Regenerative Medicine is dedicated to accelerating stem cell treatments to patients with unmet medical needs. Irving Weissman is the director of the Stanford Institute for Stem Cell Biology and Regenerative Medicine, the Virginia and D. K. Ludwig Professor for Clinical Investigation in Cancer Research, professor of developmental biology, and by courtesy, of biology.

Chapter 10: Pam Matson

68. Ward Woods graduated from Stanford University in 1964. He served on Stanford's Board of Trustees from 1996 to 2006 and is a former chair of the Stanford Management Company's Board of Directors.

    Jay Precourt earned bachelor's and master's degrees from Stanford in petroleum engineering and went on to have a successful career in the oil and gas industry. He has extensive experience as a board member of publicly traded companies in the industry.

    Barton "Buzz" Thompson is the Robert E. Paradise Professor in Natural Resources Law. A global expert on water and natural resources, he focuses on how to improve resource management through legal, institutional, and technological innovation.

Franklin "Lynn" Orr was the Chester Naramore Dean of the School of Earth Sciences from 1994 to 2002. He has been a member of the Stanford faculty since 1985 and holds the Keleen and Carlton Beal Chair of Petroleum Engineering in the Department of Energy Resources Engineering. He served as undersecretary for science and energy at the U.S. Department of Energy from December 2014 to January 2017.

69. Dan and Rae Emmett made a $10 million gift to endow E-IPER and a subsequent $7.1 million gift to further develop the institute. Dan Emmett earned his bachelor's degree from Stanford and is chairman of the board of directors of Douglas Emmett Inc., a company that owns and operates commercial and residential real estate properties.

70. Perry McCarty is the Silas H. Palmer Professor, Emeritus in the Department of Civil and Environmental Engineering. He has been a faculty member since 1962 and helped develop Stanford's environmental engineering and science program. He served as department chair from 1980 to 1985 and as director of the Western Region Hazardous Substance Research Center from 1989 to 2002.

Nobel Prize–winning economist Kenneth Arrow (1921–2017) was professor of economics, statistics, and operations research at Stanford from 1949 to 1968 and from 1979 until his retirement in 1991. In addition to his pioneering work on economic theory, he co-authored the 1997 "Economists' Statement on Climate Change" about the risks of global warming and co-authored many papers with biologists, environmentalists, and other experts on the topic of sustainability and ethics.

Harold "Hal" Mooney is the Paul S. Achilles Professor of Environmental Biology, Emeritus, in the Department of Biology. A pioneer in the field of physiological ecology, he is an internationally recognized expert on environmental sciences. His research focuses on how plant species and groups of species respond to their environments.

Chapter 11: Deborah Stipek

71. The Haas Center for Public Service inspires Stanford University to realize a just and sustainable world through service, scholarship, and community partnerships.

Head Start began in 1965 as a federal program targeting low-income, preschool-aged children and their families for comprehensive education, health, and parenting services.

The Corinne Seeds University Elementary School, now the UCLA Lab School, is an innovative school for children ages four through twelve and is part of the UCLA Graduate School of Education & Information Studies.

The Urban Education Studies Center is where nationally recognized scholars work together with educators and administrators to foster a better schooling system for California children.

72. The John W. Gardner Center for Youth and Their Communities aims to bring together a variety of community groups and government agencies, in addition to schools, that impact the health, emotions, social connections, and safety of youth, as well as their education.

     Milbrey McLaughlin is the David Jacks Professor of Higher Education and Public Policy, Emerita at Stanford University. She is the director of the John W. Gardner Center for Youth and Their Communities and director of the Center for Research on the Context of Teaching.

73. John Levin co-founded the San Francisco–based law firm Folger & Levin and served as its chairman and managing partner for nearly thirty years. He has an MA in education from Stanford and a JD from Stanford University Law School. He served as a trustee from 1999 to 2009.

     Madeline Stein is an active fundraiser and community volunteer.

74. Phil Halperin is the president of the Silver Giving Foundation and is the chairman of the San Francisco School Alliance Foundation Board. He is a member of the National Advisory Board of the Haas Center for Public Service.

75. Dan Schwartz is the Nomellini-Olivier Professor of Educational Technology and is the James Quillen Dean of the Graduate School of Education.

76. Linda Darling-Hammond is the Charles E. Ducommun Professor of Education, Emeritus at Stanford University. She was the founding president of the Learning Policy Institute and has been an influential figure in U.S. education policy and practice, especially in the areas of school restructuring, teacher education, and educational equity.

     Aspire was founded in 1998 with the mission of opening and operating small, high-quality, college-prep charter schools in low-income neighborhoods. Aspire now has thirty-six community-based schools serving over 15,300 students in California.

77. Stanford New Schools was a nonprofit public benefit corporation that partnered with the Stanford University School of Education to sponsor East Palo Alto Academy (EPAA), a K–12 elementary and high school chartered by the Ravenswood City School District.

78. Jonathan Osborne is professor emeritus in the Graduate School of Education. His research focuses on policy and pedagogy related to science education.

79. The Stanford Center for Education Policy Analysis brings together scholars from various disciplines to obtain a better understanding of educational context, promote the innovative use of data, and engage in rigorous analysis to develop solutions to real-world problems. Scholars develop strategic partnerships with educational practitioners and engage with policymakers to ensure continuous improvement for all students.

     The Center to Support Excellence in Teaching (CSET) aims to solve persistent problems of practice by improving the quality of instruction, keeping instructional equity at the center of the work, and developing leading teachers.

80. Claude Steele, a social psychologist who joined the Stanford faculty in 1991, served as dean of the Graduate School of Education from 2011 to 2014. Since 2014 he has been the executive vice chancellor and provost at UC Berkeley. From 2009 to 2011, he was the provost of Columbia University.

Chapter 12: Larry Kramer

81. The co-chairs of the search committee were John Etchemendy and Dick Craswell.

82. Mark Kelman has been a professor in the Law School since 1982 and has served as vice dean since 2004.

83. John Sexton was the dean of New York University Law School at the time.

84. David Mills is professor of the practice of law. He teaches classes in criminal law and white-collar crime, and founded and served as the first director of the school's renowned Clinical Education program.

   Paul Brest is professor of law, emeritus and served as dean of the Law School from 1987 to 1999.

85. Professor of Law Lawrence C. Marshall was associate dean of Clinical Education and the David and Stephanie Mills Director of the Mills Legal Clinic from 2005 to 2013.

86. Elizabeth (Liz) Magill was the dean of Stanford Law School from 2012 to 2019.

87. Diane Chin is the associate dean for public service and public interest law and was the director of the John and Terry Levin Center for Public Service and Public Interest Law.

Chapter 13: Richard Saller

88. The "nine provosts" meeting included the provosts from Harvard, Yale, Princeton, Columbia, Penn, Cornell, the University of Chicago, Stanford, and MIT.

89. Richard Saller's wife, Tanya Luhrmann, was a chaired professor at the University of Chicago who had been elected to the American Academy of Arts and Sciences. John Etchemendy made it possible for the Department of Cultural and Social Anthropology to hire her.

90. Lloyd Minor is the Carl and Elizabeth Naumann Dean of Stanford University School of Medicine. He was the provost for Johns Hopkins University from 2009 to 2012.

91. Hanna Gray is professor of history, emerita at the University of Chicago.

She served as president of the University of Chicago from 1978 to 1993 and as provost of Yale University from 1974 to 1978.

Geoffrey Stone is a law professor at the University of Chicago, where he served as dean of the Law School from 1987 to 1994 and as provost from 1994 to 2002

92. Barry Weingast is the Ward C. Krebs Family Professor, Department of Political Science, and senior fellow at the Hoover Institution. He served as chair of the Department of Political Science from 1996 through 2001.

93. Adam Daniel is the vice provost for planning at the University of Virginia. He served as Stanford University's senior associate dean for Finance and Administration in the School of Humanities and Sciences from 2008 to 2016.

94. Gary S. Becker (1930–2014), Robert E. Lucas Jr., and James J. Heckman all received the Nobel Memorial Prize in Economic Sciences when they were faculty members at the University of Chicago.

95. Thomas Hansen is the Reliance-Dhirubhai Ambani Professor of Anthropology at Stanford University. He directed Stanford's Center for South Asia from 2010 to 2017.

96. This is still the case. In 2020, Stanford was still ranked number one in the world for arts and humanities.

97. The Stanford Institute for Economic Policy Research is Stanford University's thought leader for understanding the economic challenges, opportunities, and policies affecting people in the United States and around the world.

98. Chaitan Khosla is a professor of chemistry and chemical engineering at Stanford. He served as the Baker Family Director of Stanford ChEM-H from 2012 to 2020.

99. Carl Wieman was awarded the Nobel Prize in Physics in 2001. He holds a joint appointment in the Department of Physics and at the Graduate School of Education, where his current intellectual focus is on undergraduate physics and science education.

Alvin Roth is the Craig and Susan McCaw Professor of Economics at Stanford University and the Gund Professor of Economics and Business Administration, Emeritus at Harvard. His research focuses on game theory, experimental economics, and market design. He shared the 2012 Nobel Memorial Prize in Economics.

Chapter 14: John Bravman

100. MIPS is an acronym for microprocessor without interlocked pipeline stages, a system architecture that was a focus of John Hennessy's research at Stanford. In 1984, he founded MIPS Technologies to commercialize his work.

101. James Sheehan is Dickason Professor of the Humanities, Emeritus. He is a

scholar of German history and former chair of the Faculty Senate and the History Department.

102. Ramon Saldivar is a professor of English and comparative literature and the Hoagland Family Professor of Humanities and Sciences. He served as the vice provost of undergraduate education from 1994 to 1999. President Barack Obama awarded him the National Humanities Medal in 2012 and appointed him to a six-year term on the National Council on the Humanities in 2013.

103. Think Again was a component of the Campaign for Undergraduate Education aimed at reacquainting alumni with the university.

104. Alumnus Charles Schwab, a pioneer in the discount brokerage business, and his wife, Helen, have made many generous donations to Stanford, including a significant gift to construct the Schwab Residential Center for the Graduate School of Business.

   Jerry Yang is a computer programmer, internet entrepreneur, and venture capitalist. He is the co-founder and former CEO of Yahoo! Inc.

105. Jim Fox was an associate professor of anthropology at Stanford who specialized in historical linguistics and the languages of Native Americans. He died in 2019.

106. Robert Sinclair is the Charles M. Pigott Professor in the School of Engineering. As a materials science scholar, he studies microelectronic and magnetic thin film microstructure.

107. Stanford's undergraduate student enrollment was 6,366 in fall 2020; the average class had approximately 1,591 students.

108. John Hennessy has been married to Andrea Berti Hennessy since 1974.

Chapter 15: Harry Elam

109. Carlos Morton is a playwright and professor of theater at the University of California, Santa Barbara.

110. Students established the Committee on Black Performing Arts in 1969 as a cultural resource for Stanford and surrounding communities by hosting artists, creating master classes and workshops, and staging productions. The committee also published a literary journal, *Black Arts Quarterly*.

111. The Institute for Diversity in the Arts is an interdisciplinary program in the humanities in which students study culture, identity, and diversity through artistic expression. It merged with the Committee on Black Performing Arts (CBPA) in 2005. Its mission is to engage artists, students, and members of the local community to create performance and visual art that examines the intersections of race, diversity, and social action.

112. John Bender is the Jean G. and Morris M. Doyle Professor of Interdisciplinary Studies and professor of comparative literature, emeritus, at Stanford. As a scholar, he explores the relationship of literature to the visual

arts, philosophy and science, and the sociology of literature and critical theory.

Timothy Warner is vice provost for budget and auxiliaries management at Stanford University. He is responsible for overseeing the university's $6.5 billion annual operating budget and several line operations, including Residential and Dining Enterprises, Institutional Research and Decision Support, and the financial side of the Athletic Department.

113. The Haas Center for Public Service was established in 1985 to connect Stanford students with service-oriented opportunities. Service is an essential feature of a Stanford education, and the Haas Center facilitates this by coordinating community-based research programs, fellowships and internships, education partnerships, leadership programs, and distinguished visitor programs.

Chapter 17: Ann Arvin

114. The Stanford Center on Longevity was established in 2007. Its mission is to accelerate and implement scientific discoveries, technological advances, behavioral practices, and social norms to help people live healthy and rewarding lives well into old age.

The Center for Advanced Study in the Behavioral Sciences (CASBS) was established through a grant from the Ford Foundation; it began operations in 1954, inviting selected social science and other scholars for yearlong fellowships. It became part of Stanford University in 2008.

Scholars at the Wu Tsai Neurosciences Institute explore how the brain gives rise to mental life and behavior in states of both health and disease. It began as the Stanford Neurosciences Institute in 2013.

Chapter 18: Carla Shatz

115. James Spudich is the Douglass M. and Nola Leishman Professor of Cardiovascular Disease in the Department of Biochemistry in the School of Medicine. Lucy Shapiro is the Virginia and D. K. Ludwig Professor in the Department of Developmental Biology and director of the Beckman Center for Molecular and Genetic Medicine. Channing Robertson, a chemical engineer, is the Ruth G. and William K. Bowes Professor Emeritus in the School of Engineering. Charles H. Kruger Jr. (1934–2017) was a professor of mechanical engineering at Stanford. He served as the vice provost and dean of research from 1993 to 2003. Richard Zare is the Marguerite Blake Wilbur Professor of Natural Science in the Department of Chemistry.

116. Technology entrepreneur James Clark was an associate professor of electrical engineering at Stanford from 1979 to 1984 before starting several major technology companies, including as Silicon Graphics, Netscape, Healtheon, and Shutterfly.

117. MIT's Convergence Scholars Program cultivates an integrative vision of science and technology and provides postdoctoral trainees opportunities to further their experiences and skills beyond the research laboratory. The program, administered jointly by the Marble Center for Cancer Nanomedicine and the MIT Center for Precision Cancer Medicine, was founded in 2017.

118. Matthew P. Scott is professor of developmental biology, emeritus at Stanford University, and emeritus president of the Carnegie Institution for Science. He was the director of Bio-X from 2001 to 2007.

119. Dan McFarland is a professor in the Graduate School of Education. He studies the intellectual, social, and institutional dynamics of educational systems.

120. Sir Norman Foster is the founder and executive chairman of Foster + Partners, based in London. Foster + Partners also designed the Center for Clinical Science Research (CCSR) at Stanford. Appointed in 1995 and completed in 2000, CCSR integrated state-of-the art modular laboratory and office space.

121. William Newsome is the Harman Family Provostial Professor of Neurobiology in the School of Medicine and the Vincent V. C. Woo Director of the Wu Tsai Neurosciences Institute. As a renowned scholar in systems and cognitive neuroscience, he has advanced our understanding of the neural mechanisms underlying visual perception and simple forms of decision making.

122. Heideh Fattaey became the director of Bio-X operations and programs in 2004 and was promoted to executive director of Bio-X operations and programs in 2010. She has a PhD in biochemistry and molecular biology.

123. Stephen Quake is the Lee Otterson Professor of Bioengineering, professor of applied physics, and the co-president of the Chan Zuckerberg Biohub. He has invented new DNA sequencing technologies that have enabled rapid analysis of the human genome, microfluidic automation techniques that allow scientists to efficiently isolate individual cells and decipher their genetic code, and new diagnostic tools including the first noninvasive prenatal test for Down syndrome.

124. Launched in 2008, NeuroVentures focuses on stimulating and accelerating interdisciplinary research on the brain. It has helped develop new technologies and approaches requiring novel interdisciplinary collaborations between neuroscientists, engineers, physicists, and other members of the Stanford community.

125. In 2001, Clark had withheld $60 million from his originally pledged donation of $150 million to support the creation of Bio-X. Together with the $90 million he gave, this commitment of $60 million brought the total donation to up to the originally promised amount of $150 million.

126. The Innovative Medicines Accelerator is designed to speed the translation

of Stanford research discoveries into new medicines for everything from deadly diseases like cancer and COVID-19 to rare disorders overlooked by most pharmaceutical companies.

Chapter 19: Jeffrey Koseff

127. Widely recognized as one of the world's leading climate scientists, Stephen Schneider joined the Stanford faculty in 1992. He died in 2010 at the age of sixty-five. The book referenced is Stephen H. Schneider, *Global Warming: Are We Entering the Greenhouse Century?* Sierra Club Books, 1989.

128. Paul Ehrlich is the Bing Professor of Population Studies, Emeritus and president of the Center for Conservation Biology at Stanford. His research focuses on the dynamics of insect populations, the evolutionary interactions of plants and herbivores, the behavioral ecology of birds and reef fishes, and human cultural evolution.

129. The Stanford Woods Institute for the Environment's Environmental Venture Projects program provides seed grants of up to $200,000 for interdisciplinary research projects that seek to identify solutions to pressing problems of the environment and sustainability.

130. Valentina Zuin completed her PhD with the Emmett Interdisciplinary Program in Environment and Resources (E-IPER) at Stanford University in 2014.

131. The Stanford Realizing Environmental Impact Projects provides next stage funding to principal investigators to move existing interdisciplinary environmental research projects toward adoptable solutions and implementation by external stakeholders and partners.

132. E-IPER, the Emmett Interdisciplinary Program in Environment and Resources, develops the knowledge, skills, perspectives, and ways of thinking needed to understand and help solve the world's most significant environmental and resources sustainability challenges.

Nicole Ardoin is the Sykes Family Director of E-IPER in the School of Earth, Energy, and Environmental Sciences. She is an associate professor in the Graduate School of Education and a senior fellow in the Stanford Woods Institute for the Environment.

133. The Natural Capital Project aims to improve the well-being of people and the planet by motivating greater and more targeted investments in nature.

134. The Center for Ocean Solutions catalyzes research, innovation, and action to improve the health of the oceans.

The Center on Food Security and the Environment aims to generate innovative solutions to the persistent problems of global hunger, poverty, and environmental degradation through a focused research portfolio and an interdisciplinary team of scholars.

135. Initiated in 2011, the Stanford Rising Environmental Leadership Program helps graduate students and postdoctoral scholars hone their leadership and communications skills to maximize the impact of their research.
136. The David and Lucile Packard Foundation works with partners around the world to improve the lives of children, families, and communities—and to restore and protect the planet.
137. Jenna Davis is professor of civil and environmental engineering and the Higgins-Magid Senior Fellow at the Woods Institute for the Environment. Her scholarship sits at the nexus of water, economic development, and public health, particularly in low- and middle-income countries.

Chapter 20: Randy Livingston
138. Charles A. Holloway is the Kleiner Perkins Caulfield & Byers Professor of Management, Emeritus in the Graduate School of Business. At Stanford since 1968, he is a leader in the study and teaching of entrepreneurship, supply networks, and technology management.

Chapter 21: Bob Reidy
139. Curtis F. Feeny joined the Stanford Management Company in 1992 as executive vice president of real estate. When he left Stanford in 2000, he was executive vice president and director of university land and buildings.
140. Frederick Law Olmsted (1822–1903) was a pioneering figure in American landscape architecture.

INDEX

Photographs are indicated by an italicized page number. Notes material is indicated by the page number followed by "n" and the note number.

reflections on Hennessy,
328–330
as senior associate vice provost
of undergraduate education,
317–318
undergraduate curriculum,
323–324
Electrical Engineering Department (EE), 18, 19, 146, 149, 150
Emmett, Dan, 219, 469n69
Emmett, Rae, 219, 469n69
Emmett Interdisciplinary Program in Environment and Resources (E-IPER), 219–220, 402–403, 408, 411, 476n132
endowment
during global financial crisis, 44–46, 94–96, 126
for GSB, 175, 187, 188
management of, 422–426
per capita comparison to other universities, 286
for School of Medicine, 205
Stanford Endowment Market Value, x–xi, 459
energy delivery system, 450–452
entrepreneurial culture, xx, 110, 202, 245
Environmental Ventures Projects, 397–398, 400, 407–408
Escondido Village Graduate Residences, 339
Etchemendy, John W., *7, 33, 52, 68, 290*
PROVOST, xii, 33–54
built leadership team, 37–39
commentaries on, 121, 165, 200, 218, 221, 224, 227, 233, 245, 274–276, 283, 289, 297, 329, 332, 334, 351–352, 428,

445, 455
development of role as provost, 36–37, 52–54, 192–193
financial aid program, 47–48
funding for building projects, 43–44
during global financial crisis, 44–46, 113–114, 126–128, 224, 425
Hennessy's partnership with, 4–7, 27, 35–36, 38, 39–40, 47, 51–52, 74–75, 91–92, 107, 134–135, 136
incentive funds for diversity in hiring, 223
needs assessment process, 40–41, 91–94
press coverage of campus sexual assaults, 48–51
as recipient of Cuthbertson Award, 55
as senior associate dean for humanities and arts, 34
Stanford Challenge, 212
structures to support collaboration, 41–43
as vice-chair of presidential search committee, 34–36
vision for university, 39–41
Everett, Shirley, 339–340
excellence, achievement of, xx–xxi
executive education, 188, 239

F

faculty appointment process
fundraising campaigns for, xi
joint appointments, 17–19
quality of, 27
spousal faculty members and, 39
tenure and, 19–20, 22–24

of women, 8–10, 223–224
Faculty Senate, 208, 209, 332,
349, 356, 357–358, 364, 365,
394, 427
Faculty Staff Housing Office,
57–59
Fattaey, Heideh, 381, 475n122
Feeney, Chuck, 129, 465n42
Feeny, Curtis F., 438, 477n139
FERPA (Family Educational
Rights and Privacy Act), 50
financial aid program, 47–48, 66,
87, 95, 107, 114, 126, 130, 188
formula schools, 197, 200, 429,
468n63
See also Graduate School of
Business (GSB); School of
Medicine
Foster, Norman, 378, 475n120
Fox, Jim, 305, 473n105
Freeman Spogli Institute for Inter-
national Studies, 125, 130–131,
283, 359, 403–404, 407, 465n40
free speech issues, 70
Freshman-Sophomore College
(FroSoCo), 305–306, *306*

G
Gardner, John W., 186, 467n61
gender research. *See* Michelle R.
Clayman Institute for Gender
Research
General Atlantic, 123
general use permit (GUP), 98–99,
203–204, 454
Georgia Tech, 148
Gibbons, Jim, 146, 161, 466n45
global financial crisis (2008–2009),
impacts on Stanford, 44–46,
94–96, 113–115, 125–127,

152, 224–226, 264–265, 278,
307–308, 424–426, 433, 446
Golde, Chris, 343
Google stock, 66, 463n24
Gordon, Robert Aaron, 183,
467n57
Gordon-Howell Report (Ford
Foundation), 183, 467n57
graduate education
quality of, 187
review of curriculum, 176–177
student enrollment, 336
See also Gumport, Patricia; Joss,
Robert L. (Bob)
Graduate School of Business
(GSB), 21, 42, 43, 172–188, 258,
445–446
See also Joss, Robert L. (Bob)
Graduate School of Education
(GSE), 229–246
Gray, Hanna, 275, 279, 471n91
Green, Anika, 343–344
green buildings, 218–219
Gressens, Sally, 338
Gumport, Patricia, *331, 345*
VICE PROVOST FOR GRADUATE ED-
UCATION AND POSTDOCTORAL
AFFAIRS, xvii–xviii, 331–354
advisor relationships, 345–347
background and assuming vice
provost role, 332–333
diversity in graduate education,
341–345
early period, 333–335
expansion of what's possible in
graduate education, 335–336
graduate student funding and
affordability, 337–338
leadership approach, 349–351
prioritization of graduate stu-

Made in the USA
Monee, IL
15 April 2023

e8176231-7a57-48a5-86c4-b9a09d77fa6cR01